—TH ARCHER'S BOW

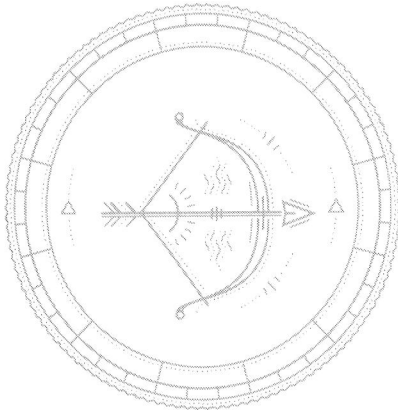

A BOOK THAT WILL FOREVER CHANGE THE WAY YOU THINK ABOUT PARENTING

VIRGINIA SKROBISCH

Cover and Interior Design: Jasmine Hromjak

ISBN 978-1-7358599-0-3 (trade paperback)

ISBN 978-1-7358599-1-0 (epub)

Printed in the United States of America

Acknowledgements

*This book is dedicated to my family; in particular, my sister, Liz, invaluable sounding board and unfailing source of support, for her part in making this book a reality. I also want to thank Margot Bennett-Mathieson, lifelong friend and committed trailblazer, whose support and belief in me have been unwavering over the years. The two of you inspire me with your passionate dedication to making this world a better place. There are other friends, too, and although I won't mention them here, they know who they are. Special thanks go to Maria Luisa Mansergas, whose wisdom I continue to treasure, and who taught me almost everything I can say I know about human beings. Last but not least, I want to thank my son, Sergi, the inspiration for this book and trusted source of input and encouragement. I continue to be humbled by your honesty and clarity of vision, and above all, by your willingness to challenge yourself, continue to grow, expand your knowledge and stretch your boundaries day after day.

Contents

· · · · · · · · · ·

On Children

(FROM *THE PROPHET* BY KHALIL GIBRAN)

And a woman who held a babe against her bosom said,
  "Speak to us of Children."
And he said:
Your children are not your children.
They are the sons and daughters of Life's longing for itself.
They come through you but not from you,
And though they are with you, yet they belong not to you.
You may give them your love but not your thoughts.
For they have their own thoughts.
You may house their bodies but not their souls,
For their souls dwell in the house of tomorrow, which you
  cannot visit, not even in your dreams.
You may strive to be like them, but seek not to make them
  like you.
For life goes not backward nor tarries with yesterday.
You are the bows from which your children as living
  arrows are sent forth.
The archer sees the mark upon the path of the infinite, and
  He bends you with His might that His arrows may go
  swift and far.
Let your bending in the archer's hand be for gladness;
For even as he loves the arrow that flies, so He loves also
  the bow that is stable.

Preface
· · · · · · · ·

*W*hen I first started thinking about writing this book, I wanted it to be more than a series of rules to be followed. In a much broader sense, I wanted to create an awareness around what it is we do as parents that empowers (or conversely, discourages) our children in becoming all that they can be, based on the premise that we all have a calling; something that is uniquely ours to achieve here on this planet.

The title of this book is inspired by the wisdom of Kahlil Gibran's poem "On Children", which turns out to be as true in the 21st century as it was when the poem was written. It speaks deeply to me and my understanding of the power we have as parents to enable our children to become the best they can be.

In my work as a life coach, and in the course of my own personal growth, I have learned that, as adults, it often takes years of grappling with our own fears and self-perceived limitations to break free, to learn to trust ourselves and go for what we really want.

What if we could stop the cycle of negative imprinting, and the frustrating loss of human energy and potential that it entails? Not to mention the time and money spent later in trying to recover what we were never allowed to have in the first place: our right to reach for our dreams.

I thought: what if, instead of our *calling* being a lofty quest to be pursued upon reaching adulthood, we could allow our children from an early age to begin to be aware of their own nascent potential and unique gifts by creating the conditions for these gifts to emerge naturally from within?

Drawing attention to what we as parents do and, beyond our best intentions, the impact that we have on our kids, this book offers a glimpse into how, as parents of children who are born into an era very different from our own, we can find an authentic way to support them in becoming happy, fulfilled adults, according to their own definition of whatever that may be.

I wanted to share what has been an enlightening journey and learning experience, often based on intuition, sometimes on luck, and frequently, with the sense that I was travelling without a map.

With the clarity of hindsight, I look at my son's upbringing and the person he has become. There are a few references to the city of Barcelona, Spain where he grew up, although that does not in any way change the message for readers of this book. I am convinced that at a very essential level, parents everywhere share the same concerns, hopes and desires for their children.

I also want to make it clear that, although the ideas and insights I offer on these pages have emerged as a result of my training as a coach, most of the journey – in fact, the first 18 years - took place before I knew anything about the profession.

In owning up to the fact that as a parent I was inexperienced and unprepared, relying only on trust and my belief that children are indeed perfect, my intention is to encourage parents to trust – above and beyond whatever information they may glean from parenting literature – that they, too, have the knowledge within that can enable them to be the best parent ever for their child.

In the parenting process we try, sometimes fail, and eventually learn to do things better, just as our children do. There is an entire chapter on letting go of the need to be perfect parents. The point is, our parenting can be flawed and still be right for our kids. Imperfection is a great quality that we can model for our children to learn from, and indeed, cherish.

Seeing children as naturally perfect just as they are is the starting point. Helping them to learn what they need to know to function in the world, enabling them to trust their own gifts and learn what they have that is uniquely theirs to contribute to the world is, I believe, the genuine contribution of parenthood, and the greatest source of joy and gratification.

VIRGINIA SKROBISCH

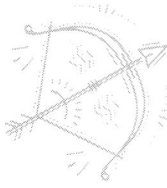

CHAPTER 1

. . . .

The Knowledge Within

We all have within us the knowledge of what we need and what we want.

The knowledge is within us, and yet… there are times when we may think we don't really know what we want, or we may feel confusion around what it is that we want.

Most of us have undergone the conditioning of school, society and our own families or parents who, in all fairness, probably feel they have our best interests at heart. It may take us years to discover that, in retrospect, what we thought was our goal for ourselves was really an expectation planted in us by other people, at a time when we were unable to discern our own wants from those that later became lodged in our mind as the things we *ought to want*, or *ought to be doing*.

Interestingly, many of the things that our minds tell us we *should* be doing come from sources outside of ourselves. The knowledge within – our most authentic and immediate knowledge – is that of the heart.

When we imagine something we love doing, we feel it in our heart. Those positive feelings confirm that whatever that something is, it is connected to who we really are.

What is the impact on our children when we impose on them our own ideas of how they should be?

To use a metaphor, every individual is like an ecosystem, coexisting with other ecosystems in our world. We know that ecosystems maintain a delicate yet dynamic balance, within themselves and with other ecosystems around them.

When we decide for our children who – or how – they must be, the ideas we plant are like foreign "species" introduced into their ecosystem.

Some of these "species" will find a hostile environment and will fail to thrive. Others, if they find fertile ground, may virtually do away with the original species that were native to that ecosystem. It's important to know that the stand we take as parents will have a lasting impact, positive or negative, on our children. That is precisely what makes consciously choosing the way we want to be as people and as parents so powerful.

A Radical Act

My intention is not to paint an apocalyptic picture of the way we influence our children. I would, however, suggest we take an honest look at our own lives: how we were influenced by what was put into our heads at some time during our childhood, and the choices we made as a result. We may not be unhappy with the results, yet most of us – even those of us raised in a comfortable environment, with doting parents – could probably say there is a thing or two we might have changed.

We get to decide what we want to keep - because it is meaningful to us - and what we want to let go of, or perhaps exchange for something else that is more aligned with who we are. We become happier people and better parents when we get rid of this excess baggage.

This mental "housecleaning" process is frequently hindered by a belief that choosing a different path somehow means disappointing, or even discrediting, the parents who set so much store by our successes (or the anticipation thereof) based on their admonitions and encouragement.

Acknowledging that our parents did their best to give us what they thought we needed, and recognizing that "well-meaning" does not necessarily mean "right" or "better", is a first step toward consciously letting go of certain learned beliefs that no longer serve us so that we can rediscover who we really are – and what we really want. It is a process that is often emotionally charged, and for many, a challenge that can take years to resolve.

What if our children never had to go through this process?

We could save our children the often monumental task, as they grow older, of untangling their own wants and desires from those that were considered "better", or "more appropriate", or more "realistic", if we were willing to let go of the need to know *for them* what it is they should do, or how they should be.

Doing so is a radical act. It means being willing to trust and accept that our youngsters contain within them the knowledge that they need, and that it is as good as any other dream we might have for them. They will probably not identify it immediately, and of course we can suggest areas for them to explore, but why not just be honest with our kids and tell them that we have hopes and dreams for them – because we see them as capable of being and doing so many things – but that they get to choose?

We can learn to strike a balance between setting limits and instilling values – providing our children with security, discipline, and the willingness to work for what they want to achieve – and standing back and allowing whatever it is that they want to be, or become, to emerge. Because no two individuals are alike, some may know when they are quite young what it is they want to do later; others will take more time, perhaps even embarking on one path before deciding to switch to another.

Learning is Everywhere

From our standpoint as onlookers, our kids may appear to be squandering the time, effort and, possibly, money invested in one course of study when they abandon it for another that they feel more drawn to, or when they decide they need to take time off from their studies to do something completely unrelated. Yet nowhere is it written that human beings – our children or ourselves – are meant to be consciously aware from an early age what their calling will be.

Of course, many of the stories that most appeal to us are those of individuals who have not followed a single, unswerving path throughout their lives to where they ultimately end up. We point to people who have taken "risks", occasionally leaving a well-paid job or comfortable social status to do what their heart told them was their calling. Or youngsters who – unable or unwilling to "fit" into the demands of the educational system – ended up finding a path of their own outside of the traditional educational route of high school, university and graduate school. Some become artists or athletes; others, such as some very successful dotcom entrepreneurs, make their way without completing a college education, often blazing new trails for others to follow.

Okay, we might counter, but those are just a handful of people who latched onto something that could make them a living – often quite successfully. Isn't it better to have a college degree to hedge our bets, regardless of what we want to do in life?

As someone who grew up in a very academic environment with the certainty that I would go to college (it honestly never crossed my mind that I might *not*) my answer some years ago would have been "yes". Yet as time has gone by, my view has shifted: society itself has evolved, and the Internet, among other developments, has opened up a plethora of possibilities to people wanting to learn.

I'm still a firm believer in learning, curiosity, and – as part of our evolution as human beings – the search to expand our knowledge and understanding of both ourselves and the world around us: it is, in fact, the foundation upon which my work as a coach resides. Curiosity and a questioning mind are among the greatest gifts that human beings can possess: they feed our creativity and problem-solving abilities and inspire us to grow and evolve as individuals and as a society.

What has changed for me is the format in which learning takes place. When we know what it is we want to do, we can obtain learning from an institution of higher learning, in a pottery shop, or on the ski slopes (as did the son of a colleague, who despite his now proud parents' repeated admonitions, eschewed University to follow his dream, becoming an expert skier and ski coach, traveling the world competing and teaching the sport that is his passion). There are a million and one options open to people of all ages nowadays, including different forms of self-study and experiential learning.

If we can withhold our judgment about what is "worthwhile" for our kids to do; if we can trust that as they move forward, they – by experimenting and seeing what does, or doesn't, work for them – will connect with the knowing within that will enable them to create for themselves a fulfilling life, we can genuinely be of service to our children. In this way we can give them the benefit of great parenting that sets limits based on meaningful values in the form of ground rules, but also, and more importantly, posits that anything is possible.

The great benefit is that, once we believe that anything is within our reach, we throw the doors wide open to all kinds of possibility in our lives. We may have heard, or read, that quantum physicists affirm that our quantum brain attracts to it what it focuses on, and that the key is consciously and intentionally focusing on what we want, rather than what we don't want. We may not yet know how to do so for ourselves, particularly if we grew up with the idea that things *happen to us* rather than being *created by us*. Yet dreaming, feeling, and believing is something our children do naturally if we let them. The good news is that even if we don't quite know how to do it for ourselves, our children *do* know: they are very good at conjuring up and imagining what they want!

A Harbinger of Things to Come

I did not arrive at this conclusion from day one. A lot of observation, and a willingness to go with the flow with my own child, led to this conviction *after the fact*. I was also navigating without a map, relying on my own inner compass to keep as much as possible from allowing what I suspected were my own biases, or limiting beliefs, to seep into my son's upbringing.

Unsurprisingly, it took me years to learn what my son has grown up knowing intuitively. While it's true I've done many things in my life, there have also been times when I've found myself assailed by doubts or uncertainty which, had I been more firmly connected to my purpose, I would not have experienced. Curiously, it was by watching my own son that I learned to start reconnecting with something that I was no longer always in touch with: my own ability to believe in the things I wanted, and make them happen in my life.

What happens to the knowledge within? There are so many things we know when we are young that we forget or are expected to dispense with as we grow up. The innocent curiosity and the dreams that we are encouraged to have when we are children no longer seem appropriate as teens or adults. A lucky few get through the gauntlet of naysayers and come out the other end with their creativity and dreams intact, or with the resolve to find out what it is they really want. Many more of us swap our dreams for something that looks "realistic", and we end up creating a life that looks the way we *think* it should (or our parents think it should, or our friends think it should......) rather than interrogating the voice within.

Cognizant of my own fortunate circumstances – I drifted into almost every job I got until I was well into my 40s, when I began to realize that I could actually believe in and get what I wanted if I allowed myself to – I decided that, in the case of my own child, things were better not left to chance, since I didn't know whether "drifting" would work for him as it had for me. Instead of encouraging him to "focus" on what he wanted to do, however, I allowed him to give full rein to his dreams.

In part, it was because I didn't want to shut down his creativity by suggesting he couldn't achieve the things he imagined himself doing. I figured if it turned out it wasn't for him, he would discover that for himself. But it was also largely because I had already begun to suspect that dreams are not a mere figment of our imagination, but the expression of some deeper desire to create something that is uniquely ours. In that sense, it is both a harbinger of things to come, and the seed from which we create.

At some level, it felt to me as though the bright, fresh dreams of a youngster, uncorrupted by outside attempts to dismiss them, had the potential to come true. I was curious about how they would play out. In fact, a part of me suspected that believing in one's dreams from a place of authenticity, untainted by the opinions of others, was the secret to making them happen.

Apart from the certainty, from childhood, that I wanted to live abroad, I never really knew, back when I was growing up, what my own dream was – maybe because I had forgotten it, or convinced myself that I was already doing other things that interested me (*so it didn't matter*), or even convinced myself that I didn't have a dream (*so no need to feel bad if by some chance it didn't come to pass......*). Who knows at what point in our lives the dream gets packed away like clothes that don't fit us anymore, forgotten in the back of our mental/emotional closet.

The very fact that we can, if we so desire, pick up the threads of the dream where it lies within us, seeing the stuff of which it is made and exploring it anew, is the confirmation of our resilience and resourcefulness as human beings. Indeed, we don't always need to know our destination when we set out; what we need is an open mind and the willingness to set aside the dictums that may not work for us any more as we discover our own way forward.

Dreaming is Serious Business

One way or another, however circuitous the route, or the path we take at each crossroads we encounter, if there is something we are meant to do we can somehow get there, regardless of our age. In my work as a coach I have seen so many people, typically in their 40s, who tell me there is something missing in their lives. Often they say they don't know what that "something" is. In fact, the underlying fear that finding out what that "something" is, and acknowledging it, might overturn the carefully built, organized structure of our lives, is often enough to cloud our minds, keeping us from perceiving what it is that's missing.

The point is, I didn't want my son to have to spend years figuring out what his dream was, and how he could find personal fulfillment after a lifetime of pushing it away. As time went by, I began to understand that dreaming is an essential and necessary part of our nature as human beings.

I thought: Instead of assuming that dreaming is an amusing but inconsequential pastime in which children engage – a kind of innocent sport – how would it be if we could imagine that children dream and play at inhabiting their dreams — being a princess or a doctor or astronaut – the way animal young play with each other as a way of honing their skills to become self-sufficient adults as nature intended them to be? We know that animals, domesticated or in the wild, play to learn what they will need to know in adulthood. Our children, through innocent play, learn things such as problem-solving, sharing, and other social skills considered important for their development. They also spend a large percentage of their time creating from their own fantasy, the stuff of their dreams.

The conclusion I have reached is that dreams are in fact the human equivalent of baby animals' stalking and pouncing on each other and learning to catch their prey: the skills that, as adult animals, will ensure their survival. In the same way, our dreams nurture our soul and contribute to our fulfillment as human beings well into adulthood, allowing us to tap into the extraordinary creativity that each of us possesses. Indeed, we feed our children's innate creativity when they are young, reading them fairy tales and buying them educational toys or perpetuating the tradition of Santa Claus. We encourage them to dress up as a princess or a butterfly or Zorro, celebrating the fun of pretend.

So at what point do we decide that pretend is okay for Halloween and creative writing class, but not for our real lives? After all, "*Stop daydreaming*" is a common reproach wielded by parents, one they may well have been subjected to as children themselves. How do we anchor the dreams in reality without stifling the dreams themselves?

Reality is a Perspective

Perhaps we should consider what "Reality" is. Quite conceivably we may have ended up believing that Reality is something external to us. So strong is this notion, indeed, that we may have difficulty relinquishing it, at least in the Western world where the basis for Reality is those things we can see and touch and experience for ourselves.

What if what we consider to be Reality were actually no more than a perspective that we have chosen, a lens through which we see our own (and others') lives? We may have chosen the perspective that life is hard: that much effort is required to achieve what we want; that we have to fight in a world of cutthroat competition and that we will find it difficult to get ahead. Or we may be in a perspective around life that tells us it is easy: that things flow when we allow them to; that anything is possible; that we can be whoever we want to be.

In fact, either of these perspectives is true, if we believe it. Highly publicized works by respected authors, including neuroscientists, quantum physicists and authorities on meditation, have enabled an age-old concept once empirically known, and now scientifically proven, to work its way into the general culture in the form of a new awareness: that what we put out into the world, in the form of ideas and beliefs, comes back to us in ways that confirm what we already most deeply believe to be true.

Our Inner Compass

In the case of people for whom life is easy, things may seem to just happen, or *to flow* (to others, these individuals may appear to be "lucky"). The reverse is also true, because when we believe life to be hard, we are constantly beset by obstacles that repeatedly remind us that we are right.

What's more interesting is to observe the lives of people who started out in difficult circumstances and were able to achieve what they most wanted. Instead of concluding that "life is hard" and throwing in the towel, they were able to consider their difficult circumstances as just that: circumstances. Their desire to achieve something greater enabled them to rise above their circumstances, because they were so strongly motivated to go for whatever it was that they were inspired to do, or achieve.

Different obstacles may appear in our lives in the form of adverse situations, yet being able to hold on to our dream, or our vision of what we want to achieve or how we want to be, will enable us to circumvent the obstacles to find what is often a new path to wherever we're going. When we pursue our vision it acts like a compass, indicating that we are on the right track.

If we were actually to take a compass and try to find our way northward, for example, the compass would not tell us that there is a lake or a mountain between where we are and our destination. It would mark a direction for us to take, and we would find our way around the natural obstacles that appear between our current location and our objective. We would not assume that we must remain on the shore of the lake or at the foot of the mountain because the only way to move northward would be by traversing that lake or the mountain in a direct line.

Yet in our own lives, what we do is often precisely that. We see a mountain, and we conclude that the mountain is keeping us from getting to our destination. We see that the compass is pointing north, but our conclusion is that if the mountain is between us and where we want to go, there is no way to get there. We may even point to the mountain and bemoan that fact it is there. Were we to take another route, with our eye on the compass, we would reach our destination, perhaps by a more circuitous route. Who knows what we would have observed and discovered along the way?

Connecting with the "Nudge"

The title of this chapter is "the knowledge within", but it could well have been, "the feeling within". The nudge, the urge to go for what we want, comes not from our head, but from our heart. The expression, "to follow one's heart" indeed conjures up a very different image from "following one's head", although great emphasis is placed, in Western society at any rate, on having rational reasons for doing things. The problem with rational reasons is that they don't take into account the differences between you and me and what drives or motivates each of us, or anyone else on this planet.

Here is where the proviso comes in about passing off our own experience as "Reality". Based on our own experience, many things may appear difficult or impossible to achieve. We may subsequently tell our children that there is no point in trying, that their dreams will get them nowhere, or that they need to prepare for the "real" world. Perhaps we will remind them that they should set aside their pipe dreams and put their nose to the grindstone.

Interestingly, when youngsters are interested in something, they will devote hours to learning about and gaining proficiency in whatever it is. The *usefulness* of their endeavors – or of the subject on which their attention is focused – is no more than a judgment call that we make, one that is as subjective as our own view of Reality.

Neuroscientists know that the more experiences we have, the greater our creativity and chances for having a satisfying life will be, since our creative and problem-solving capacities come from the unconscious piecing together of bits of experiences acquired throughout our life. Childhood is now known to be a seminal period of life because of the number of neuronal connections that are created at this time.

When we shut down these avenues to creativity we are closing down opportunities for our children to feel, identify and explore what moves them, what drives them, and where their passions lie. We may ourselves be able to think back to a time when we had a longing to do something that we were told was "unrealistic", "inappropriate", or "a waste of time". Our own well-meaning parents were undoubtedly attempting to guide us instead down a route that, based on *their own experience,* would get us somewhere in life and would make us happy (according to their own subjective idea of what happiness was).

It's difficult to get from infancy to adulthood without acquiring some subjective biases along the way (hats off to those of you who can honestly say you haven't!). So while we may find it difficult or well-nigh impossible to simply toss aside our learned preconceptions (even once we have become aware of them), we can offer our children the opportunity to grow up in a world untainted by our perspective of Reality, allowing them to create their own Reality in a natural, authentic way.

To do so, we have to be willing to acknowledge that our view of

Reality is no more than a *perspective*, one acquired or drilled into us at some point in our lives. Perhaps it works for us, yet the assumption that our experience of Reality is the best (or the only!) interpretation of what constitutes Reality, and that it is best for our children as well, might prompt us to try to guide them along a path that we feel will serve them, but that may not be right for them at all.

It may be difficult to relinquish the need to know, or be the expert, where our youngsters are concerned. Naturally, there are areas in which we do know what is best: establishing a healthy lifestyle, encouraging a love of learning, and so on. However, if we want to genuinely support our children, we may have to admit that their way of learning may be different from ours, and that they may be interested in learning, or doing, something different from what we might have imagined for them — possibly even something for which we can see no earthly use.

Children, if allowed to, will naturally be drawn to areas that interest them, be it drawing, or numbers, or airplanes, or sports. It is our fear that they may end up with a passion for something that we feel will get them nowhere that prompts us to steer them elsewhere as they grow older, since when children are small, almost everything they take an interest in is encouraged and applauded by their parents.

What would it be like to just stand back and watch them explore? Kids naturally connect with "the feeling within", and follow it spontaneously. As they grow, if they have many interests they may find it difficult to decide where to set their sights. When they are given the chance to discover naturally where they are headed, they will ultimately find a connection with the feeling, or "nudge" that – like a compass — will take them where they need to be. Prompted by whatever that urge may be, in a process of trial and error, their inner feeling of what they want will take them around the mountain and lead them to wherever their own internal compass guides them.

Alternatively, we can simply join forces with all the other naysayers, assuming that – because we are the parents – we have the right to decide for our kids what is right, or appropriate, for them to want or pursue. We all know of parents (perhaps including ourselves) who tell their teenagers, in all seriousness, *"First go get a college degree; then you can go do what you want"* (or some version thereof). The implication is that what counts is having a traditional seal of approval for an achievement, not whether one's son or daughter ever really hungered for that course of study.

There are many young people who actually complete their higher studies and get a degree to please their parents, and then take off and do something radically different with their lives - probably what they would have done to start off with, had they felt free to do so.

Gratitude and Faith

The knowledge within can be nurtured. For children, as for adults, learning gratitude for what we have is a great step toward creating happiness and fertile ground where creativity can blossom. There are many things to be thankful for, including health, relationships and our material circumstances, but also, importantly, the unique gifts that we were born with and that are ours to use and develop.

When my son was about 7 or 8 years old I had him collect all of the used toys that he wasn't playing with anymore. We packed them into the car and drove to an orphanage – the first time he had ever been to such an institution. I had explained to him ahead of time that the children at this orphanage did not have their parents, and in addition, that many were from disadvantaged families.

Although we had talked about the fact that these youngsters didn't enjoy luxuries and didn't have a lot of individual possessions, I don't think my son was prepared for the excitement generated among the children at the orphanage at receiving toys and games in which he no longer had any interest himself. The realization that things he had always taken for granted were prized by others had an impact on him, and enabled him to understand better what I meant when I spoke to him of gratitude, and cherishing the things we are fortunate enough to have.

Still, and even though in our heart we may know what we want, and feel gratitude, it is our faith in what we want to do that will eventually get us there. The faith in our vision is what will enable us to keep believing, when it isn't immediately or clearly visible to ourselves or others that we will get there. How many times do we not tell others about something we long for, for fear of spoiling it or somehow keeping it from happening?

Even kids who grow up with the freedom to believe in themselves may encounter the challenges represented by "realists", pessimists and "doubting Thomases", of which there are plenty in our lives. Most friends and relations will willingly volunteer their advice in our best interest, which includes attempting to discourage us from almost anything that they can't see coming about.

As my son would say, "*What's difficult is not the hard work or energy you put into doing something you really want. What's hard is continuing to keep the faith that you'll achieve it even when others criticize what you're doing or dismiss it as impossible, and when you yourself don't know how you're going to get there."*

So many rules have been made up and their origins forgotten, like someone locking a set of beliefs in our head and throwing away the key. There may be a legitimate reason for some of the rules we go by, but there are some whose validity has lapsed, yet are never questioned.

Rules that act like a corset often stifle the knowledge within. Staying aligned with who we are, and keeping our faith in ourselves and our kids, means heeding what our intuition tells us, rather than what we are "expected" to do.

If my focus here has been on who we are as parents, it's because we set the stage for how our children will grow up. We get to choose whether to simply reproduce old, discordant models, or dare to create something new. I'm totally convinced that if we allow ourselves to connect with our children rather than our fears, we can be truly great parents!

Just as creative inspiration comes to artists, inventors and entrepreneurs, there is a nudge that parents get that guides them in raising their children. Indeed, were parents given a course to prepare them for child-rearing, it would probably look a lot like what they would have done if they had been able to tap their intuition, with no outside interference at all.

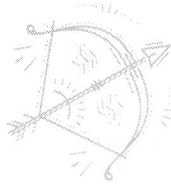

CHAPTER 2

· · · · · · · · · · · ·

The Archer's Bow

The Journey

We accompany our children on their journey from birth through adolescence and into adulthood. As traveling companions on their voyage, much of our delight in them comes from witnessing their excitement and enthusiasm at visiting the special places along the way that we already know and love.

For those who observe such traditions, Christmas or Hanukkah shared with children has a different flavor and meaning to it than when spent on one's own. In different cultures, other holiday celebrations with their rituals and traditions are proudly passed on to children, who in turn learn to cherish and honor them.

When we look at our children and witness in them the wonder of discovery: taking their first steps, learning to read and write or putting together a puzzle for the first time, we enjoy and celebrate these achievements with them the way we enjoy sharing a special and treasured place or moment from our own personal journey with someone we love.

The Intangibles (love, confidence, support and faith)

Our role as parents of the new generations of children born and growing up in changing times is to be reliable companions as they set out on their voyage; we are here to point out the sights and celebrate the discoveries along the way! We need to be aware that our kids will take in the scenery in their own way as they go forward. Some will be careful and meticulous; others will rush in with enthusiasm to experience things firsthand. Each will have his or her own way of exploring what life has to offer.

Despite the widespread belief that the challenges and perils of an evolving society require that we keep an ever firmer hold on our children, I'm convinced that our children are already prepared for the new world that awaits them; our role as parents is to cultivate and foster their potential so they can flourish and grow, finding fulfillment in whatever it is they have to contribute to the world.

If we want this to happen, we need to trust our children. If, from the moment they come into this world, we trust that they are here to do something that is uniquely theirs and that they are perfectly equipped to do so, our role becomes that of horticulturist to a climbing vine: we provide the trellis upon which the plant can grow and thrive. We water and care for it, pruning it judiciously from time to time, then standing back to admire its beauty… whose potential was in it from the time it was just a tiny seed! The purpose of all of our ministrations is to allow the plant to thrive, and to enjoy the abundance of leaves and blossoms that nature intended it to have.

Some plants will flourish more readily than others. The soil and sun to which they are exposed are important, and tellingly, the care we lavish on them will also make a difference.

I still remember a scraggly looking azalea plant that my own mother once rescued from a piece of property that was being bulldozed to make way for new homes to be built. It was barely more than a long, skinny twig with a few leaves still attached, but she carefully prepared the soil and planted it behind our house, near our back door. In time, the plant began to grow and thrive, and we were all amazed to see how the original weedy-looking branch she had planted had been transformed; in its place was a robust, burgeoning plant, heavy with blossoms in such abundance that they appeared to outnumber the leaves. It was her care that had made it thrive.

As it turns out, what we give our children is actually less tangible than we think it needs to be: love, confidence, support, and the discipline that will teach them to persist at what they really want to achieve. Like a trellis guiding their growth, we set limits while supporting them in what they want to do.

Sometimes we don't really understand or agree with what they say they want to do. Our first inclination may be to redirect them toward something we feel is more "realistic" or "useful". Yet by not allowing them to dream and explore the things that most appeal to them, we shut down the possibilities that are naturally triggered by dreaming big.

How can we trust that it will all be okay? Since to a certain extent society places demands on our children that they must be prepared to handle, social skills and an ability to deal with challenges and frustrations are important strengths for them to acquire. At the same time, we have to keep sight of the bigger picture: their lives, understood as the projection of who they are into time and space.

We don't know who they are meant to be or what they are meant to do in their lifetime. It takes faith to believe that they have something unique, large or small, to bring to the world. We may have grandiose hopes for our children: that they can do as well as we did; that they can do *better* than we did… but they are here to live their lives, not to fulfill our hopes.

Often we will be called upon to support them even when we don't understand their choices. Building trust from when they are small creates the safety net over which they, like circus acrobats, occasionally teeter. It creates room for maneuver, leeway to succeed and at times, to fail.

For our children, being allowed to fail, and get up and try again, is essential to discovering their own path. If they feel coerced into acting a certain way or aiming for certain goals merely because that is what is expected of them, they may never find what it is that they are here to do.

Withholding our Opinions, Reconsidering our Beliefs

To those who assert that young people nowadays lack passion, I would suggest that youngsters who are allowed to freely explore and pursue whatever it is they want to do, knowing that they are valued by their parents for who they are and not merely for what they achieve, express their passion in a multitude of ways.

Will their passion be expressed in a more *traditional* way? Or will it take an unconventional turn, veering off the well-worn path of what we, deep down, may wish for them? It takes great courage to be able to withhold our opinion when our children express the desire to do or be something that we esteem to be offbeat or unorthodox.

Of course, what is unorthodox is subjective too. The child of parents who are Wall Street brokers may be faced with a different set of expectations from one whose parents' lives were devoted to the performing arts. Other parents, who feel they never had a chance to excel, and see life as a series of missed opportunities, may see their children as a way to vicariously redeem themselves.

So, often we want them to do better than we did… or alternatively, to follow in our own footsteps. But what does "better" really mean? Do our ideas about what will make our sons and daughters happy and successful – two other subjective notions – reflect what they feel inside?

A common justification for our expectations is our own hard-earned experience, held up as the yardstick against which our children's performance is measured. In raising children it's inevitable to refer to our own experience, because it's what we know best.

So how can we hold back from "imposing" advice while feeling we are offering our children the best opportunities from our view?

One way is to invite them to consider our suggestion as another alternative that they might try. In this way, we open up possibilities rather than shutting them down, because we've added another option rather than insisting that ours is the *only* option. In addition, kids like taking on responsibility for choosing, and are more likely to consider something that is offered than something that's imposed.

We're also more effective if we give advice on the things they need to know, and hold back from giving our opinion on the things they need to find out for themselves. It can take a lot of restraint for us to allow our children to discover things on their own, resisting the temptation to discourage them – albeit with the best of intentions – from embarking on a course of action that our experience tells us will result in failure. Our thought process appears to be: help them leapfrog over all of the trial and error so they can just understand and get on with things, and we'll save them time and distress in the process of getting where they want to go.

What appears to be a time-saver in our fast-paced, information-dominated world (with so much to learn, we feel justified in helping them gain time by spoon-feeding them the solutions that we have already acquired) is not always useful. They may or may not follow our admonitions, but the greatest value for them lies in making their own discoveries, complete with all of the mistakes along the way.

In this regard, there is something I like to call *JIT advice-giving*. Many people are familiar with the original JIT concept from manufacturing, where JIT, or *just-in-time*, production makes it possible to improve quality and efficiency, and reduce waste in the production process. The JIT concept has since been applied to many other areas, including education: in this context, learners identify their own learning needs, and then acquire knowledge from a range of sources on a "need-to-know" basis.

In a similar way, *JIT advice-giving* is delivered with an eye to efficiency. Advice overload is actually unproductive, just like excess inventory in a manufacturing process. In this case, it may be that the person receiving the advice (here, our child) has asked for advice. More likely we are offering it unsolicited, something we may consider part of our parental role. (Our warnings to our children about real and perceived dangers are a different matter, touched on later in this chapter).

In *JIT advice-giving*, JIT stands for: Judicious, Impartial and Timely. **Judicious**, because the content should be what our child needs. Nothing more. A good rule of thumb might be: think of the advice you want to give; then withhold about 90% of it. **Impartial** means it is judgment-free. In other words, it is not our agenda for them, but a response to what is needed by them at that moment. And **Timely** means it should be used sparingly, on an as-needed basis.

We tend to give far more advice than is really necessary. In fact, if we pay attention we may catch ourselves dispensing advice liberally not only to our children, but to friends and colleagues as well. The best approach, if we can't resist giving our opinion, is to come clean and say that it is just that: our *opinion*. Most of the time children do far better discovering things on their own.

Discovery, Creativity and Resourcefulness

Our children need the opportunity to make their own discoveries. The trial and error involved in finding things out for themselves develops their problem-solving capacity and stimulates their natural, open-minded curiosity. It's something that doesn't happen when ready-made solutions and opinions that come with the seal of parental approval are fed to them as Reality.

From this standpoint, it's easy to see how we grow up with biases and limiting beliefs as a result of what we were told as children: when our parents asserted that things were a certain way, we believed them. Many such messages are assimilated and become the basis for the way we lead our lives when we are adults.

We may pass on some of these "inherited" beliefs to our own children, never questioning their basis in truth. An illustration of such a message would be the belief that *life is hard*; or: *other people are to blame for how I feel*. We can see how such categorical assertions – essentially *opinions* – have conditioned us, and can condition our own children as well, if conveyed to them as fact.

An example of the importance of fostering open-mindedness, and of prompting rather than discouraging discovery, can be found in the scientific community. Scientists will tell you there is no such thing as scientific "truth", since what is initially understood to be "reality" actually turns out to be something else as more is understood about it and it becomes possible to perceive it in ever greater detail. What we like to think of as scientific "truth", is actually something that shifts and evolves.

Were scientists to have accepted at face value all that was known about molecules in the early 20th century, none of the great achievements of the later 20th century and 21st century would have occurred. Can anyone imagine what our world would look like today had that happened?

When as parents we try to dissuade our children from something they want to do because *our own experience* tells us it will be unproductive, we inadvertently shut down the possibilities that might emerge for them if they actually gave it a try, doing it their own way.

Many of our arguments come from our comfort zone: the place where things are predictable and familiar, based on our experience of what we have learned

In the face of our child's desire to do things differently, our first reaction may be resistance. Rather than getting curious – being willing to learn more and perhaps consider another option – it may feel more reassuring to tuck ourselves away in the perceived safety of our unshakable beliefs. As time goes by we pass on to our children the same staunch beliefs that have kept us feeling safe, like a life raft meant to take them unscathed through the choppy seas of the unknown: their future.

Why do we do this? Curiously, human beings are the only creatures that fear the unknown. A cat will venture fearlessly into the dark, relying on instinct, its superior night vision and its senses to tell it whether danger is near. It does not fear danger lurking behind a corner if its sight and hearing do not inform it that danger is really there. Not being able to see, bats rely on their radars when they fly, never fearing that their radar might someday fail to work!

Humans have learned – often through received messages – to fear the unknown, and frequently, to anticipate the worst. We ruminate about the past and worry about the future. For many parents, worrying about their children is a way of life. Paradoxically, it is often our "worry" about what might happen to our children that inadvertently holds them back from being all they can be.

In contrast, children who are allowed to enjoy the excitement of discovery and dreaming learn that they can shape their future: they are the navigators of their own lives, staying their course and occasionally changing tack when need be. Instead of fearing the unknown, they learn to embrace it as a path to self-fulfillment.

As human beings, we will inevitably be faced with life's circumstances, *regardless* of whether we believe we have a choice in creating our own future or not. The difference is, those who understand what it means to create and take responsibility for their own future can use their *creativity and resourcefulness* to weather the storm… and create learning in the process. The curve balls that life throws at them are seen as challenges or opportunities that can take them further, rather than a calamity that jeopardizes their sense of well-being. For children such as this there is excitement, rather than fear, in stepping outside of their comfort zone.

The Calling

So how can we as parents best relate to our children? What is our part in "making" them who they will eventually become?

Children, on the whole, appear to have a part of them that is "inherited" from one or both of their parents, another part that they acquire as they grow, and another that seems to be just *theirs*. Perhaps that is why parents are so often struck by just how different their children are from each other. "*We raised them the same!*" parents exclaim, at a loss to explain why their daughter is a social butterfly while her brother spends hours engrossed in the mechanical workings of any contraption he can find. Or: she is a studious overachiever, voted by her classmates as "most likely to succeed", and his driving passion is to hitchhike around the world.

In fact, we as parents are not responsible for everything our children become. It has also become clear to me that our children are not strictly "*ours*". I have heard mothers of older children speak nostalgically about a sense of closeness, or "oneness" that they experienced during their child's infancy, that somehow shifted as time went by. The feeling is real, yet the sense of a loss of "oneness" that may accompany our child's growing independence is the product of an illusion generated by the physical dependence and strong bonds knitted in the first years of life.

To me it is clear that our children are on loan to us, in a manner of speaking… while they gain what they need to know to move on. Our children come into our lives, and we create the nest into which they settle. We then enjoy the privilege of overseeing their development, stewarding them through infancy, childhood and adolescence until, at a time that is right only for them, they are ready to leave.

For them, gaining what they need to know is not necessarily done while living in a perfect world. Some of the most resourceful individuals have come from dysfunctional families, or families beset by poverty. Some lost their parents and were adopted into new families, or grew up in foster homes. Some endured war and hardship, while others were raised in comfortable homes and sent to schools where they could excel, attending extracurricular classes to cultivate their artistic sensibilities.

Here, I want to make a plea for children, and childhood itself. I am aware, as I write this, of the starkly contrasting circumstances faced by many youngsters throughout the world. Yet I hold that ideally, childhood would be the halcyon, predictable time when youngsters could gain a sense of confidence because they would know they could always rely on certain things being the same way. There is an order and reliability to such a life that is reassuring and breeds confidence. Depending on the family, this life could also involve travel and adventure, where there is a common thread of knowing "this is what we do" as a family, a confirmation of things that are a certain way.

Most parents want to provide their children with what is best for them. We are urged to create a context in which children have freedom to use their creativity; we are also told to set limits for them. Often confusion arises as to how constraining the limits must be, or on the contrary, how much freedom is advisable, and whether the two can be reconciled at all. Some parents err on the side of being too restrictive; others are liberal to the point of being lax.

Parenting, for many adults, may be the most challenging job we ever undertake. It can also be the most gratifying. It's interesting how, even as we guide our children, we are called upon to grow and push our own comfort zone by learning to do what does not necessarily come "naturally". For some of us, stretching ourselves as parents consists in being more permissive; for others, being stricter. Perhaps some of the frustration parents feel comes from seeing that a unilateral parenting style – solely restrictive or solely permissive – doesn't yield the most satisfactory results.

The good news that emerges when we step back and look at the big picture is that children can learn from models that are more lenient as well as from those that are more firm-handed. We see it all the time: healthy, well-adjusted young adults who come from a wide range of different family backgrounds. Nevertheless, there are still ways, if we are open and willing to learn and adapt, that the parent-child relationship can be of greater benefit to our children than ever before.

Being a parent is in many ways a learning process. At the same time, it's a job for which many feel ill-prepared at best, and – let's face it – just wanting to have a child doesn't guarantee that all will go smoothly along the path from infancy to adulthood. In fact, when seen in this time frame, child-rearing can actually appear quite daunting!

As parents, we will undoubtedly be called upon to stretch ourselves. That is a fundamental part of the learning process for us. What we learn from our children may not be as direct and straightforward as what we give them: things like good manners, an interest in reading, sports and other activities, and parental advice that is intended to smooth out the bumps that appear along the way and avoid frustration and heartache for them. We want to give them the benefit of what we know in order to spare them the disappointments that we ourselves have experienced.

The best thing we can give our children is the tools they can use to explore what they want to do with their own lives, and discover who they are meant to be. It's like being the stage manager for our children, who are the stars of their own lives. There are a lot of rehearsals before they take center stage. But at some point they will take off and the spotlight will be on them; it will be their show.

So what is needed to prepare our children to fly with their own wings? To an extent it will depend on each child, but there are some givens. Curiously, what children need from us is not so much the information we provide them to guide their steps as it is the love and confidence in them that will enable them to step out and own their place in the world. When they take center stage in their lives, what transpires will look different depending on who they are and where their passion takes them, but in preparing for their own stellar performance they will benefit from having the confidence and willingness to explore and discover what life holds for them.

Perceived Dangers

Is it a well-worn path that they must find and follow? Those children who veer off the well-traveled path may be seen as ingrates, rebels, or losers intent on jeopardizing their future by ignoring the advice that their parents and society-at-large proffer with their best interests at heart.

We might consider… What kind of advice are we giving them? And why is it so important that they follow it?

Setting rules that create safety and discipline is an indispensable part of parenting, but where does this essential task encroach upon our children's own ability to find things out for themselves? Indeed, telling them what to do is often necessary, and a way of providing guidance… yet equally important is the space we allow them, to explore and make discoveries on their own.

Giving our children the freedom to learn on their own not only develops their ability to investigate and find out what they need, but enables them to establish a kind of *intuitive relationship* with what is around them that will serve them in good stead, both in childhood and as adults. Rather than giving them a road map with Start and Destination on it, we offer them a compass with which to chart their own course.

My experience is that *it is our fears* that keep us from allowing our children more freedom to make their own discoveries – and mistakes – even though we know that doing so will offer them opportunities for creativity and learning. Although use of their creativity and imagination is generally accepted as necessary – and indeed, encouraged – when they are small, the idea of our children running the risk (or taking the time) to explore as they grow older, when it feels safer and more expeditious to feed them the answer ourselves, may go against the grain.

What about discipline? In terms of the rules we set, a part of us knows the difference: it can distinguish between the significance of a parental warning to look both ways before crossing a street, and a warning that our child's Nintendo will be taken away if they fail math.

In the first case we provide our children with a rule intended to protect them from injury, and we often express it to them that way. In the second case, many other aspects come into play... such as whether the child has been struggling with math from the start of the school year or has routinely been misbehaving in class; whether removing a privilege is useful at all in correcting a behavior, assuming that it is about conduct in the first place... and of course, the consideration of whether depriving a child of a Nintendo is in any way related to their poor grade in math, or likely to have a bearing on it.

How about advice? There are things we tell our kids to do that we know they will ignore and do anyway, because it's natural for them to do so. *"Don't run on the wet pavement; you'll slip",* is an admonition usually only followed as long as we are there saying it, and when they do slip and fall, the echo of our words of caution may ring briefly in their ears, bringing home the importance of heeding our advice. But it is the doing and slipping, and skinned knee, that bring home the learning.

I'm not suggesting that we not give such advice. As parents we are trying to help our kids navigate the hazards, large and small, that they will encounter from babyhood onward. Warnings are a way of doing just that.

But what about perceived dangers? Or our own biases?

When we serve up our beliefs in the form of advice meant to facilitate a decision on the part of our youngsters, something gets lost in the process: our children's ability to tap into their own creative problem-solving skills. In the same way we provide admonitions to protect our children from physical harm, we may be brandishing our advice as a shield to protect them *(and ourselves)* from another kind of hazard: the risk of perceived disappointment that could come from making mistakes.

Advice-Giving and Authority

As said earlier, advice that is offered in the form of "just one more option" to choose from opens up a gamut of possibilities for our kids. It's when it conceals an implicit judgment that it no longer serves them. Compare the blanket statement beginning with the words: "*You should do (...)*" with the suggestion: "*What if you tried (...)?*" Of course, the question can't be merely rhetorical, and our tone of voice has to be aligned with our message. Language plays an important part, and the impact when we offer something to our children will be different depending on the way it is expressed.

Again, I've discovered that advice-giving on the whole is most effective when it's done on an "as needed" basis, as opposed to constant nagging, or worse, pontificating. As parents, a lot of what we do is counterproductive. We know our children tune out when we nag, but we do it anyway. We insist on winning the skirmishes instead of saving our ammunition for the battles that count.

Of course there are many things we know but don't always do. We're actually aware that enlisting our youngsters' cooperation is the most effective route, but we all know there are times when we don't have the energy or inclination to humor them: it is at such moments that we may find ourselves losing our temper or resorting to authoritarian tactics.

Although I believe in being firm, in my own home there were situations in which I opted to allow my son greater leeway. Sometimes it just didn't seem to be worth an argument, and I would save my comments for a time when I sensed they would have more impact.

It was as though I had my own little *"nag-ometer"* that let me know when I was becoming heavy-handed in my remarks about whatever it was my son was supposed to be doing: cleaning his room, running an errand, doing his homework, etc.. I also trusted that I would have the opportunity to drive home the importance of what I had asked him to do, if not at that very moment, then certainly later, and that perception invariably proved to be true. The only thing I never budged on was his being respectful, of us as his parents and of other people, whoever they might be.

What about pontificating? Eventually, of course, all the rhetoric – otherwise known as *"hot air"* – proves to be a lie. As adults we realize when someone is pontificating, and it doesn't take children very long before they do too. Right up alongside parents who pontificate are those who pretend to be right when they aren't, and those who won't admit to making a mistake.

So where does our authority come from? Can it be attributed to our physical size, or the fact that our children totally depend on us to provide for their needs during their early years? Is it the fact that we know more than they do, have more experience than they do, or have the benefit of having spent more years on this planet?

In my experience, authority comes from humility. Young children rely on their parents' knowledge and discernment…while frequently resisting them. At the same time there's a natural inclination to love and want to admire one's parents. The strength of this desire is evidenced by the fact that it often persists into adulthood, when we find ourselves perpetuating the belief we first harbored as children – so much so, in fact, that admitting our parents' flaws may seem like a breach of loyalty. Perhaps part of what makes it so hard for some parents to admit to making mistakes is the fear of losing that admiration; the fear of disappointing our children and tarnishing the image we imagine they hold of us.

The range of parent-child interactions in this regard is a world unto itself. We all know of parents who assert their authority adamantly, assuming that their children will passively accept empty pronouncements passed off as parental "wisdom". And so those children do, for many years. Until they don't anymore. When disparities begin appearing between what a parent says and what a child perceives, the first chink in the facade has emerged.

A Line of Communication

Similarly, there are parents who appear to assert opinions and proffer advice as a way of filling a conversational void. Instead of a calm discussion between parent and child, with the parent asking questions about their son or daughter's thoughts or opinions, interactions between the two generations take the form of a parental monologue, or complaints and admonitions that predictably trigger an argument, generating anger and frustration and never really addressing the issue at hand. In older children, this breakdown in communication often takes the form of heated exchanges followed by stony silences; something that has come to be considered "typical" teen behavior.

There are also parents who feel it's finally time to sit down and "have a talk" with their children when they become adolescents. Before that, children are treated like second-class citizens; they are told what to do, but no one ever really takes the time to find out what makes them tick. Of course, by the time they are adolescents they have no incentive to share something that no one has shown an interest in before.

Mind you, the aforementioned children may have no other real complaints. In fact, they may enjoy a very comfortable existence, with toys and gadgets, a hefty allowance, and other creature comforts. Or they may have none of the above; my point is that it's not a problem that is resolved with more *things*. There is a real need for an open channel of communication.

Why does this path sometimes appear to be so hard? I find myself observing soon-to-be mothers, excited at the prospect of having a child. Often it's something they've longed for, and their emotion is heartwarming. I look at the mothers of school-age children, stretched thin as they try to handle their youngsters' needs together with the pressure of being a "good mother", and wonder: how is it that the excitement and optimism at the birth of a child can morph into such a sense of stress and overwhelm – mitigated, fortunately, by moments of enjoyment and satisfaction – as their child grows older?

Couldn't the enjoyment and satisfaction be present always? How would it be for parents to have the sense that they are giving their children exactly what they need, in terms not only of material "things" but of the support and guidance that they know is going to be fundamental to helping their kids grow up into healthy, happy adults?

When a baby is born, parents go to great lengths to meet its needs, often acquiring a truckload of paraphernalia, including crib, playpen, stroller, toys, bibs, room decorations, and more. The first signs of insecurity have yet to appear. At this stage, while some new parents may still feel unskilled, most are not assailed by doubt. Making use of basic guidelines, even first-timers quickly become proficient at caring for their infant, and a great deal of love and attention is lavished on their baby in the process.

At some point the baby becomes a toddler, who becomes a schoolchild; before parents know it, they have a tween who is turning into a teenager. What worked for the infant no longer does for the schoolchild… and certainly doesn't for the teenager!

So when do things change so radically? Where does the line of communication break down? Is it that children suddenly become difficult and obstreperous when they are teenagers, as many adults like to insist? Mothers and fathers who previously felt sure-footed in parental territory may suddenly find themselves on slippery ground. Indeed, there exists a kind of unspoken alliance amongst parents of teenagers. A roll of the eyes and a sigh say it all when referring to children at that *difficult* age.

Perhaps it is that, what we parents understand as "communication with our children", from an early age, is actually one-sided and deficient, given all of the potential that they really have and that we may be unaware of because it lies somewhere outside of our comfort zone. What frequently occurs is that parents end up as *givers*. We *give*: love, attention, food and even (quality) time, but it often doesn't occur to us – or we don't really bother – to *receive*. Yet the secret (the *magic*, I would say) is in the receiving part.

Our children tell us their stories, share their fears, and express their emotions. How many of us really listen, rather than going on automatic pilot: do we catch ourselves saying their story is *nice* without really having heard it, reassuring them without really taking the time to find out what else is there? It is as though we focus on what we know how to do, never venturing into the uncharted territory that soliciting their input would require. We do things to bring out their potential: read books to them, sign them up for art classes and ferry them to soccer practice or piano lessons, yet we spend precious little time finding out what our children are really about.

There is in fact no specific age at which it becomes important to solicit our child's input. It is something that can and ideally would be there from infancy, but whether or not it happens will depend on us because it is we who hold the key. When we invite our children to share their ideas and opinions, we insert the key into the lock that opens the door to a healthy, satisfying parent-child relationship in which trust and confidence can flourish.

But where does it all start?

Respect, Moral Authority, Authenticity

I believe respect to be a basic human desire and, in so many ways, the cornerstone of child-rearing. I see proof of this in the fact that even small children know when they are not being respected, well before they themselves have assimilated the importance of showing respect for others. Nevertheless, there appear to be some differences of interpretation with regard to what this notion actually represents.

There seems to be a general agreement that children should respect their parents. It is one of the tenets of parenthood, emphasized by experts and seen as a linchpin of our educational system and society as a whole. Much is written about the implications of a loss of respect of young people toward their elders, including the degradation of such institutions as family, school, and law and order, to name just a few.

Some years back, this expectation appeared to be a fairly straightforward matter. Children had to respect their parents, period. Authorities were to be respected, and that included teachers, police officers, religious institutions, and basically, just about anyone older than oneself. At some point in time, coinciding with the emergence of a new sensibility, things changed. It was thought that children should be given more of a say in family life, be able to express themselves freely, and enjoy new liberties.

With this change in sensibility came a wave of insecurity experienced by parents that persists to this day. What was once simple and unequivocal (children were seen and not heard) gradually morphed into a maze of possibilities that kept parents constantly guessing and fretting over whether they were doing a proper job of raising their kids.

Corporal punishment was out; humoring your child was in. The long-held notion of *spare the rod and spoil the child* was overturned, and in its stead came a plethora of works by experts in the field, aimed at parents with children at different ages of development.

Some offered wonderful advice. One of the great pioneers of modern child care, Dr. Spock, invited parents to trust their own instincts, encouraging and empowering them to have a supportive relationship with their children. It was a far cry from the long-held notion that paying attention to children was tantamount to spoiling them.

Children today are far more aware and evolved than ever before, and at the same time need the same, if not more, support and guidance from their parents than kids have always required. Parents may implicitly recognize that their children need something different from them, but are frequently unsure as to what that is, let alone how to provide it. Our sense, sometimes only vaguely or subliminally perceived, that doing so would require a part of us to change as well, may be one of the biggest hurdles for adults looking for a new way to relate to their children.

To their credit, most parents would like to be the best parents they can be for their children. The change, and the new paradigm, involves seeing our children as complete and whole from the moment they are born, at the same time as we create a safe space for them to grow and flourish. Safety is created by providing discipline and guidance and making the corrections to their behavior that we feel are necessary. In this safe space, if we allow it to happen, their creativity can blossom. It's possible to be firm without being rigid. We're providing a context of security and stability through the values we convey, which will likely include, among other things, making sure our children are polite and respectful of other adults, as well as their own peers.

Yet combining the notion of "discipline" with "respect for the child" is disconcerting to many people. It may be difficult to comprehend for parents for whom the idea of "respecting" their children conjures up images of pampered brats who rule the roost.

Respect for our children does not mean we cannot disagree with them, correct their behavior or tell them that we know best, as may indeed be the case. It includes, however, a willingness to allow them to be who they are, with the understanding that they are unique and will find their own way to be in this world if we let them do so.

But this approach also demands a new awareness on our part. The more we are willing to show up as who we are, as real and genuine, the more respect we'll earn from our children; in turn, giving us the moral authority to demand that they do the same with others.

What does moral authority have to do with it?

As our children grow older, there will come a time when that will be pretty much all we have left to count on in engaging with them.

The real issue – much dreaded by parents perhaps for this very reason – comes not when children are 4 or 5 years old, but at the age of 14 or 15, when they have long since become aware of our failings even if we have vehemently denied having any. The same qualities we want to see in our kids: honesty, openness, and truthfulness, we can model for them. And where we fail to be models, "telling on ourselves" is usually the best policy.

When children are small they haven't got much of a grasp of our shortcomings. Our imperfections only appear to them gradually (fortunately so, some might say..!). However, small things, such as saying we're sorry for blowing our stack or not delivering on something we promised, lay the foundation for empathy and sincerity in them when they are older, and build trust. The more honest we are about who we are, the more we will inspire honesty in our kids.

In fact, wouldn't it be great to be appreciated by our children for our authenticity? If we stop to consider it, our greatest feelings of satisfaction in whatever we do come from being authentic. And is that not a model that we can hold up to our children? Part of being authentic means having the ability to acknowledge our shortcomings. Our children are keenly aware of when we are being authentic and when we aren't. When we have the courage to admit that there are things we don't know, or that sometimes we wished we could do better, they respect us for our authenticity and learn from it.

It also gives them permission to be less than perfect themselves, something that is not only liberating, but surprisingly, allows them to do far better, because the stigma associated with failure isn't there holding them back. Indeed, there is so much we can learn – or relearn – from our children if we allow them to be who they are. Redefining some of the words in our own vocabulary (*"failure"* is only one) could be one of the benefits we enjoy as a result.

To paraphrase *The Prophet,* our children are the arrows that are sent forth by the Archer's steady hand, and as parents, we are the bow that must bend to provide the momentum that they will need to go swift and far. Yet it is not we who decide how they will reach their mark, or even what that mark will be. We usher them into a future that they themselves will create, and it may well be a future that is far beyond our wildest imagination.

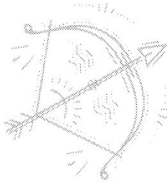

CHAPTER 3

Living in
the Place of Possibility

O ne day my seven-year old son said to me, "What if a child asked you, 'How did you get to do all the things you wanted to do?' What would you tell them?"

I replied, "I would say: 'You know when you dream about what you want to do or be… when you're in that dream, and in it there's no one telling you that you can't do it? Keep on dreaming that dream.'"

We have all had the experience of being in a wonderful dream. Yet so often, in our own lives and in our children's lives, we close the door to dreaming.

We are taught at a young age that our dreams are not an option. We're told, and eventually become convinced, that dreaming is an unproductive use of our time that will only get us into trouble. So we learn to put away our dreams on a back shelf somewhere, like so much memorabilia to be looked upon with nostalgia as we grow older: the vestiges of our childhood innocence.

Much of our attitude toward dreaming appears to be based on the unquestioned assumption that time spent dreaming is time wasted. So, I ask, why have we as human beings been given such a special ability to dream? For what was this particular ability intended? And just when did dreaming get a bad name?

Children dream naturally. Often incipient and undefined in early childhood, our youngsters' dreams become invested with greater depth and meaning as they mature, if not discouraged along the way. Like stem cells that are initially undifferentiated and only gradually evolve into the function for which they have been programmed, our children's dreams may appear diffuse at first, but gradually begin to take on a recognizable form, specific to each child.

Indeed, if we can see beyond the temptation to shut the dream down, and allow it to blossom in its own way, we allow our children to manifest their own particular expression of godliness in this world.

I take the stand that our dreams are an expression of who we are: a manifestation of our essence. Despite this essence quality of our dreams – or perhaps because of it – a vast many educational and social norms conspire to keep us small and flat, discouraging us from ever actually "running the risk" of going for our dreams.

Fear and Disappointment

Fear is one of the biggest obstacles to living our dreams, and a force to be reckoned with. So much of what we tell our children – ostensibly, to "protect" them – is prompted by our own fears. When we discourage them from believing they can do certain things so they "won't be disappointed", it's often because we ourselves fear disappointment and what we think it represents, both for them and for us. Our unwillingness to let our children pursue their dreams – indeed, to allow ourselves to pursue our own dreams – is generally fueled by an aversion to the disappointment we sense it will bring.

So what is it about disappointment that is so bad that we need to protect our children from it?

What if our perception of disappointment were actually keeping us from seeing the same situation in a different light: as an opportunity, an achievement, and cause for celebration!

The label "disappointment" is like the seal on a door that can't be opened for fear of treading the unknown territory that lies on the other side. Many wonderful projects are imagined but never materialize, essentially because their creators convince themselves that they aren't viable or worthwhile. The ability to convince ourselves that we shouldn't / don't need to / don't really want to do something is often our response when fear of failure begins to loom.

We are set up for this belief in childhood, when we are taught that making mistakes is to be avoided at all costs.

A New Perspective

Disappointment is no more than a perspective. When our children go for their dream, they may not achieve it at first. In that case, more often than not, they will attempt to achieve it some other way, or the dream itself will shift. But the steps they have taken toward their goal have brought them that much closer to where they are headed, be it their original goal or something different. They don't experience this natural shifting and honing of their dream as a disappointment, unless they are taught that it is. As adults we use the word "failure" a lot to describe what is essentially a process of trial and error: something that in many settings is in fact encouraged as a useful and necessary part of the process of achieving a goal.

We also know that children – that is, until they learn to take on our mannerisms and, yes, our fears – often see things differently than we do, from a place of openness, curiosity and opportunity. If not told to do otherwise, small children will investigate and eat bugs, climb onto or over anything that looks challenging, and find in the most mundane objects the props they need to stage their own fantasies.

In fact, what young children take away from their encounter with reality is more often the "wonder of discovery", than "disappointment". And yes, the games they create are full of winners and losers, and endless competitions among themselves to determine who is the fastest, strongest, and bravest.

What would happen if we actually encouraged them to fulfill their dreams?

From my training as a coach I learned the importance of dreams as the motor that drives us toward action – and action is important because just wishing for something isn't enough. Yet as we grow, we often come to acquire the belief that we can't have our dreams. In fact, what coaching does, in great measure, is give us back the capacity to dream and experience wonder that we relinquished on the way to adulthood.

Imagine if we never lost this ability in the first place! Even if we as parents were not allowed to follow our own dreams growing up, we can offer this gift to our children. We can allow them to imagine all of the possibilities – in fact, encourage them to do so – and not be the straightjacket that forces them into the straight and narrow… into a model that makes us feel comfortable because it's aimed at doing away with the guesswork, or at the very least, the nagging worry about how they are going to succeed in a world which we are aware is fraught with uncertainty.

How we look at uncertainty will of course depend on our perspective. There are many of us for whom uncertainty is exciting. Not knowing what comes next makes us feel alive. For others, it's scary. Such individuals frequently prefer predictability. Yet there is an inherent contradiction in wanting for our children a safe, predictable future that would avoid the vicissitudes of our own past experiences, and at the same time wanting them to grow and blossom into creative, fulfilled beings.

It is the nature of humankind to learn through experience. Indeed, the real learning that makes us grow as human beings comes from encountering challenges, at which we often fail and occasionally succeed. When everything is made safe and foreseeable, learning doesn't happen; that is, until something we can't control – such as a health problem or financial difficulties – arises to present a challenge from which we can learn and grow.

Creativity also springs from a place of curiosity, or the need for change. *"Necessity is the mother of invention"* is the popular wisdom intended to remind us that we tap our creativity to the utmost when the going gets tough. It's a maxim that alludes to the importance of circumstances in forcing us to stretch ourselves (since human nature itself is often resistant to change).

So what does this have to do with our kids?

It's about making it okay for them to try and fail, mess up and start again, and to dream up what they want to do. If children, from their earliest childhood, learned that trying and failing were an opportunity instead of a setback, they would be prepared to seize opportunities that arise rather than shrinking from them to avoid disappointment. They would know that, regardless of the outcome, there is always something valuable to be learned.

Starting when my own child was very small I made a habit of showing him how to turn setbacks around. When he would come home from school, upset because he had gotten a bad grade on an exam when he thought he had studied what he needed to know, or when he was careless and broke something he loved, or when he said something to a classmate that he realized had made that boy angry, I would say to him, *"if you want to take some time feeling upset, go ahead, take ten or fifteen minutes and be mad or upset about what happened. Then think about what you can learn from it, so you can do better the next time."* What I didn't do was tell him *"never mind, it doesn't matter"*, or *"just forget about it"*, or in some other way try to get him to pretend that the situation wasn't important.

Getting him to think about what he could learn from a negative situation changed it from being one in which he was a "victim" of his circumstances to one in which he gained control, because he got to decide what to do with the experience: in this case, get learning from it.

I never added, *"...so you can get it right the next time"*, because it often happens that we make the same mistakes (or versions thereof), more than once before we finally learn to avoid or overcome them.

The Power of Choice

In fact, it didn't feel honest to set the expectation that by learning from the experience he would automatically prevent similar situations from occurring in the future, since learning is a gradual process that builds on previous experiences. My son might make a mistake, decide to learn from it and do better, and still make another similar mistake because there was something else to be learned, or the learning needed to be repeated to sink in.

What was most important was the element of *Choice*. He got to choose how to turn the experience into learning, as opposed to just getting upset.

A bit of history is worthwhile here, because this technique is useful for adults and children alike. I actually developed this way of thinking before my child was born, to combat my own natural tendency to fret – or occasionally obsess – when things went wrong. I discovered it was a great way to regain control by replacing the bad feelings that the experience brought on with the determination to change whatever it was, for the next time.

Nevertheless, for first-timers wanting to apply this strategy, I feel I must share the difficulty I encountered in the beginning, trying to push aside the negative thoughts that would assail me while I was trying to latch on to what I could take away that would be positive. Whether an interview went badly, or a less-than-ideal conversation with a colleague created a rift, or I unintentionally scraped the side of my car and was faced with a hefty bill to repair the damage, I would likely be invaded by the negative feelings of: "if only I'd done it differently... *Now* what will I do?" ...and in the case of a relationship gone awry, "How will this affect me in the future?" to name only a few of the feelings that typically surfaced.

What I now know is that I can't know how it will affect me in the future, since all I have is right now; I can't do it differently because it's already done (so it's a waste of time even thinking about it), and "what will I do now?" has changed from being a source of worry to becoming an inquiry about what I want to do with the experience.

It wasn't easy at first, because the negative thoughts were persistent. Just as I later taught my son to do, the tactic I finally adopted when invaded by negative thoughts was first to allow myself some time – say, ten or fifteen minutes — to actually dwell on them and feel the impact they had on me.

Next I would imagine a sliding door or curtain pulled across my mind to shut those thoughts out, turning my attention instead to what I could take from the negative experience that would be useful and serve me in the future. At first it was a clear, two-step process; an initial, almost physical movement of sliding a door closed to shut out the negative thoughts; then a clear, intentional focus on the positive: What is my learning from this for the future?

However, there was an unexpected benefit that accrued from this strategy as I continued to use it. There came a time when I no longer needed to give myself permission to dwell on negative feelings before pushing them away. Switching from negative to positive became quicker, easier, and finally, automatic. At some point I was finally able to skip the first part of the process altogether.

Choice as Part of our Lives

It boiled down to: "so what am I going to do with this now?" It was something I'd taught myself, but by the time my son was a teenager he had already surpassed me in his ability to receive "bad" news and take it in stride. The ability to choose became a theme for us. Emphasizing choice turned out to be a way of getting him to take charge of his decisions, and generated an awareness of his freedom and responsibility in choosing, irrespective of the circumstances.

One example was the conversations we had about our family. I would tell my son, still a youngster, "your father and I both have some very good qualities, but they're different. And of course we're not perfect. But you get to pick the best from each of us. You get to choose which things you get from your father and which you get from me."

Now, growing up I'm quite sure no one ever told me that I could decide for myself how I would be by consciously choosing the parental traits that I liked the best, but I do know that what usually happens when one unconsciously adopts parental traits is that the good ones come with a lot of less desirable ones. Children experience both in their parents, so what an eye-opener it is for them to be able to value the good, and consciously leave aside whatever is going to become excess baggage for them later in life!

Of course, the first step is being able to admit to our kids that we aren't quite perfect. The difficulty in doing so may come from our own reluctance to step down from our lofty perch on some imagined pedestal, but – news flash – our youngsters eventually become very aware of their parents' shortcomings anyway, even though they may not actually voice this discovery at first.

Understandably, while my son was still young, the opportunity that he enjoyed at home to make choices was mostly taken for granted. It would never have occurred to him that he was fortunate in that respect. Indeed, he tended to think that a lot of his friends had it better than he did. So-and-so went on fun holidays, others got to stay up later in the evening than he did, and so on.

One day he came home from school telling me that his teacher had given the class the homework assignment of writing about their family. Jokingly, I said, *"Okay, but you'd better write only about the good things,"* to which he responded, eyes wide, *"What* good things?"

Clearly, for him good things meant treats, or frequent trips to the movies, the amusement park or the bowling alley. The fact that we regularly conversed as a family and involved our youngster in our discussions, allowed him considerable leeway to express himself and took an interest in what he did, was just "business as usual".

With time, he learned to value the opportunities he had at home to make decisions in matters that concerned him. Within the boundaries that we set for him, and which expanded as he grew older, he was always given some freedom to choose.

One example would be his penchant, when he was still young – perhaps 10 or 11 years old – for signing up for extracurricular activities: essentially sports.

Recalling my own placid life in the suburbs of New York, back in the days when nothing ever really happened, or was expected to happen, and our free time after school and on weekends was spent outside climbing trees, playing softball in the street, or going to a friend's house – or, in winter, skating on the pond near our house or playing board games – I was a bit concerned at the number of activities that were filling his free time.

I could see that in addition to his long school day – which as in most Spanish schools, went from 9 am to 5 pm – he needed time to do homework… and, I thought, sometimes to just do nothing. Thinking back I remembered, as a child, lying on the grass in the front yard looking up at the sky, and spending – what was it, minutes, hours?…. watching the clouds float above me and change shape, or lying face down on the lawn to explore the teeming life that scurried between the blades of grass.

The point was not so much what my youngster would actually do with his free time. Rather, some of the articles on child-rearing that I had read warned of the dangers of overloading children with guided activities and depriving them of the necessary downtime in which to give free rein to their creativity and imagination. At that point I knew that reading was not one of my son's favorite activities, but I did think that downtime just to play with friends would be beneficial. I had some concerns about how full his days had become.

At one point, when he was about ten, he was going to soccer practice twice a week, to the swimming pool three times a week, and to ballroom dancing class on Thursdays and Fridays after school. There were also piano lessons on Tuesdays, and on most Saturdays there were soccer matches and, occasionally, swim meets, since he had begun competitive swimming as well. In the summer he signed up for tennis, which he continued to practice on many weekends throughout the year.

Apart from the occasional overwhelm I felt in the role of chauffeur as I raced from soccer field to swimming pool, I worried that he was taking on too much. It certainly seemed so to me… even granting that I was not as energetic as my indefatigable son, who always had endless stamina for the things he loved to do.

Physical activity was something he enjoyed, and in most of the sports he took on, he excelled. We could always count on his grade in gym to bring up the overall grade average on his school report card; he was just one of those kids who took naturally to sports. I occasionally wondered whether, had we gotten him to concentrate on any one of the many sports he tried out, he might have reached a level of professional competence. But he was not interested in focusing on a single sport, and when the coaches at his pool asked him to commit to training every day of the week – reflecting the additional demand placed on young people competing in individual, rather than team sports – he decided to abandon competitive swimming entirely.

My concerns about his becoming overloaded turned out to be unfounded. In the beginning, his natural enthusiasm and curiosity prompted him to take on many different types of activity; however, eventually the choice occurred naturally. When he reached the stage where his different interests began to conflict, he made the decision to pull out of some of his activities in favor of others.

Underlying all of the above, of course, was the fact that his grades were reasonably good. Could they have been better? Most certainly they could have... We of course knew it, and it was something frequently repeated by his teachers. Still, when I think about the balance between academic achievement and extracurricular activities –and with the perspective that time affords – I am convinced that engaging in activities outside of the school environment has a positive influence.

I was also aware that part of the reason he didn't get better grades was that, like many kids, he didn't make an effort in the areas that weren't his strengths, and the school system – as is unfortunately often the case – wasn't particularly geared toward making academic subjects more compelling for youngsters who weren't initially drawn to those particular areas of study.

In that respect, my conclusion that his grade average was not directly related to the time spent on activities outside of school prompted me to give my son more leeway in deciding what he wanted to do. Had he really been struggling at school I would undoubtedly have asked him to choose activities that allowed him additional time for schoolwork. The choice of where to focus his energy would ultimately have been his, though he would also have had the responsibility of demonstrating that the activities he chose didn't keep him from his studies.

Labeling Them Shuts an Open Door

It's common for children to do well in subjects that come easily to them, and to lag in those areas that they find dull or uninteresting. My child was no different. His excellent grades in math were offset by his poor grades in history and social studies.

I'm still convinced that if history or social studies were taught in a way that engaged children's imagination, he and a number of other children like him would have gotten "hooked" and fallen in love with it. The proof is that in high school he had a teacher who for the first time conveyed to him the joy of learning about history. This teacher turned history into a story, engaging his students' attention and imagination… (which suggests to me that he undoubtedly had a good time teaching it too..!). It became one of my son's favorite classes.

Without entering into a discourse on the shortcomings of our school system, I want to challenge the temptation to categorize individual students as "good" in some subjects and "poor" in others. This kind of label actually predisposes kids to shy away from certain subjects that, under other circumstances, they might actually find compelling.

The truth is, interests can develop in any area. It's something I learned in my early years working as a conference interpreter, a profession in which hours are often devoted to studying technical subjects to prepare for a job. I discovered that if one approaches a subject with an open mind, some of the driest subjects are potentially interesting. I tried to pass on this curiosity and love of learning to my son as I encouraged him in his studies.

Typically, I was the one looking up a word to be sure of its meaning, or checking something in the encyclopedia to get it right. For many years my child didn't appear to want to be bothered picking up a dictionary, preferring to "get the idea", as he said, rather than taking the time to find the precise meaning of a word. For me it was clear that "getting the idea" was a euphemism for "I can't be bothered looking it up".

When, more often than not, he decided he didn't need to check a word that he didn't know, I would say something like: "Well, *I want to know* what it means so *I'll* look it up" (and then would share with him the definition I had found), or as was more often the case, if it was a word I knew, I would tell him what it meant, jokingly adding something like *"I can't believe that my own son doesn't want to know what a word means... you must be adopted!"* I never made an issue out of it, although I confess I secretly wished he would find religion (mine...!) and fall in love with words.

My own curiosity and interest must have rubbed off on him at some point. Although it didn't become apparent until he was in high school, my son was finally bitten by the "learning bug". Now, he is the one perusing the dictionary and debating nuances in meaning. There isn't enough time in the day for the things he wants to study, and he undertakes new learning challenges with enthusiasm and a sense of purpose.

As I've already mentioned, there is a clear tendency to categorize kids, who are often labeled as "more science-oriented", or "more artistic". Subjects that come more easily to children appear to point to the route that they are predestined to take. Some youngsters may struggle with studies in general – which, again, I take as an indication that some things in our school system need to change – and a few appear to excel at whatever they tackle. But the great majority appear to have a natural inclination for some area of study while finding other areas more of a challenge.

I remember, when my son was about ten, being told by his guidance counselor that he was definitely a science and math type. I myself had thought as much because when he was small he loved solving simple addition and subtraction equations, and often, en route to his child care center in the mornings, it became a way to pass the time. He would ask me for a "problem", I would say something like, "13 plus 38" and he would come up with the answer. He thought it was great fun, and always asked for more.

Nonetheless, although there appeared to be a definite bias in favor of numbers, other abilities began to emerge along the way. Interestingly, when the guidance counselor issued her prediction that he would pursue math or science, she also added that his gifts apparently didn't lie with languages or the humanities. Despite the evidence that supported her statement, her remark struck me as a rather sweeping pronouncement. My child clearly had a flair for math. He also (to my dismay) had at one point categorically asserted that reading was not for him. Since I had already reconciled myself with the fact that he might never find a love of reading, I didn't make it into an issue, although a part of me continued to harbor the hope of a potential interest in language and books lying dormant in him, one day to emerge!

As it turned out, in addition to growing up speaking three languages (which, I should note, in itself didn't indicate a "gift" because no particular effort was expended in learning them; they were spoken at home) he went on to pick up some French, and to gain a good command of conversational Italian at the age of 19, when he took 5 months off from school to work on an Italian cruise ship. He subsequently decided to further pursue his studies in Italian, and then French. Of particular note, his interest not only in language, but music, prompted me to consider how stereotyping our children can ultimately deprive them of learning experiences that would enrich their lives.

The Potential Yet to Appear

On the one hand, it seems to make sense to encourage children to use their natural abilities to the full, pursuing studies and activities in areas they take to naturally. On the other, by encouraging them to explore other areas that may initially appear more challenging, we help them to broaden their range and discover new fields of interest that can make their personal and professional lives more satisfying.

Living in the place of possibility means that we are open to the potential not only of what is immediately apparent (in my son's case, his affinity for numbers), but also, of those abilities that have not yet come to the fore. By refraining from categorizing our kids, we allow them to investigate areas that would otherwise be ruled out as unworthy of attention.

To some extent it is logical and natural for us – and our kids – to focus on the things that come easily: for some it will be drawing; for others, dreaming up inventions or learning a foreign language. However, the tendency to dismiss other areas ("I'm no good at math", or "history is boring") may have to do with the perceived need to be *good at"* something for it to be interesting. The prevailing idea is: devote your energies to what you're good at; don't waste time pursuing subjects at which you're not naturally gifted.

This emphasis on focusing on what we are best at is a corollary of the idea that it's important to excel at whatever we do. Much like the quest for perfection (dealt with elsewhere in this book), the need to excel – something qualitatively different from the notion of "doing one's best" – results in many lost opportunities to explore other potential areas of interest.

It is indeed true that great satisfaction is obtained in using our natural talents, but if we were to take away the pressure of having to be "good at" whatever it is and replace that with the enjoyment of discovering something new, I believe we would unearth many new areas of interest that not only would engage us, but would make use of abilities that might otherwise languish. By letting go of the need to excel and being willing to work at something because we really want to learn, we can indeed not only learn, but occasionally... even excel! The unspoken influence of a society – and often, the complicity of parents and teachers – that measures children by their degree of accomplishment, is a powerful force to contend with, because it makes other pursuits unrelated to the child's main abilities appear to be an unproductive use of their time.

On the one hand, at school children are required to study different subjects and are pushed to get good grades. On the other, it's often assumed that if they do not have an innate interest in a particular subject they will toil to get a passing grade, and that the only reason they are studying it in the first place is to fulfill a requirement; implicit is the assumption that they will neither take an interest in it nor further pursue it once it ceases to be mandatory in the curriculum. For many teachers it is easier to "sell" their course to the talented few who take to the subject easily than to engage the attention and enthusiasm of the remaining lot who persist in finding it tedious and uninspiring.

Granted, teachers have a lot to cope with given the diversity of most student bodies and the demands of the school system and challenges that our society has generated. However, we can all hopefully remember at least one teacher who inspired us, whose love of the subject they taught was contagious, kindling our interest and curiosity, making us want to know more. If, despite the constraints, more emphasis were placed on the joy of learning rather than solely on meeting curricular requisites, children might actually be able to enjoy learning subjects at which they do not initially excel.

Taking the pressure off means that children's self-esteem is not on the line when they invest time in something without an immediate return in the form of "good grades". By making it not about achievement but about the learning process itself, children might separate the learning from the result, and acquire good study skills to boot. Of all of the study skills I have seen, there is nothing that beats curiosity. Children have naturally inquisitive minds; it is the judgment that lies behind their perceived ability – or inability – to master a subject that dampens their enthusiasm and "turns them off" whatever that subject might happen to be.

If teachers and parents could take the pressure off so that learning were enjoyable rather than being, as is so often the case, perceived as a chore; if education, rather than playing consistently to the willing, motivated few, also embraced those who lag behind, not only allowing but encouraging them to dream, our educational system – indeed, our entire society – would look quite different.

Why and When did we Change?

We actually know how to embrace our children in this way. When they are still small, before they have entered the competitive, grade-based school system (and perhaps excluding the offspring of some particularly achievement-driven parents), there is little or no pressure on them to be better at one thing than another, nor to do much more than discover whatever is new to them – and of course, challenge themselves, as they naturally do.

Parents cheer their toddlers on and extol their achievements; children respond by mustering their best drawing, or running their fastest race, or throwing themselves wholeheartedly into whatever it is that they are up to. For the parents of these tots, the results don't count as much as the child's individual sense of achievement. Granted, there are parents who begin early trying to pinpoint their toddler's budding talents, but most adults are simply happy and eager to celebrate their children's feats, however big or small.

Then, at some point, we forget to be enthusiastic. It becomes all about finding out and capitalizing on what our kids do best, and picking a good, safe course of study.

How does this happen to us? Just when does our transitory experience of the place of possibility morph into a quest for security and dependability?

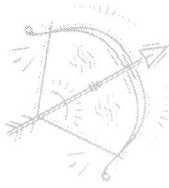

CHAPTER 4

· · · · · · · · · · · · ·

A World without Fear

O ne of the things that make small children so engaging is the curiosity and fearlessness they bring to trying new things. Children constantly challenge themselves to do things that are "out of their comfort zone", as we like to say, starting with the very act of walking. Can we imagine an infant, after falling several times while attempting to stand, deciding that she might as well remain seated because it's the safest option? And as we all know, children will seldom walk if they can run.

Children not only challenge themselves; they show off shamelessly for their friends as well: *"Look what I can do!"*, or *"Bet you can't ....
(fill in the blank)"*, in a spirit of competition that pushes them to try things beyond what they already know. Kids will call attention to themselves *("Look, mommy, look!")* as they jump off the diving board for the first time, do their first cartwheel, or try to balance a ball on their finger.

We cheer our children on as they take their first steps, clapping our hands and urging them on with encouraging words. Our child's first random scribbles on a piece of paper are received with exclamations of enthusiasm and praise. We show inordinate delight in every accomplishment of our little ones, setting the stage for future achievements that are bigger and more ambitious.

As they get older, children naturally seek out obstacles to overcome.

How many of us have seen a child that is running along, comes across a lone object – such as a log or a piece of fencing that is in the way – and then deliberately clambers over the obstacle rather than skirting it? There is something about trying, succeeding (or failing), learning and progressing for the next time, that children seem to know how to do naturally. It's something that many of us as adults no longer know how, or allow ourselves, to do.

I have given this observation much thought. When my child was small, his natural enthusiasm seemed boundless. I noticed it was something that all children, whether they are bold or shy, slower or quicker, appear to have: an insatiable curiosity and innate desire to stretch their own limits.

More than once, when practicing piano, instead of doing scales properly my son would race through them, little fingers scrabbling hastily over the keys as he rushed to see how fast he could play. The presence of an observer – particularly someone his own age – only made the challenge more rousing.

It felt wrong to curb this natural zest and enthusiasm. I wanted to be clear on the limits, yet allow space for my child to give free rein to what came to him naturally. Because these were things that all children did, I suppose I assumed that they were natural and important, and that they were *meant* to be done this way by playful youngsters.

Of course, as our children grow they expand their abilities: "graduating" from a baby seat to an adult chair, and from the "kiddy rides" at the amusement park to those with an age or height requirement, are rites of passage. Climbing trees, racing bikes, and outdoing and outperforming friends and playmates are challenges they love. Even squeezing cookie dough through a press and decorating and baking their creations are opportunities for our youngsters to test their skills.

With children, there is a shamelessly unselfconscious desire to excel, and also, little time spent dwelling on minor setbacks. Small children who are put in an environment with a new language quickly adapt, using nonverbal communication to express themselves until they eventually gain verbal proficiency, without once feeling embarrassed about making grammatical errors.

It seemed to me, intuitively, that if children were so naturally able to challenge themselves and adapt, this quality was certainly one that was important to keep. I also knew that, despite having had loving parents myself, I had my own share of fears and limiting beliefs, acquired along the way to adulthood. How could I keep the same thing from happening to my son?

Stilling the Fears

Some of my fears for my child (will anyone reading this book recognize them?) were: What if he *fails*? I let my child grow up blissful, and then he encounters the difficulties of *real life*. He's going off with the

Boy Scouts to bike around the island of Majorca and he's only 11. *What if something happens?* The school has sent out a note informing parents that children over the age of 12 can no longer ride to school on the charter bus; they must take public transport (or be driven) to school. *What if something happens along the way?*

Almost as big as those fears was my concern that thinking and obsessing about them would somehow make them actually happen, so I put a great deal of effort into trying *not* to think about them. Here I give credit to my son's father, who was much more relaxed about letting him do things on his own, and as for my tendency to worry, well, I chalked it up to having grown up in New York … but then again, I grew up in the relatively placid suburbs, so where did my fears come from? I can't remember either of my own parents instilling great fear in me about strangers, or about my being off on my own or with my playmates.

I even grew up at a time when, on Halloween, we would go off to *trick or treat* on our own, venturing far and wide in our costumes, armed with pillowcases to load up with (hopefully) candy and (less thrillingly) apples. We would actually even manage to come home and drop off our first payload before heading off to visit more houses before it got dark. No one ever fretted that something bad might happen to you; you were in the neighborhood, and everyone knew you … (not that anyone would have recognized you anyway under that sheet or in your skeleton costume !).

So again, where did those fears emerge? More importantly, was there any way I could avoid passing my own fears on to my son? Here, I almost wrote "my own *unreasonable* fears", but then it came to me:

What is *unreasonable?* Perhaps what needs to be conveyed to kids is not fear, but reasonable caution. Such as: if strangers stop a car to ask you directions, take a step back, rather than towards the car, before you answer. That kind of thing.

I don't think we are aware of how many negative messages we voice, in the guise of good advice, all given with the best of intentions. A part of me wanted to preserve my son's mischievous spirit and playfulness. There was a wholeness that I wanted to keep… like seeing a perfectly decorated cake, and knowing that once sliced, it will never be as perfect again. It will be different. It felt as though there was something precious there to be safeguarded.

In retrospect, not instilling fear in my child was probably the best thing I ever did. Although I didn't want to make him unnecessarily fearful (and therefore bit my tongue more than once when the words that wanted to come out were *"don't do that; it's dangerous"* or some variation thereof, when he attempted something new), I didn't realize the extent to which not instilling fear actually allowed him to keep much of the confident, trusting disposition that he had as a young child.

Years later, friends of his would be surprised at how he achieved things seemingly effortlessly. If he needed to find someone to help him on a project, that person would somehow materialize. If contacts were needed, he would not only find them, but obtain from them what he needed. More importantly, when working on projects with classmates in secondary school, and later at university, he would willingly dispense any information that could be of use to them, and would freely share his creative ideas with others.

I initially wondered if he was being naive. He "gave away" some very good ideas, never appearing to feel proprietary about any of them. The notion of being possessive about his own ideas never seemed to cross his mind. Even when he was older, he would be disarmingly forthright in asking others' critical opinion of his thoughts on a particular project. Where someone else might have remained close-mouthed, my son would openly discuss his views.

Over the years, I've been impressed with how his straightforward, candid manner has garnered results that run counter to the "common sense" learning that we acquire from childhood, whereby we must jealously guard our own ideas and be vigilant toward those who might "steal" them. On the contrary, his enthusiasm and openness have attracted to him not only people who have been interested in supporting his projects but, I would venture to say, the situations in which his projects could take shape and flourish.

Our Experience vs. Theirs

One day, over at the local gym, I came across a couple and their daughter, about age 3, in the swimming pool. I watched with interest as the little girl gleefully made her way around the pool unaided, wriggling and paddling with great energy between her mother and father. I remarked to the mother how impressed I was with her daughter's confidence.

The mother responded with a smile, *"Yes, she's always game to try anything that's fun…"* She then added, with what appeared to be a touch of resignation, *"…though sooner or later she'll learn things aren't so easy."*

I was struck by her answer. Clearly, the underlying message was that life's hard lessons would eventually divest this child of her pluckiness, which was endearing in a three year-old but wouldn't survive the transition to adulthood.

Her words got me thinking, again, about how we respond to our children's natural enthusiasm and eagerness to test themselves.

I wondered… Does "managing our children's expectations" do anything other than put a lid on their aspirations and the joy of pursuing their dream?

When we assume life is hard, and prepare our children to deal with it (so it won't be so painful……), are we actually *setting them up* for failure? Do our well-intentioned warnings about the limitations and risks they will face in life in fact create a mold into which they will ultimately fit? What is more, when we warn them about the limitations they will face, are we actually taking clean, untouched ground and erecting barriers that, rather than holding the dangers out, will keep our children caught inside?

Perhaps our own setbacks, and the painful experiences that have shaped the way we look at the world, are no more than just that: *experiences*. The picture of Reality we paint for our children is actually the sum total of our own experiences, ups and downs, frustrations, and grievances. What if their Reality were to be something entirely different?

Of course, that notion flies in the face of our acquired prejudices. Innocence is charming in the very young, but considered a liability as one grows older. What would it be like to keep the innocence… or at the very least, the fresh, candid gaze that pre-dates our assimilation into the *prevailing view of Reality*, which holds that for the great majority of people life is just plain hard?

What if the obstacles and setbacks that naturally occur in life, rather than being the barbs of a hostile Reality, were in fact the raw material from which we grow and develop? Very little is learned, indeed, unless we are put to the test; it's the way we humans progress and thrive. Ultimately, I get to choose: I can see "failure" as the calamitous proof that *I'm not good enough*, or embrace it as an opportunity to *expand my learning and grow*.

Fear of Success

I will probably never know how much of my son's confidence came from his personality type, and how much from his upbringing. He may be the best judge of that. However, regardless of whether our children are outgoing or introverted, daring or timid, we can help instill in them the belief that they have something that is uniquely theirs to discover and develop.

From the time my son was in grade school I would tell him that he had gifts, including intelligence and talents, that were his to use. I would add that those gifts did not make him better than anyone else, though they in some way characterized him. He got to choose whether or not to use his talents, just as other people could choose whether to use theirs, but I stressed his responsibility for using them. Why else would he have been given them if not to realize their full potential?

At the age of 7 or 8 he appeared oblivious to this reasoning, still getting into trouble at school on more than one occasion for his monkeyshines in class, while resisting our attempts at making him more aware of the importance of buckling down and applying himself to make the most out of what there was to learn.

Leaving aside the shortcomings of a school system whose determination to feed all students into a common educational hopper has in many ways become outmoded (certainly a topic for another book..!) we felt that he could be getting more out of his studies instead of simply coasting through subjects he liked, where his grades were good, and trying to devote as little time as possible to those he did not, where his grades were borderline.

It must have been in his early teen years when he finally voiced his concern with being seen by his classmates as stuck up or conceited if he pursued his interests to the full. Outside of the family environment, where he was encouraged to make use of his abilities, social pressure not to stand out appeared to have generated a reluctance to be seen as excelling at things that came to him more easily than to his classmates, and certainly didn't motivate him to work harder at those that didn't.

He appeared to perceive that making the most of his talents was an affront to those who didn't have the interest or motivation to do likewise. The result appeared to be a kind of internal tug-of-war that accompanied him for a number of years.

It wasn't until the age of 19 that he learned about a concept now commonly known as "the law of attraction". This notion, widely understood to be a way of manifesting things in one's life, actually rests squarely on an underlying principle, which is that this is done by connecting with one's essence or "authentic self". My son understood at last, from someone other than his parents, that when you are the best you can be, you're not competing with anyone else because each person has a unique combination of gifts and talents, and his or her own way of using them.

It didn't matter how this epiphany came to him; it was simply the right moment for him to take it in. What was important was that it hit home, striking a chord that resonated; connecting him with something that he undoubtedly knew deep down but had been reluctant to give voice to, out of "deference" to those around him.

It's common for fears to surface when we take on (or *contemplate* taking on) something that involves a risk of failure. In this case, it was the risk of being *successful* and possibly offending friends, who might perceive him as "pretentious", that were at the origin of my son's reluctance to use his talents to the full. It dawned on me how most of us live our lives squeezed between the two constraints: don't fail, don't win. We find our lives reduced to something that is acceptable to others, then feel obligated to find justifications to explain why we haven't done better for ourselves. This belief that starts in childhood persists long into our adult years.

Fear of failure often goes hand in hand with another limiting belief, already mentioned: the accepted wisdom that life is hard. This notion, which holds that only the fortunate or very gifted few ever really make it and that our circumstances determine our possibilities of success, keeps us squarely in our comfort zone. From here, we relinquish our responsibility for making our lives better or achieving the success that we dream of; it's easy to point to "the way things are" as though they are written in stone. The logical conclusion is: if the odds are stacked against us, why try and risk failing? Why risk trying to change something that we have decided doesn't depend on us? Our fear of failure gets the better of our desire to succeed.

How many of us have passed on this very same notion to our children, exhorting them to play it safe, *just in case*?

How We Disempower Ourselves

But from the standpoint of who we are, and more importantly, who we are becoming, why should we categorize anyone as better, or more fortunate or successful than ourselves, based on what we perceive as the advantages that they enjoy? Why should people be considered – indeed, why should we consider ourselves – to be *deprived* or *privileged* depending on the circumstances of our lives? There are people who have grown up under adverse conditions who openly admit that it shaped their character and their determination to succeed. Was that person actually deprived, or privileged?

The circumstances exist. What we do with them is our choice. The circumstances may be benign and advantageous, or arduous and troubled. Nevertheless, we are always deciding, making the choice to be run by, or go beyond, our circumstances.

We may find ourselves falling prey to feelings of inadequacy, the result of our tendency to compare ourselves to others. Indeed, our feelings of dislike or aversion toward certain individuals are frequently no more than a reflection of how we feel about ourselves, and what we perceive to be our shortcomings and failures, seen mirrored back to us by them.

How often do we find ourselves observing and judging from the sidelines, admiring some, vilifying others, yet never taking steps toward our own dreams? We allow circumstances to run our existence, and become bystanders in our own lives.

There is indeed something perverse about a belief that keeps us in the confines of what is familiar, safe and small, instead of allowing us to stretch out and touch our dreams, making them ours to own. We want our children to succeed, yes, but we also instill in them the limiting beliefs – often disguised as values and guiding principles – that hold them back. It is like irrigating a garden with polluted water and expecting the flowers to thrive.

By the time they reach adulthood, many young people have become "realistic", relinquishing their dreams or postponing them to some unspecified future date. Some turn to professional help to find out what is missing in their lives.

How many of us know of young people who showed a promise that never quite blossomed, or remember those voted most likely to succeed who faded into the comfortable recesses of a humdrum life? Or those who appeared destined for a great life, propelled forward under a momentum driven by someone else's hopes for them… a trajectory that ultimately proved unsustainable because it was fueled by aspirations that weren't their own?

A Safety Blanket

So what role do parents play? And how can parents stop inadvertently contributing to a problem that they themselves may subsequently lament? How can we stop reproducing in our children the very patterns that have so often engendered dissatisfaction in ourselves? So many of us have come to believe what we were told first as infants, then as youngsters growing up, then as young adults… until the message was thoroughly instilled: *"Your dream is impossible; you can't do it. Do something you know you can do (even if it doesn't inspire you); do something that will guarantee you a safe future."* Safety becomes an end in itself.

… Sometimes we even turn the message around, and make it: *"They won't let me do it."* On a cultural level, it becomes, "the government won't let me; society won't let me; the economy is bad……" It is our own fear that stops us, and we become victims by blaming our circumstances for our own failure to move forward.

Some of the words we use to describe our propensity for sitting on the sidelines and watching our life go by are things such as "having common sense" and "being realistic", which are the culturally acceptable terms used to refer to the way we accept the limitations that we have been given and taught to cling to, believing them to be there to keep us safe, when in fact they are the walls that keep us from going out and living our lives to the full.

How many of us grow up failing to express our own gifts for fear of being seen as different, smug or conceited? Or because there is no "future" in pursuing that particular path… Or we limit ourselves to doing something we know we are good at because it's expected of us, even if our hidden dream is something completely different? It's so much easier to blend into a crowd and take the same road as everyone else than to explore another path and strike out on one's own, particularly when doing so runs counter to the norm!

How can we avoid re-creating this situation with our own children?

As I reminisced and thought about the way my own youngster was raised, I began to wonder how much of what we tell our kids they *must* or *must not* do is really necessary. Observing other parents, I began to see how much of what we tell our children is an attempt to control them, or more aptly put, to avoid losing control. It might be the fear that our children will turn out very different from us, or alternatively, the fear that they will be just like us. After all, we know our own short-comings, and we want something better for them...

However, child-rearing all too often revolves around changing our children's inclinations, rather than exploring them. We may attempt to shape our children, as though they were made of some kind of pliable clay, modeling them to fit what we feel will help them become "well-adjusted" and *"realistic"*.

As I stress in another chapter, I'm not saying that parents shouldn't guide their children, set limits, and establish rules. Quite the contrary: these will be like the trellis upon which the young plant will grow. But the need to control our youngsters often springs from our fear that we will not know what to do if they are allowed to believe their dreams; to want things that we see as unattainable; to challenge the norm that we ourselves may have come to accept. We control them not, as we like to imagine, in order to ensure that they will get a better start in life, but because their dreams and wants connect with the longings, dreams and wants that live deep within us, but that we have pushed away.

The same fear that kept us safe, the fear that kept us from going for our own dreams, is triggered by our children's unbridled desire to live fully – something small children do very well. It's something we enjoy in them while they're very young – just as it was once enjoyed in ourselves – but often try to curtail as they get older. Teaching them "the facts of life" (including the fact that their dreams are unrealistic and unattainable) is usually done with the best of intentions: to prepare them for life as adults and give them what we feel will be a better shot at success.

What We Believe to be True

There is a common belief among parents that if they don't control their children when they are small, these children will be uncontrollable when they are adolescents. The problem with this line of thinking is that merely saying *No* to everything when children are small does not produce willing, obedient teenagers. Parents who control their children out of the fear that they themselves feel, say *"No"* far more often than they would if they were simply aiming at getting their kids to adhere to the ground rules that have been set up for their family. In the first case, the word "No" has become synonymous with control – becoming the end rather than the means – the unfortunate corollary being that not only its impact, but its power to control, diminish over time.

So how can we resist controlling our children out of fear, perpetuating the cycle of fear and resignation that so many of us have experienced ourselves? Even if we grew up with limiting beliefs, we can make a conscious choice to avoid reproducing the same limitations in our

children. We can keep the good controls: the respect, the discipline...
yet allow them to strive for more than we ourselves can imagine, in
ways that we might not even understand.

Doing so requires a conscious effort on our part. It means insisting
on what is important to us, and making it clear what that means. At
the same time, it means keeping many of our doubts to ourselves. So
many of the doubts we harbor are the result of having grown up hesi-
tating to try new and challenging things that seemed way beyond our
reach. If we take a closer look, we can see that much of what we hold
to be true is in fact the product of the assumptions we were taught,
and unquestioningly believed.

"It's a hard world out there" is a classic example of the kind of well-intentioned brainwashing that most of us underwent at some stage in our
lives; if not by our parents, then by our peers (themselves brainwashed)
or by society. We are asked to look around ourselves to see proof of this
truth everywhere; talented people getting nowhere; people who devote
long hours to a thankless job, never getting promoted; still others who
don't like what they do, but see no way to change and go for what they
really want (here the excuse will probably at some point include the
remark that they are "being realistic", or something to that effect).

A Leap of Faith

Even those of us who actually do what we love may not be able to see
the path that our children want to carve out for themselves. It would
have been easy for me to try to convince my son to continue studying
architecture rather than going for music full time, which is what he

felt he wanted to do. He actually enjoyed architecture; he just had a bigger dream that he was following, and music appeared to him to be the path to get there.

I could have argued with him based on my own values having to do with the importance of higher education, backed up by the fact that all the way back to his great-great grandparents, getting a university degree was considered an important and necessary achievement. It was a stretch for me to contemplate the idea that my son might never finish university. When I told him, "go for it", I knew that I was supporting him in what he really wanted to do. Yet a number of people – as I could have predicted – subsequently said to me: "Do you think it was a good idea to let him drop out of university? What if he decides not to go back and finish his degree?"

Had my son chosen to switch from music to architecture instead of the reverse, I'm sure the questions would have been different. Quite frankly, for many of us, architecture studies rate higher than music on the prestige scale. Furthermore, although I told people – truthfully – that my son wanted to continue his music studies, I had no guarantee that he would continue his studies at his music school, since he had already given indications that while he was finding it useful, it was also limiting him to a certain extent in terms of what he wanted to do.

So essentially, telling my son to *go for it* was a leap of faith on my part. At the same time, as I considered the different possible outcomes of his decision – knowing that one can never contemplate all of the outcomes, and that often, it is precisely the outcome we have not contemplated that ultimately transpires – I could not see how I could do otherwise. There was no way for me to be true to what I believed and at the same time ask him to turn back from his decision.

It took me back to the time when he was about 7 or 8 years old, and we were walking down the street together, talking about what he would do when he got older, and I heard myself say, *"Sergi, whatever you do, always follow your heart"*… catching my breath at the sound of the words I had just uttered as I wondered whether I would live to regret a statement that had emerged so naturally from a place of sincerity and love.

Years later, as my son and I talked about his decision to leave university, I saw that his conclusion had not been reached hastily. He had considered it for some time before making his choice. It was also apparent that the verdict came not so much from his head as it did from his heart. He *felt* that it was the right choice. His conviction that he needed to follow his dream was stronger than the initial drive to follow a career that incorporated many of his talents and interests.

Now, everything I've learned has taught me that decisions that come from the heart – conveyed by our feelings – are the ones that are most true to who we are. Our mind is good at many things, but not at telling us which choice will make us happiest. My son's heart was not in architecture – at least for now – and if I were to honor another value of mine: *be true to your values and to your heart*, I could not in all good conscience tell him to continue doing something that no longer interested him.

What I've just described is something I call a *"red flag moment"*; the kind of juncture where as parents we can find ourselves with the temptation to *sell out*. Some important values of our own may take a back seat to what we believe to be more practical, "realistic" concerns. Or we may feel divided: one of our values may be to see our children happy, and at the same time – as in the case I have mentioned – there may also be another strong value around the importance of getting an education.

When we hit this crossroads, what do we do? Depending on the circumstances, and assuming we don't feel completely confident in our child's ability to choose, the next step might be to explore both values further: to learn what might *really* make our children happy (perhaps we have some assumptions about their happiness that we have never actually checked out with them), and to get curious about what actually constitutes an education, in their eyes and ours.

For example, is an education necessarily the knowledge attained in an institution of higher learning? This question provides an opportunity to consciously examine our own assumptions, since as is often the case, those assumptions may actually be limiting what is possible for our children rather than expanding those possibilities.

I should add that learning about what will make our children happy, when one has always been open and listening for what resonates with them, is not all that difficult. It most often becomes hard when what makes them happy does not jibe with what we want for them. When we continually insist that we know better than they do what is good for them, and steer them toward that goal, they finally lose interest in sharing the dreams that we are not prepared to hear.

A few more words on the *"red flag moment"*: In fact, what this crucial moment often signals is a blurred distinction between two sets of parenting values, in which parents (a) want their children to be happy, accomplished human beings, and (b) want to ensure that their children can make a good living and provide for themselves and their families as adults.

The desire to see our children succeed in life – whatever that may mean to us – often makes us assume that some of what they want, when it doesn't dovetail with our own, or society's, perception, is pointless or fanciful. We use our own life experience to back up our assertions of what is important for them to know and to do.

The change of mindset that is required from parents in this regard has to be one of the most challenging aspects of parenting. How do we effectively oversee our children's upbringing, yet leave them the freedom to be who they are and follow their dream? How do we provide reasonable guidance, yet avoid letting our own fears hold them back? How do we keep from instilling in them the fear that will keep them from going for what they really want?

Part of the process involves what I call "suspension of disbelief": a willingness on our part to "not know" and just be curious about what our children really want. It means sometimes not expressing our doubts, or turning them into unbiased questions instead. Rather than a dubious "*Now, how do you ever think you're going to do that?*" a curious question might be, "*So, what would it be like to do that?*"

I confess that there were many times when my son talked about becoming a singer and I didn't see how he was going to get there. It would have been easy for me to express what was in my thoughts: mostly doubt, combined with a feeling of apprehension at the thought that he might end up disappointed. It took some self-management on my part to express only interest and encouragement while in my head my "rational" mind was busy questioning whether his goal was actually achievable.

There are also aspects of his dream that have yet to materialize. He had a vision that went beyond what was immediately present – in this case, a pleasant, but still untrained voice – indeed, beyond what either of us could actually imagine at that point. I willed myself to trust that, one way or another, whatever came out of his drive and determination to become a great singer would take him closer to where he was headed, and to accept that I might not be able to see that myself.

The Dream and Its Facets

We may never fully understand another person's dream, even when it is our children's. Yet we can explore gently to see what is underneath the dream, bearing in mind that the doubts we experience may stem from our own notion of Reality, whatever that is. When our children's dream changes, as it well might, rather than seeing it as proof that it was pointless and insubstantial, or that they "failed" at their dream, we can get curious about what is new and different about their dream now.

Getting curious also means suspending judgment. We may have our opinion about what our child wants to do, but it is easy for an opinion to turn into a judgment, often based on our own assumptions. The interesting thing about assumptions is that they are often biases, disguised as common sense. We have lived with them for so long that we take them to be true, and we deliver these truths with conviction. It is the way such assumptions are perpetuated.

When we withhold our assumptions we can find out more about

what is actually there under the surface; what really makes our kids tick. We can also see how invested our children are in their dream by their willingness to go after it. I would qualify that statement by saying that children who have continually been discouraged from even contemplating their dream may not feel confident in going after that goal – if they even remember what it was! When no credence has been given to any ambition of theirs that deviates from what we find accept-able, our children's vision of what they most desire becomes clouded.

In my son's case, had he just spent his time lounging on the sofa dreaming about being a great singer, I would have asked him whether he was really serious about achieving that dream. At the same time, as I discovered with him, dreams do have their periods of latency: not all is action, and indeed, some time devoted to imagining what it would be like to actually have that dream in reality is an important part of making it come to pass. Another thing is: Is the dream we are hearing about the ultimate goal, or is it more of a step along the way? We can't know unless our children tell us, and they may need first to experience it before they discover the answer.

Perhaps, looking back at our own lives, we can see the different steps that got us to where we are now. We may not understand how it all happened, yet in retrospect, we can see that it makes sense.

How much more powerful would it be if this path were taken in-tentionally? Of course things happen unexpectedly along the way in our lives – that is the magic that we experience when we are *on course* – but the path is much clearer when it is intentional. It is as though, instead of hacking our way through the forest to reach the castle of our dreams, a path opens up magically before us, beckoning us there.

In fact, a surefire way to know whether we are on or off course is to see what obstacles appear before us. Coming across countless, seemingly insurmountable obstacles is a clue that we may have to recalibrate our aim. When things flow – and we have all had experiences in which everything flowed, seemingly effortlessly – it is a sign that we are on course, being true to ourselves and to our purpose.

Indeed, our dreams may be the harbinger of our life's purpose. We may not immediately identify them as such, and they may be like the most distant twigs on the branches that lead back to the trunk of the tree that is our purpose and meaning in life. Our dreams are nature's way of making us experiment to exercise the gifts, and acquire the abilities we will need, to be fulfilled human beings.

In my son's case, I could see that he had a gift for music, and particularly, for composing. As he grew he gained confidence not only in his own abilities, but in the realization that each of us is unique – himself included – and that we are here to express what is singularly ours to offer. In doing so, he discovered the message that he wanted to bring to the world.

So while the only part of the dream I was aware of for some time was his desire to sing, I gradually began to see that it was a means rather than an end in itself. By that point his ability to dream and imagine his future far exceeded my own. His conviction was so powerful that for me, hearing him talk about what he planned to achieve was like a vicarious trip to a land of promise. I became totally convinced that he would achieve whatever he set out to do. His vision was contagious. Most of all, he himself is so utterly confident that he will achieve his dreams that it feels they are somehow destined to happen.

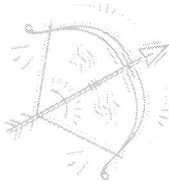

CHAPTER 5

· · · · · · · · · · · · ·

Creating from Trust

*T*he strongest relationships we have are based on trust. For most of us, that means trusting our siblings and close friends, our parents, certain relatives, and some coworkers as well. We also want to trust our children, and in turn, we strive to make them honest, trustworthy individuals. By the same token, we probably take it for granted that our children will trust us too.

Undoubtedly, we will try to endow our children with common sense and good judgment as they grow. As their parents, we support them with our love and our experience, building bonds with them that will last a lifetime. In the process, as we help our children learn to exercise good judgment, dispensing admonitions to watch out for things that can harm them, how can we keep from instilling *unnecessary* fear and generating distrust?

Even for us as adults, it's important to retain some of the childlike trust we had as infants. That means learning to distinguish the real dangers from the looming figments of our imagination that often conspire to hold us back, masquerading as… real dangers!

The Power of Trust

Our children, when they are raised not in fear of the unknown but in curiosity about it, have access to all of the potential they hold within as they boldly step out onto the stage of life to bring their dreams into reality. For all of us, as human beings, the potential we hold within is no more than that – potential – until it is realized; something that can only happen when we interact with the circumstances we encounter, often creating new circumstances as we go.

It's true for us, and it's true for our kids. With so many inputs, from family, society, friends and acquaintances, bidding them to tread carefully – or discounting their ideas as pipe dreams – our children often reach adolescence with the message that they cannot trust in the world, or even in themselves. The result may be, finally, that they fear straying from what they perceive to be the safest path. We ourselves have likely been the recipients of such well-meaning, cautionary messages.

To me it came as a surprise to see how naturally my own son embraced the belief – or should I say, the conviction – that he would achieve whatever he wanted, even before I'd managed to shift my own thinking from uncertainty to fully believing that I could accomplish what I really desired in my life. Yet well before I attained any level of confidence or trust in the universe with respect to achieving my own goals, I was aware of consciously restraining myself from voicing any concerns about what he said he wanted to do, to avoid tainting his conviction with my own hesitation and doubts.

I suppose there was a part of me that felt it was wrong to discourage him before he'd even tried, but I was also struck by the energy and confidence he put into the things he wanted to do, starting at a very young age. Even when I couldn't see how he was going to do something, I would tell him, "OK, sounds great!" or something to that effect. I then watched from the sidelines, like a bemused bystander, while he accomplished the things he had set out to do.

There were times when the things he had set out to do changed. Something that had previously been an objective no longer appeared so important. Rather than chiding him for throwing in the towel, I noticed that things were taking him elsewhere. He did not persist obstinately in attaining his initial goal, but was receptive to what came up, and as events unfolded, his priorities sometimes shifted as well. I also observed that had he not taken the first steps toward his original objective, the subsequent events that took him elsewhere would never have transpired, and that by taking those initial steps he had set in motion a series of circumstances that actually took him to a new place, providing him with new information as he moved forward.

My son never saw such changes as a defeat but, rather, as a clarification of his desire. As he describes it, sometimes what appears to be the goal is actually more of a representation of what we really want: something that emerges in greater detail as we devote time to imagining it. In fact, allowing our children to dream is a way of letting this process unfold naturally.

Yet in order for our children to manifest their own gifts in this world – and for those gifts to be fully expressed – there needs to be trust, not only in the things that, if they are fortunate, they will be able to take for granted (a roof over their head; their parents' affection), but in the things they cannot necessarily grasp, but can eventually recognize: their uniqueness and their singular contribution to the world.

Lest anyone imagine that believing oneself to be unique is a recipe for arrogance and vanity, I would again emphasize that *"unique"* doesn't mean *"better than"*; just *different*. As I raised my son, I encouraged him to study and to use his talents because they were his unique combination of gifts, but I would always remind him: *"It doesn't make you better than anyone else; everyone is different and has different things to contribute, so use the abilities you've been given, because only you can do it in your way."*

Of course the underlying credo is that we are in a creative universe, and that the reason we are here is to use the gifts and aptitudes with which we were born – in addition to developing other capabilities if we so choose! For some, the gift may be the ability to bring joy to people around them; for others, it may be to become a researcher who discovers a cure for a disease. The difference between the two is a value judgment that we make; there is no such thing as "large" or "small", if it is what we desire to create. The beauty of it is that in the process of learning to express our unique gifts, we discover who we are.

Although it appears a statement of the obvious, I feel it's important to point out that creativity cannot arise from distrust in the creative process. Where there is a firm bed of trust, the river of creativity flows freely. For those whose parents did not allow them to give free rein to their imagination, it's possible to recover that innate gift by connecting with the creative source within, deciding how we want to be, and how we want to be with our children. *We always have the freedom to choose.*

Trust from Infancy

Building trust begins in the first days of life. When our baby cries and we react by soothing her or picking her up, we're letting her know that she can trust us to respond to her needs. Our infant is learning that she can have an impact on the world around her, an experience that also builds her confidence. Upon reaching adulthood, this trust and confidence form the foundation upon which she can actively create the life she wants, trusting that the universe will fulfill her needs and realize her dreams.

Having given much thought to this process and its origin in our childhood experiences, I am more than ever convinced that the widespread and perverse notion that infants will be spoiled if they are picked up when they cry should be struck from the precepts of parenthood. Considering that a newborn, whose language skills are as yet undeveloped, has a limited range of resources for communicating with its parents, it seems unfair to presume that "crying to get attention" has other connotations besides a desire for physical contact and communication. The fear of "giving in" to our infant is oddly incongruous, as though infants somehow had the ability or need to manipulate the full-fledged adults who are their parents. To me, a newborn's demand for attention is the legitimate expression of a need for affection and well-being.

Ultimately, human beings are social animals, and it's natural for our infants to want to feel the warmth and comfort of our arms. That doesn't mean we have to tote them everywhere (although in some societies babies are indeed carried about on their mother's back, accompanying them in their activities throughout the day), but it does suggest that we be attentive to what our baby is trying to tell us… including a demand for *"social time"*.

In Spain I was faced with in-laws and relatives who were firm believers in allowing a baby to cry to "exercise its lungs". They assured me that my infant would grow up spoiled if I attended to him whenever he cried. Such arguments, faced by first-time parents who do not have the benefit of any previous experience of their own, can be disconcerting. In my case, I fortunately had a mother who assured me that responding to my infant would do nothing but instill more confidence in him, and it was something she encouraged me to do.

Since I felt a natural urge to respond when my infant cried (and here I believe I speak for many parents), I was happy to take my mother's advice and do something that felt right to me. My son's father, whose initial reservations were quickly overcome, fully supported me in this parenting decision. If I heard restless sounds coming from the crib I would go over, place a hand on my infant, and rock him gently, with some soothing words. Often that alone was sufficient. If the fussing continued I would pick him up and find a way to comfort him until he quieted down and could fall sleep.

Interestingly, and blowing away the dire predictions around me that picking my baby up would prompt him to cry continuously and demand more attention, quite the opposite turned out to be true. My child in fact cried very little. In a world where you are taken into account, there is little need to clamor for attention. A sense of security and trust is generated from the beginning.

For the benefit of the naysayers who conjure up images of a babe in arms turning into an albatross, I would recall the fact that there comes a time when children are far more interested in crawling around, exploring and getting into things, than in being held in our arms. On the contrary, they may fuss and protest when we want to *hold* them, when far more interesting things await exploration in the immediate vicinity!

Trust through Honesty

Trust is also fostered in our kids when we are honest with them, without pretense. One example that comes to mind occurred during a visit to the pediatrician when my son was a toddler. Our usual doctor was away and we had been given an appointment with a substitute. I felt uncomfortable with this doctor, whose professional manner was brusque. As he poked around with his stethoscope, my child, who had been quiet up until that point, began to cry. Instead of finding some calming words, the physician remonstrated with him: *"Stop that now. Your mother's going to be cross with you."*

I can't remember exactly what I said. I do recall pointing out to the doctor that gentle handling would have worked better. I found myself particularly annoyed by his expectation that I would automatically defer to his authority and show displeasure rather than sympathizing with my child.

I refrained from getting into an argument because I didn't want to undermine the authority of medical professionals as a whole in my son's eyes, but when we left the doctor's office I said to my still tearful toddler: *"I'm sorry honey, that wasn't a nice doctor. He didn't know how to be gentle. We won't go back to him again."*

Rather than scolding my son for not being cooperative with a doctor whose manner was inconsiderate, I showed my child that I understood his feelings, and ruled out that particular doctor for future appointments. I didn't hide my own sentiments or feel compelled to issue a pronouncement that "doctors are always right", to avoid criticizing an authority figure. Instead, I acknowledged that my toddler was upset, while reassuring him that it was not his fault. The authority of doctors as a whole was never questioned.

Such an experience exemplifies just one of the ways we build trust with our kids, by acknowledging their feelings. It's not always possible to change a situation, but we can show that we understand. In this case, I was able to assure him that there would be no more visits to that particular doctor.

A Word on Meltdowns

Trust is also built through our skill in handling challenging behavior, such as when our youngster has a meltdown at home or – more embarrassingly – in public.

I don't remember having to deal with more than a couple of tantrums. But it happens to all kids, and how their parents react can vary considerably. The way I see it, a tantrum is not so much a challenge of adult authority as it is a loss of emotional control by our child. Something that starts out as our toddler insisting: *"I want (…whatever…)"* (to which we have, perhaps in a calm, firm voice, responded: *"No, you can't"*) inexplicably slips out of control and escalates: we suddenly find ourselves, possibly in the midst of strangers in a busy shopping center, with a screaming child who resists all our efforts to pacify him.

Despite my initial consternation and uncertainty as to how to handle the situation, when it did occur it felt right to be supportive rather than reproachful. In doing so, I learned that using reassuring words and speaking soothingly to an overwrought toddler lets him know that we understand he has lost control, and ultimately helps calm things down. At this point, a hug and kiss, assuring our child that everything is okay, restores normalcy sooner, and reinforces his knowledge that we trust him and empathize with him.

As parents, we may be tempted to see such outbursts as a sign that we're not doing our job right. We raise our child in a loving, understanding manner, when all of a sudden that child goes over the edge, oblivious to our attempts to communicate rationally even when that line of communication has appeared to work before. Yet when you think about it, meltdowns are a pretty natural outlet for small people who haven't yet mastered their emotions or learned to articulate what they feel.

Nevertheless, some parents appear to perceive tantrums as a battle of the wills; their toddler pitted against them. Determined to keep the upper hand, these parents follow a different logic. The inner dialogue appears to be: *"I won't give in to the tantrums and crying, because if I do, my child will become more demanding and I'll lose control. I'll nip that in the bud by simply ignoring the crying, demonstrating that I am indeed in charge."*

This stance, and the view of authority that it reflects, raises a question that is at the heart of so many parenting decisions: whether, ultimately, we need or want to engage in a battle for control with our children.

It's useful here to distinguish between two different aspects that characterize tantrums. On the one hand, our child wants something he cannot have. The point here is not to cave in and give him whatever it is that happens to be the object of his hysterics, because we've told him *No*, and he needs to learn that we mean it – even though in his head at that moment there is nothing more important to him than getting whatever it is that he wants. Never mind that he will undoubtedly have entirely forgotten about what it was shortly thereafter.

On the other hand, his tolerance for frustration – the boundaries set by us, his parents – is still undeveloped, and on occasion a meltdown will occur. He loses control and doesn't know how to regain it. Here, he will benefit more from empathy and understanding than from exasperation and threats.

As I've so often been able to confirm, ranting at a child while he's in the throes of a tantrum, or ignoring him as a way of showing disapproval, is an ineffective way of demonstrating our authority. Besides, why would we need to play tit-for-tat with a child? Even with toddlers it's possible for us to establish a moral higher ground by firmly saying no, and then showing that we love and care for them by taking their side emotionally.

Once again, it's an opportunity for us to model for our children the behavior we hope they will eventually adopt. We set the stage for the future: our child feels loved and supported by his parents, and learns to distinguish being loved from getting whatever he wants. We build trust.

Trust and Responsibility

Trust is fostered in other ways as well.

In our family, the relationship with my son was always built on the trust that he would do his part. I used to tell him our family was a team. In fact, even today, I tell him how great it is to be on his team!

One way to consider families – large or small – is as an interconnected unit in which everyone plays a part, and everyone is affected by what the others do. Each of the members has rights and responsibilities, and we all contribute in some way to making our family thrive. We gain our children's trust because we also trust them to do their share.

This way of seeing our family is not vertical and authoritarian, but horizontal and participatory. It appeals to children's desire to be recognized as important too, and makes them feel that their contribution matters. There are times when they fall down on the job, of course... The bed doesn't get made, a chore doesn't get done, an errand is forgotten... But it means we can appeal to their sense of responsibility: they understand that the reason they are expected to pitch in is not merely because they are to do as they are told, but because they are making an active contribution to the household: "We are all in this together".

This approach is as effective in children as it is in adults. As adults, we know that we're far more willing to apply ourselves when we are aware that what we're doing is important.

Interestingly, one of the great ongoing debates in society is about how to bring more meaning to the jobs people do, not least because it imbues employees with a sense of purpose, and raises productivity.

The same is true for the rest of us. In the case of children, when they are given a task that has meaning for them, they rise to the occasion! Children love having responsibility, although they may not always do an exemplary job right away. As they get older, we can also ask them to suggest a good way to do something: soliciting their input is a great way to bring them on board, and children love being able to contribute ideas and win parental endorsement.

And yes, when kids realize that being involved means actually having to do their bit, they may also protest. It's far more interesting to play a game with one's friends than to straighten one's room! But while we can negotiate how and when they will clean their room, the principle that they are to make their contribution to the household, just the way their parents do, prevails. We trust them to do their bit, and they gradually learn to exercise responsibility in living up to that trust.

The level of responsibility that children take on depends upon their age, but *participation* is a great learning template; one that also helps them to become responsible young adults. There are tomes written on how to cope with teenagers and make them responsible individuals. In this regard, there's everything to be gained by starting when kids are young. Responsibility is progressive, and parents who never enlist their children's cooperation and sense of responsibility when they are small may subsequently find themselves with the dilemma, when their children reach their teens, of how to transform their insouciant youngsters into responsible adults.

Trust in Adolescents

With all of the changes they are going through – no longer children; not yet adults; shifting hormones often determining their mood – teenagers naturally "have their moments", as we like to say, although with humor and understanding, our relationship with them is far easier. When my son was still a pre-teen I told him that I knew that as he became a teenager he would be experiencing such mood changes, and that it would be normal for him to feel crabby and uncooperative at times.

Since we had already talked about it, when he became grumpy or stubborn I would say, "Right, it looks like one of those teen moments. Don't worry, it's normal" and would basically ignore the behavior he was showing at that point. This lack of resistance on my part appeared to take the wind out of his sails, and it was not long before he was back to his usual good-natured self.

Again, it's important to bear in mind that adolescents, like all kids, want to be trusted. A relationship based on trust means that from childhood kids learn that there are certain expectations of them in return for the privilege of being included as a full-fledged family member and being given *the benefit of the doubt:* i.e., we will trust them to step up to the plate and do their bit, be honest, and do as they say. In giving them the benefit of the doubt – even bearing in mind that they may occasionally let us down – we have laid the foundation for what we want our relationship with them to be, and set a standard that will serve to guide them in their own lives.

An example of how the matter of trust was dealt with at home is exemplified by the subject of my son's allowance. We began by giving him a small amount of money each week. In my opinion, the sum we had allocated for pocket money was symbolic compared to what some of his friends were receiving, but to him the fact that it was a trifling amount didn't seem to matter. It must have been when he was around 10 years old that I went to give it to him one day, and curiously, he told me he didn't need it.

I remember my own tiny allowance as a youth, made purposely small to give me a sense of frugality and teach me the value of money. It didn't seem to work with me because I never managed to save any, and it took me until well into my adult years to find a positive relationship with money. I was curious about what was going on with my son.

In his case, he just didn't appear to need much. What finally happened was, I would ask him to tell me what he needed, and then would just give him the money. I don't remember what he actually used it for, but it was usually for something he required for school or sports, or some small purchase. He was not hooked on brands, although his aunt did occasionally send him brand name T-shirts from the States, which he loved; he just didn't think of them in terms of the brand. What we finally did was, when he thought he needed something he would just ask me, and I would decide whether he should have it. Usually it was something reasonable, and I had no objections.

Interestingly, when he was going out with friends and asked for money (say, for an afternoon at the bowling alley) he would generally request some inconsequential amount, like 2 euros (about 3 dollars at the going rate back then). I would tell him he might need more, suggesting he take 8 or 10 euros instead (Barcelona is a big city, after all, and I figured he might run short of cash). He would refuse the money, saying he didn't need it, and I would insist that he take it just in case! That same scenario would repeat itself whenever he went out and needed money. Inevitably, the two of us would end up laughing at ourselves and the silly argument we were having.

People I knew whose children never stopped pestering them for extra cash thought I was incredibly fortunate to have a son who never appeared to need money. I once told him that my friends thought I was lucky to have a son who didn't ask for money. To which he replied, "Well, my friends think I'm lucky to have a mom who always wants to *give me* money!" It became our standing joke. It got to the point where if he needed cash I would tell him to just get it out of my wallet. If he was buying something I would ask him to bring me the receipt, but the underlying principle was always trust. My son was matter-of-fact about being trusted with money, perhaps unsurprisingly, since trust had been a theme since he was small.

Trust through Love

Here again, what comes to mind is how, for my son, trust grew over the years from knowing he was loved, even when he occasionally messed up – something kids are bound to do – or when he did things that got on my nerves and drove me crazy. I remember my own mother, one of the most supportive parents I've ever met, telling me that when her children were young she loved them to death, but there were times she would have chucked us all out the window! (Even now, transported back to my childhood, I think: "Who? You mean ME??") Perhaps at this stage I should include a warning for parents. You know… *this package may contain traces of nuts.* Throwing your kids out the window in moments of overwhelm is not advocated by this book.

Regardless of how good a relationship we have with them, our kids can be trying at times, and we don't always have the patience to distract their attention or deal with them with aplomb. Yet as parents, even when our children are being difficult, we want to avoid sinking to their level and getting caught up in a childish altercation that can go nowhere.

I remember one occasion – my child must have been about 5 or 6 years old – when I refused to acquiesce to something he had asked for, and he defiantly asserted, *"I don't love you."*

Now I know, because I've seen this tactic employed, that when children misbehave, one of the ways some parents attempt to get them to obey is to imply that love will somehow be withheld until the expected behavior is produced.

Of course parents know it's not true that they don't love their child, but it's something children take to heart. It's an unfair manipulation that teaches youngsters that their parents' affection depends on what they, as children, do, rather than who they are.

In this case, when he said, *"I don't love you!"* my son was repeating what he had heard other parents say to their children, or what those children had answered back. He certainly hadn't heard that at home. I calmly responded, *"Well, that's okay, because I love you anyway."*

The honesty of this reply put an end to the argument. In retrospect, getting into a reproachful exchange about why my child was saying he didn't love me, telling him: *"That's not nice!"*, or *"What do you mean you don't love me!"* would have gotten us nowhere. Furthermore, such an altercation quickly degenerates into a battle of the wills: we as parents trying to prove that we are right and that our children are wrong.

Interestingly, withholding love is a stratagem that, once learned in childhood, may well repeat itself in adulthood. Its impact on our beliefs and expectations is far-reaching. A short synopsis of what the battle is actually about would be: love is at stake; the fight is to see who has the power to take it away. Even infants, apparently, realize that love is important and that people will go to great lengths to keep from losing it.

As I have found with so many other parenting situations, sidestepping an apparent provocation and continuing to be firm but loving is not only conciliatory, but very effective in getting kids to cool down. That means, of course, that the parent cannot be intent on wielding power at all costs by making their child wrong. In fact, when we realize that we are actually role models for our children, empathy becomes far more important than proving that we are right and they aren't.

I'm not saying I never lost my temper with my son – I think he can attest to that – but I rarely resorted to shouting at him, and on the few occasions when that did happen my patience had been tried to the limit. I then usually apologized for shouting, but I also made it clear that when he didn't listen to me there was a point where I might very well blow my top! It seemed to sink in, eventually; the truth is, my son and I don't really have arguments nowadays. Of course we sometimes disagree, but we talk about things rather than arguing about them.

As for my son's share of responsibility, he learned early on that he was expected to take responsibility for his own decisions. In hindsight, it's easy to recognize that treating him as dependable and mature from a young age made him more willing to step into that role.

There were, however, times when he fell down on the job. On those occasions, expressing disappointment proved to be far more effective than becoming angry. I extended total trust to my son because it felt to me like the right way to raise him, and I expected that he would respond by living up to my presumption of responsibility on his part.

It seems clear to me that as parents, if we never give our kids the "benefit of the doubt" because we assume they'll fall down on the job at some point, we miss a great opportunity to build trust and responsibility as they grow. Of course I expected some setbacks along the way, because "failure" – in this case, failing to live up to the desired behavior sought by one's parents – is a natural part of the learning process.

In fact, I clearly remember one such occasion because of the impact it had on his perception of responsibility. My son must have been about 12 years old at the time. He was fairly cooperative, but often busy with friends and activities, and he frequently had to be reminded more than once of whatever it was he had been asked to do.

At the time I was using crutches to get around, having twisted my ankle in stepping off the curb; at home, I actually used a desk chair with wheels to go from one room to the next to avoid putting weight on my leg. As a result of my more limited mobility everything was more of an effort, and I was asking my son to do things for me that I would normally do for myself: bringing me things that I needed, or running errands.

After a while he appeared to tire of being so frequently called upon, and some of my requests had to be repeated. There was one point, however, when I realized he hadn't done something I'd asked of him – nothing big, just something I would normally have done myself anyway had I not been temporarily laid up – and in my frustration I told him I was disappointed in him. I guess I got emotional because I was already having a difficult time with not being able to get around as my usual active self.

My feeling of having been let down, together with the impact of the emotion in my voice, prompted in him a realization that he had failed to live up to a responsibility with which he'd been entrusted, in a situation in which I genuinely needed to rely on him. We had a talk about what it meant to me to be able to count on him, and my expectation that he would understand and voluntarily pitch in when needed.

My disappointment had far more of an impact than chiding him would have. It was as though an opportunity for him to show his maturity had been missed … I honestly think it was one of those *"Aha!"* moments in the learning process, where it really sank in that to earn trust, he also had to step up to the plate.

Now that he's a full-fledged adult, responsibility is a natural part of his life, and there is a freedom in our relationship that comes from having trust built into it. He will occasionally ask me for advice, or I will offer a suggestion. Many times now, indeed, I ask him for advice! Our relationship has benefited from the frequent opportunities he was given in the course of his childhood and adolescence to develop the tools, and the emotional intelligence, that would serve him in good stead and be an invaluable resource for him as an adult.

Trust and its Impact on the Future

Seeing my son now is my confirmation that children who grow up knowing they are loved, and learn that love goes hand in hand with responsibility, are better prepared to successfully ride out the ups and downs that life is bound to bring. They learn to be sensitive to the needs of others and to their own needs, a kind of field guide for survival in the 21st century. Trust builds confidence and creates adaptable children who can navigate the waters of change in the rapidly shifting currents of our society.

Going still further, it is my conviction that children who grow up being trusted and are given the freedom to be who they are, within the bounds of respect for others, have greater confidence and will more naturally learn to trust in their own ability to create whatever it is that they want to achieve in their lives. It is the same trust that I refer to elsewhere in this book, one that is created in our children when we are attentive to, and attend to, their nascent dreams and desires.

For them, as for us, *believing* that they can attain their goals is essential for them to achieve what they set out accomplish. It's something that applies to us all. Since much of the time we don't know exactly *how* we will get where we want to be, *trusting* that we will find the way makes us more receptive to the "chance" opportunities that crop up along the way. The ability to seize those opportunities is multiplied when we trust that we are held and guided by our universe.

At the same time, trust allows us to work toward what we want, and surrender to the unseen forces – often referred to as fortuitous events – that come into play to actually make things happen. We are often unaware of the power of our intention until, in retrospect, we retrace our achievements and can consciously attribute them to our desire, or determination, to make them come about. Indeed, our achievements turn out to be *proportional* to our desire and determination to make them happen.

Creating from trust is powerful. Trust gives us the confidence to stay our course when the going gets rough, and to know that there is no wrong path when we act from a place of awareness. There are, too, many actions we take without knowing why, their meaning in our life only emerging clearly many years later. Agonizing over what to study, whether to change jobs, or whether it is the right time for a certain course of action in fact has the opposite effect, as it can actually paralyze us and keep us from taking a first step – any step – that would bring us closer to where we want to go.

If we can hold back from transferring our own doubts and apprehensions to our children, we can allow them not only to be who they are, but to explore possibilities that they would otherwise be incapable of imagining. Because what happens when we think things are impossible is that they become impossible: our mind no longer goes there, our creativity is shut down and our imagination fails to take us to whatever lies beyond what we believe to be attainable.

When we instill trust in our children we prepare them to embrace what the universe has to offer them. Even if we ourselves have not been raised to trust fully that we will achieve what we most desire, we can allow our children to grow up believing that they can accomplish whatever it is they set out to do.

It is this trust that we ourselves often fail to manifest, and understandably, fail to convey to our children. However, it's not necessary to know how to do so to be able, as a parent, to allow our children to do what comes so naturally to them. Sometimes all it takes is stepping out of their way so that their natural energy, creativity and curiosity can take them farther than we can imagine. Even if we can't see it, we can let them *go for what they want,* and be curious about what they are learning along the way.

The problem that most of us face is that we try to figure out the course of events ahead of time, then fall prey to our fears when we come up with a worst-case scenario that we have included "just to be realistic". Or we take a timid step – a toe in the water – and then jump back when it initially feels cold, appearing not to be giving us the results that we want.

My son has always said he didn't need a plan B. According to him, if you really believe in your plan A, then having a plan B is unnecessary. I myself have come to the realization that when you're connected with what you want, there is no plan B: only variations on plan A. In his world, things work out – or they shift – but there is the faith that whatever happens is important because it is part of the process of getting where he wants to go. Occasionally the things that haven't worked out have proved to be just as significant to the long-term goal as the things that have. Everything is perceived as something to be learned from, and something that contributes to where he is going.

Establishing a relationship with our children based on trust lays the groundwork upon which their trust in the world around them will be solidly founded. Interestingly, trusting our world does not mean we will be defenseless or taken advantage of by others.

While the ability to think critically and exercise good judgment continue to be important, being prepared to trust and give others the benefit of the doubt is salutary, for both ourselves and our relationships.

It is our children's faith that they are always supported by the universe that, when they are older, will prompt them to take a first step when there is no "guarantee" that they will get results. Creating from trust is a leap of faith that goes beyond what already is, to stretch the limits of what is possible.

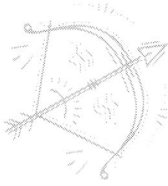

CHAPTER 6

A Line in the Sand

*W*e are often told that children need limits. Indeed, as parents, setting limits is understood to be part of what we do.

But above and beyond knowing that our children need limits, it's important to know what those limits are actually for, and how we can make our efforts count by increasing the learning component of what we as parents do.

One reason for doing so is that meaningless limits essentially fall into the same category as empty threats: ultimately, they are ineffective because our children are the first to realize it when we ourselves don't say them with conviction, or really mean what we say.

Respect

Although my own child grew up with considerable freedom to explore and be who he was, there was always an underlying theme, already mentioned in this book, which was respect. That's not at all surprising, since my own experience from early childhood was that respect for *everyone* was a given.

As I look back, it appears to me that my son learned most about respect as he grew by being the recipient of it himself. Indeed, from the moment he was born, I saw him as perfect and unique just as he was. There was always respect for him as a person, albeit a small one. It felt natural to differentiate between who he was as a human being and the limitations of his young age, which required that certain rules be set.

It has become clear to me that our children come into the world with everything they need to face the future. On their way to adulthood they "learn the ropes", acquiring the tools and skills that will enable them to adapt to family and society.

Seen this way, *respect* is for the individual, separate from any chronological age – you might call it respect for *"the being within"* – at the same time as the *limits* are for the child, for whom social etiquette and basic values are something to be learned.

Children seem innately equipped to be able to recognize and differentiate between these two concepts. They know when they are being respected (perhaps, more clearly put, they know when they are NOT being respected, or are being treated unfairly), and they also appear to grow up with greater self-confidence when they have experienced some parental limitations that they can – if not initially, at least over time – come to understand.

When I look back, I think what worked was telling my child why the rules were there. In retrospect, the fact that respect was such a solidly ingrained value in our family – something that he himself experienced – was what gave it consistency and made it work in the long run.

That's not to say that he metamorphosed into an angel from the first moment I tried to get him to understand that disregard for others was not okay. Here, what I refer to as *disrespect,* or *lack of respect,* is a broad concept that includes verbal disrespect, antisocial behavior (hitting), failing to keep promises, and so on.

My child would come home from school repeating words that he had heard from his classmates, although he already knew they were off-limits. He would divest himself of any responsibility by initiating his sentence with: *"David* said … *(add naughty word)"*. On the very few occasions that he (as a 4 or 5 year-old) ventured to push or hit me as he sometimes would with his classmates, I would tell him firmly that hitting was forbidden. There was no tolerating any kind of physical aggression, despite the fact that he was not going to hurt me, given his size. Not even *pretending* to hit was okay.

In this regard, understandably, a lot of what my child tried out at home was what he saw at school, because for certain no hitting went on in our household. Over time, I saw that small children who hit their parents when they got angry – and were allowed to do so because they were small and it didn't feel important to their parents at the time – often became rude and demanding as they grew older. The notion that hitting was off-limits had never been made an inviolable rule by their parents, and as those children became older that lack of respect manifested itself in different ways.

Looking back now, it has become clear to me that, in raising our children, some principles must be considered virtually ironclad, with parents prepared to stand by them and not budge. Respect is one, as I have already mentioned. There are also values that we have, for both ourselves and our children, that will vary from family to family.

Determining our Values

Some principles, while important in one's own household, may appear trivial to those who do not share the same values. Some parents have rules about not eating in the family car. Others, about leaving shoes at the door upon crossing the threshold and wearing slippers around the house… Trivial examples to some - though surely not to those for whom this policy is an inviolable rule!

We need to distinguish in our mind, and be clear, on what is negotiable, and where we draw the line. That line will be what indicates to our kids that we mean what we say, and that it's important to us that they observe the rules we have designed around that value. Ultimately, when we stand our ground, we show them that we are willing to stand behind the limits we set for them.

One example, taken from my own experience, illustrates the impact of taking a stand. Ostensibly inconsequential, it has to do with eating and buying candy. I use it as an example because it illustrates a value that is important to me, but not necessarily to other people.

I realize that for many families, consumption of candy is a normal affair. Both children and their parents may indulge in the habit, as candy becomes a *de facto* part of the diet, albeit one that does not appear in any of the recommended food groups.

As a child I remember eating candy from time to time; certainly on Halloween, when we made out like bandits, with a stash of it toted back home after a day of trick-or-treating, to be consumed over the following weeks (or months, depending on the quantity we had managed to amass).

I had assumed my child would probably end up eating some candy (Spain is a country that *loves* its candy), but I had decided ahead of time that I wouldn't actually buy him any, since I didn't want to actively contribute to what I foresaw as potential problems of dental health, poor eating habits, exposure to artificial sweeteners or flavorings, and any of the possible consequences of consuming candy of which I'd become aware.

I should mention that for us, chocolate was not considered candy. Furthermore, in our household the occasional cookies and cakes – preferably homemade – were not only allowed, but relished, and chocolate was considered "nutritious" (an example of how arbitrary our values might appear to individuals outside of our own family).

For me, the decision not to buy candy for my child was a no-brainer. My stated policy was: *if someone gives you candy you can have it, but I'm not buying you any myself.* As an "enlightened" former candy-consumer, my stand was that candy was nutritionally empty and if ingested in sufficient quantities, could be unhealthy. I didn't want to condone candy consumption; ergo, I would not buy any candy for my child. Since, as already mentioned, we do have chocolate and the occasional homemade treat at home, it was not a radical *"NO"* to all sweets, although that could have been another option.

I also wanted him to learn to accept candy graciously when it was offered (well-meaning adults in this part of the world will often give sweets to youngsters in a show of kindness), even if he really wasn't going to eat it. You could say that being gracious was another value of mine.

That was my policy. Of course, making a decision is one thing; contending with the environment is quite another. Supermarkets typically locate displays with packages of candy together with magazines near the cash register, where parents (and their children) come upon them while waiting for their purchases to be rung up. The result, for many shoppers, is that it's common for one or more of these items to end up in the shopping cart before all of the groceries have been run under the barcode reader.

I remember an instance, early on, when we got to the cash register and my child snatched a bag of candy off the rack and waved it in front of me, saying, *"Mommy, I want this"*. The first time it happened I simply told him that I wouldn't buy it for him, stating matter-of-factly: *"I'm not getting you candy, so don't ask."*

Not unsurprisingly, he persisted. My response, which I remember to this day because it was so unequivocal, was: *"You're wasting your breath. You can ask me all you want; I'm never buying you candy."*

In retrospect, it must have been the conviction with which I said it, conveyed by my tone of voice; but it worked. I'm not sure now, but I think he might have tried once or twice more to convince me. However, I simply repeated: *"Forget it. I'm never buying you candy so don't bother asking."* I was so categorical that he actually stopped trying. It was such a strong value of mine that it came across as unshakable, and he didn't insist. That was interesting to me, because in general my son didn't give up easily. When he really wanted something, he could be extremely persistent.

Finding our Authority

At the same time, I observed other mothers, offspring in tow, on line at the checkout. I particularly remember a situation that occurred one day as I waited on line to pay for my groceries. The child standing in front of me with his mother pulled a pack of candy from the display and threw it into the shopping cart. The mother took it out, and with a firm *"No!"* put it back on the rack.

The child again grabbed the bag of candy and clutched it to his breast. *"No, you can't have that"*, his mother repeated. A tug of war with the candy bag ensued, the mother finally managing to wrest it from her child's grasp. He thereupon squeezed his eyes shut and burst into tears, while his mother glanced uncomfortably around, manifestly avoiding the disapproving stare of onlookers.

She put the bag back on the rack and the child ran over, grabbed it, and threw it onto the groceries his mother had already begun placing on the belt in front of the cashier. He then stepped back with a pout, crossing his arms tightly over his chest, tears still streaming down his cheeks, his wails threatening to increase. His mother, employing a tone of voice that simulated a reprimand, concluded their confrontation: *"OK, you can have it… but just this once!"* At the same time, as she caught the eyes of several of the shoppers who were observing the scene, she rolled her eyes as if to say: *"what can you do with such a difficult child?"*

Her words were like magic. The tears dried up instantly as the unruly youngster was transformed into a smiling cherub. The battle was over…. But who had actually won?

It was obvious that it wasn't the first time that this scene had taken place. While acknowledging this mother for her efforts to curb her child's need for instant gratification, it seems clear that she was held hostage not only by her child, but by her own lack of conviction. Giving in after saying no under such circumstances seems to undermine a parent's authority as much as does giving in to the child's demands in the first place.

Other examples of parents relinquishing their authority are seen in public places, such as restaurants. I've seen parents feign obliviousness as their children jump up and down on their seat and throw food at each other or run around the tables, while other guests cast annoyed looks their way or struggle to ignore them and enjoy their meal. Finally, invoking the higher authority of a third party, such parents admonish their children: *"Stop that! The waiter's going to get angry with you!"*

Reinforcing their inability to manage the situation, these parents simply transfer authority from themselves to whoever happens to be in charge at that moment. Since they do not convey any values – in this case, letting their children know that misbehaving and annoying other people is off limits – no real learning, other than seeing how much can be gotten away with without getting caught, is actually instilled.

As I discovered, standing one's ground as a parent can take many forms. One such example in our household arose early on, when my son was 5 or 6 years old. We had already decided that he would not watch TV unless an adult could be with him, and often substituted videos sent by family in the U.S. for popular children's TV shows in Spain. This decision served two purposes: helping him improve his command of English, and enabling me to monitor the content of what he was watching. When I was not around and he was with the babysitter, TV was replaced with trips to the playground, or games and other play activities.

In Spain at the time, there was a Japanese animated series on TV that was very popular with the younger set, but it included considerable violence that I found inappropriate for that age (actually, for any age!). All the kids were watching it, and even my son, who was not allowed to watch it at home, would come home from school singing songs that appeared on the series.

Bearing in mind peer pressure, I wanted to find a satisfactory solution. I didn't want my youngster to feel left out of what appeared to be a fad among kids his age, but I didn't want to relent where my principles were concerned.

I finally settled on a compromise: I bought him the stickers with the portraits of the main characters in the series so that he could trade them with his friends, and an album where he could build his sticker collection. I told him that he could have the album, but that I didn't like the series "because it was violent".

He didn't seem to mind the solution we finally adopted. He didn't lose face, and I suspect his friends never realized that he wasn't actually watching the show on TV.

The Social Graces

I think most parents can attest to how long it takes small children to learn to say *please* and *thank you* without prompting, let alone behave themselves as a matter of course. Ensuring that their youngsters acquire the social graces – especially when those youngsters have seem-ingly boundless energy and the need to be constantly active – can be a particular challenge.

As a toddler, my child would very quickly become bored and rest-less unless there was something going on that interested him. Yet I had a friend who would sit her 3 year-old down with us at the table where he would happily remain put throughout an entire meal. For parents of children such as hers, my experience in learning how to deal with my own child may not be of great interest. The truth is, my son was just not one of those calm, quiet youngsters. Since he didn't know how to entertain himself while sitting at the table in company, when his interest began to wane it often became a challenge getting him to remain seated throughout an entire meal.

At home it was not such an issue: he got to participate in at least some of the conversations we had, and often that was enough to hold his interest. At some point he would be excused from the table and would go off and occupy himself elsewhere. It was more of a trial when we were at the table with other adults. On occasions – at home with guests, or at a restaurant – where it was required of him that he sit politely in company, I avoided having to constantly reprimand him by first reminding him that he was expected to be well-mannered, and then finding a way to distract him when needed so that he would end up behaving well by default.

Despite the need for frequent reminders about being patient and sitting at the table until excused, the learning that he was expected to sit politely in company was ultimately instilled. Using a tactic that might qualify as "cheating", I usually found ways to shorten the length of time that he was expected to remain in his chair so that it would be easier for him to comply. By doing so I got a higher *de facto* "success rate". On the theory that kids learn better from positivity than negativity, I figured that somehow the good results would eventually sink in and become the norm.

As for eating out, I just skipped going to restaurants with him for the most part when he was small because of the extra effort it required of me. Instead of using up all of my ammunition in reprimands, it was easier just to avoid a situation that was not particularly enjoyable for either of us. It meant I could save my admonishments for times when they were really needed rather than having them lose effectiveness from overuse.

There were other situations, too (in polite company; in a waiting room…) where I called upon my creativity to keep him occupied and generate the positive results I wanted. When drawing pictures became old hat, we engaged in other distractions, playing hangman, tic-tac-toe, or guessing games while waiting our turn. There are many parents who use this stratagem quite naturally. My own conclusion is that it requires a little extra effort, but less aggravation, to keep children occupied than to demand that they behave once they have already become fussy or rambunctious.

What I learned from these experiences, ultimately, was that finding ways to enable one's child to behave well by default is the best way to ensure that reprimands, when needed, continue to be effective. Reprimands can so quickly turn into nagging, and kids (like adults) eventually just tune it out. It's actually basic common sense: when we enable our youngsters to do well because the situation makes it easy for them to do so, we generate good behavior on their part that we can point to and praise, building the expectation that there will be more such behavior in the future.

I guess you could call it an investment in good behavior. Sometimes it took more effort to find a way to turn the situation into a positive experience than it would have to just bark orders at my youngster. He had a lot of freedom to express himself in other ways, so although I was strict with him when it came to respect, my firmness was applied judiciously and never dampened his spirit. Most of all, I'm convinced that the respect that he himself experienced from an early age set the stage for how he treated others as he grew older, although as is often the case, it took a while before the learning sank in and became second nature.

In retrospect, I was able to strike a balance between being strict, and avoiding situations in which I knew it was going to be a challenge for him to behave. It was a way of creating the circumstances in which he could be "successful" at good behavior without too much effort and I could keep my chiding to a minimum. It also avoided the inevitable attrition of parental authority that comes when our children are subjected to a constant diet of nagging and disapproval.

The Food Wars

For many of us, the dinner table may be the only place where the entire family gathers together at once. Precisely because of that, it has the potential to become a stage where many family dramas are played out. It is most certainly a place where parenting skills are put to the test.

In this regard, there is an interesting parent-child interaction that occurs at mealtime that I have dubbed *The Food Wars*. While my observations are from Spain, I would wager that, in one form or another, they hold for most developed countries where there is enough food to put on the table at every meal.

The Food Wars stem from the unrequited urge of some parents who feel duty-bound to get their child to finish every meal, frequently in the face of resistance when their youngster claims not to be hungry. I assume parents urge their children to clean their plate because it's associated in their mind with healthy eating. I have seen some parents go to great lengths to get their children to eat; their initial, well-meaning efforts turning into a kind of crusade.

One such scene still stands out in my mind. I vividly recall watching the mother of one of my son's friends pursuing her 3-year-old around the house, brandishing a spoon filled with fruit dessert, despite the fact that he had already left the table and was manifestly only interested in playing at that point. When he had finally occupied himself with a toy truck and was no longer paying attention, she tried to pop a spoonful of food into his mouth, catching him unawares. As he repeatedly shook his head and refused to take it, she tried to cajole him into eating.

Now, for those of us fortunate enough to live in a society where food is abundant, this parental concern might appear to be legitimate. Yet it has more to do with our own needs than those of our children. In this particular manifestation of *The Food Wars*, fretting that our kids won't get enough to eat can get us trapped in a battle of the wills, with consequences that go far beyond the dinner table.

A variation of the above is bargaining with our children to get them to eat, in another, ultimately counterproductive, offshoot of *The Food Wars*. *Just eat* this, *then you can have* that, we go, handing our kids a tool for future blackmail which youngsters may not be averse to using on occasion to get something they want. Not to mention the fact that pushing our kids to eat is a recipe for future eating disorders. Life at the dinner table can be so much simpler.

My thoughts on this subject became clear to me as I considered my experience with my own mom, who was herself a firm proponent of keeping food from becoming a subject of contention. *"No self-respecting child will allow himself to go hungry unless he's actually ill"*, she used to say, in what seems to me to be a paragon of parental common sense. Since most of the time when our children refuse to eat it's because they are actually not hungry, it appears to make little sense to try to force them to consume food that they don't want. On the other hand, most kids are not past attempting to blackmail their parents at some point, and food can easily lend itself to such stratagems.

I think the only time my own child attempted to sway me in this way, he was still pretty small. Perhaps he was about three years old. I do remember he was still sleeping in a crib at that stage. I had sat him down at his high chair and put a plate with his dinner in front of him. *"No, I don't want it,"* he told me. *"I don't like it."*

Now I don't actually remember what the dish was, but I'm quite sure it was nothing very different from what he usually ate. "Well, I'm sorry honey, that's all there is," I replied. "This isn't a restaurant, so I don't have anything else."

"I'm not hungry," he repeated, pushing the plate away.

"That's okay, don't worry; if you're not hungry you can get into your pajamas and go to bed," I said calmly. I scooped him up and, after brushing his teeth, brought him to his bedroom where I got him into his pajamas and put him into his crib. I gave him a kiss, read him a quick story and headed back to the kitchen to prepare dinner for my husband and myself.

Lo and behold, about fifteen minutes later a voice could be heard from his bedroom. "Mommy, I'm *hungry*."

I went in to see him. *"I'm hungry,"* he repeated.

"Honey, if you're hungry you can eat, but it's the same food I gave you before. If you want it you can have it."

He said he did, so I brought him back to his high chair where he sat down and promptly polished off the contents of his plate. I gave him a kiss and praise for eating his food; then took him to brush his teeth and brought him back to bed. I didn't need to lecture him on why he should eat; he had figured that out for himself. We had avoided a *Food War*, and he had been the one who had made the decision to eat.

In fact, my son was generally a hearty eater, but there were a few occasions, mostly when he was somewhat older, when he did actually declare that he didn't want to eat and went to bed without dinner. I would check to make sure he was well, but as a rule he seemed genuinely not to be hungry, so I didn't insist. Since all of us experience moments when we don't feel hungry at mealtime, I thought it was natural that children should occasionally lose their appetite as well. Food was something we shared and enjoyed, but it never became a source of conflict.

Ultimately, since food was never used as a reward or allowed to be the object of a power struggle between us as parents and our child, interactions around food that could have become a source of other problems, or led to unhealthy eating habits, were avoided. When as parents we adamantly insist that our children eat at all costs, it becomes *our* agenda: it's really more about ourselves and the satisfaction it gives us to see our children eat (as well as perhaps some irrational fear around what will happen if they don't) than about what our children actually need.

How our Children Blossom

The title of Chapter 7 alludes to the importance of being firm. Allowing our children to blossom as they really are happens best when it occurs within a framework of respect and a certain discipline, endowing them with the skill of "applying themselves" when that is called for. It gives them a huge advantage as they step out into the world, because it not only enables them to function effectively in society – often our main objective in insisting upon discipline – but also allows them to tap freely into their own creativity, precisely because they have a structure that serves as the scaffolding upon which their dreams and aspirations can firmly rest.

Unfortunately, as most parents will agree, believing in our children's capabilities and seeing them in a positive light does not mean they will respond by always being on their best behavior. They are learning the ropes, so understandably they will not be naturally skillful at first in adapting to what we expect of them.

Children who are taught respect for themselves and for others, a love of learning, and a willingness to work to achieve what they really want, will require time to assimilate these foundational principles. However, our willingness to view them as naturally resourceful, complete beings generates a benevolent influence that fosters their achievements and turns their "failures" into learning. "What went wrong?" can then be turned into "What can you do better next time?"

If we think about it, good behavior is such an ingrained societal value that as a rule, little attention is paid to distinguishing between well-behaved children who have been pressured from a young age to adopt a pattern of complaisant obedience at the expense of *who they are*, and children who behave, but also understand that respect is a two-way street. For the latter, there is an understanding that – within the bounds of respect for others – having the right to express themselves as they are and *having the leeway to make mistakes and be accepted anyway*, are givens.

Such children may not appear as malleable as the former, who may have learned that "being good" means "being seen and not heard", "not making waves", "doing things right" and other such behaviors that are routinely taught with the aim of creating compliant, well-behaved youngsters. From virtually every standpoint – parental, educational, societal – well-behaved children are considered "preferable" and easier to work with, at least in the ways we are used to doing so. From that standpoint, why should it matter how that behavior is acquired?

Children who learn that "being good" is the way to earn parental approval and love may, as adults, find difficulty in expressing themselves or challenging what others expect of them because the pressure on them to look good in others' eyes is so ingrained. Children brought up to *be themselves* – within the bounds of respect for others – can connect with how they feel and what they want, giving them greater access to their own creativity, even when it occasionally runs counter to the norm.

At a closer look, there are different ways of getting children to be "well-behaved". One of the most insidious ways we parents have of doing this – often with the best of intentions – is by instilling in our children the idea that when they misbehave or do something wrong, there's something wrong with them: we tell them they are *"bad"*. The implication is that they are "good" or "acceptable" in our eyes if they do what we want, or what we have determined is right.

Since all children want their parents' approval, they will assimilate these messages in an effort to conform to what we want. In the end, however, what is getting judged is the acceptability not of *what they do,* but of *who they are.* We have set the stage for their self-esteem and confidence to rest squarely on the opinion of someone outside of themselves, a pattern that repeats itself, in different forms, into adulthood.

One of the problems with this approach is the fact that there is no such thing as a fixed and immutable concept called *"what is right";* it will depend on our culture, our family, and our own experiences. Yet in conveying our sense of what is right – and to be fair, nine times out of ten it is done with a genuine concern for having our children grow up to be well-adjusted, upstanding citizens – we may end up *making our children wrong* when they don't measure up to what we expect of them, regardless of what that may be.

There are so many ideas about what is right. Our kids will grow up with whatever idea we have created for them indelibly imprinted into their outlook on life… at least until such time as they start to question it, if indeed that time ever comes. One might call it our *parental footprint.*

Indeed, if left unchallenged, that same idea of "what is right" may well be conveyed to our children's children in turn, often with the hallowed patina of traditions passed on from one generation to the next (i.e., *"In our family, this is the way we do things…"*), even if it is never explicitly worded this way.

The Illusory Goal of "Being Perfect"

I have already spoken about determining our values. It is worth taking a closer look at some values that could benefit from being redefined. Indeed, among the values that we may strive to instill as parents, there are some that do our children no service. "Being perfect" is one of them: the behavioral equivalent of a wolf in sheep's clothing.

We might ask ourselves: *"being good"* at something is such a widespread value; wouldn't that make *"being perfect"* even better? It's the case of a value gone awry, and it is all the more difficult to unmask because it's so seductive. Instead of *"doing* our best", we *"do* perfect". It seems like the ultimate value; the loftiest of goals on which to set our sights.

What happens? The search for something unattainable can condition our lives and our happiness. Being perfect can run from getting the best grades, to wearing the right clothes, to being voted class president, to having a perfect life with husband/ wife, a house, a car, and a perfect job. None of which are bad, in and of themselves; quite the contrary. It's the connotation of perfection that we attach to these objectives that gets us into trouble when it ends up running our lives.

There are many variations on this theme, but in fact, "being perfect" is a malady that causes much suffering as children grow older, become adults, and find themselves unable to accomplish all that they have set out to do. Or they accomplish all that they have set out to do, and one day realize that they are unhappy because they never actually decided for themselves what it was they wanted. They just never wanted to disappoint any of the people (parents, among others) who had their hopes pinned on seeing them succeed.

The need to be perfect is manifested in many ways. Some people never dare to try anything that would push the limits of what they believe to be achievable, for fear of not being able to do it perfectly. They set the bar low, preferring the satisfaction of achieving something predictably attainable than challenging themselves to go farther and risk not "doing it just right".

There are those, as well, who say they don't feel passion for anything, when the truth is that allowing themselves to feel their passion would be like *committing* to something – a commitment they are unwilling to make for fear of not being able to excel and be perfect at whatever it is.

The "being perfect" malady is not only widespread; it silently conditions our lives. Because the people for whom we strove so hard to do well also admire our accomplishments, it's often difficult to allow ourselves to realize that much of our life has not been devoted to whatever, had we followed our heart or the "nudge" we felt from time to time growing up, we might otherwise have done. After all, our parents are pleased, friends and colleagues pat us on the back, and our achievements are extolled.

In the case of parents, it is the unfortunate story of how wanting something for our children with the best of intentions can be completely off the mark. We may have experienced something similar ourselves, setting off on a track that we came to believe would reap us all of the things that were held up to us as desirable when we were young: recognition, approval, success. Certain courses of study might have been adopted because they would ensure we would ultimately get a job with a good income and professional recognition. We might have convinced ourselves (or perhaps, have been convinced) that a different path, one we secretly longed to follow, was no more than a pipe dream, or a pursuit unworthy of our talents.

Again, there are so many preconceived notions and judgments that float around in our world disguised as "Reality" (and the set of beliefs that goes with it) that it's generally difficult for adults, let alone children, to distinguish between what they have been led to believe is possible, and what they can in fact – through creativity, dedication, and faith – create for themselves in their lives. Even youngsters who follow a path that may not be considered socially prestigious or lucrative, such as art, theater and dance, to name a few, may embark on this journey out of love while laboring under the belief that they will never be able to earn a decent living from it.

If, when we instill respect and good behavior in our children, we continue to believe in and support them and withhold our judgments – about them, about whether what they are interested in is of any value, or about whether they have achieved anything of note on our own scale of virtue – they will be able to access the imagination and creativity that get stifled when they are simply urged to meet our expectations. They will be able to develop the faith in themselves that will enable them to achieve what they want in life, and be able to "weather the storms" in which more fragile crafts capsize.

Interestingly, it is the "mavericks" who as adults win our admiration because they have done something that most of us would never have thought of doing, let alone allowed ourselves to imagine achieving. Mavericks are found in all walks of life: business, science, the arts... Many are innovators in their field; although many are unsung heroes, a few notable individuals go on to achieve widespread public recognition.

What they have in common is their determination to follow a path that they believe in; the path that their intuition – or their passion – tells them is where they need to go. They go after the idea that no one thought of or believed in, and they are often willing to assume considerable risks to bring it to fruition. They are more creative in whatever they choose to do in life, and they are "at choice" because they make their decisions not on the basis of what is expected of them, but based on something they believe they can do, even if they are the only ones who see it. Looking back over the course of their lives, their faith in their intuition and clairvoyance is pointed to as inspirational; yet in society, and particularly in our own homes, such nonconformity is frequently frowned upon and discouraged.

Our society is not geared toward allowing such creative spirits to blossom. It is more geared toward homogenizing the masses, one might say. Interestingly, Robert Frost's well-known poem *"The Road not Taken"* is frequently quoted and discussed in schools that, in many cases, instill much the opposite, prompting children to shy from any course of action that implies some sort of risk. If we add to this context parental and peer pressure to stay on the safe and narrow, how many students ultimately depart from a path deemed safe to take "the road less traveled" that the renowned poet says was what made "all the difference"?

Modeling What we Want

It's clear to me that raising our children in a context of respect and discipline, when done without judging them, actually sets the stage for greater freedom and possibility. It's worth evoking here the common saying that "one's own freedom stops where another person's begins". In other words, our own freedom coexists hand in hand with respect for those around us. The same principle holds true for our kids.

At the opposite end of the spectrum there are parents who, in their determination to allow their children to be fully self-expressed, lose sight of their children's need for guidelines. We all know of children who have been allowed to "be who they are" with few or no restrictions by overly permissive parents who appear to feel that placing any limits on their offspring will somehow cramp their style. It does a disservice to such youngsters, who often have difficulty in discovering "where their freedom ends and someone else's begins". Such youngsters fall victim to their own frustration when they cannot have or do what they have learned to assume that they are entitled to, and ultimately – and equally important – they never benefit from a safe container in which their potential can blossom and thrive.

There are also parents who grope for, but don't find, ways to place appropriate limits on their kids as they grow. Some parents impose a strict model on their kids that is an exact replica of how they themselves were brought up. Others – either because they themselves grew up with few limits, or because they have decided to toss out the window a strict model of upbringing that didn't work for them – may err on the side of excessive permissiveness. Alongside these parents are those who are struggling to find their way amidst a plethora of advice and admonitions from experts, and the evidence that something has to change because a lot of what they are doing themselves, or witnessing being done around them, is manifestly not working.

If there is anything that we can do to help our children grow up to be happy, well-adjusted adults, it is to combine encouragement with firmness, and the belief that our children are amazing, just the way they are. Again, believing that our children are amazing does not mean allowing ourselves to be seduced into believing that they don't need our assistance, in the form of some structure and rules, and the discipline that will help them later in life.

Although there is no single template for child-rearing, I would say without a doubt that allowing ourselves to believe in our kids, even when we don't know who they want to become or how they are going to do it, is key. For us, being "real" and allowing ourselves to fail is also a model for our kids, encouraging them to keep trying even when they do not at first succeed. The old adage, *"If at first you don't succeed, then try and try again",* is oft quoted but little practiced. All too often, a first try that is unsuccessful prompts us to just throw in the towel and quit. In fact, the mere prospect of being unsuccessful is often enough to discourage us from even taking a first stab at whatever it is.

However, there's no reason why, just because *we* are not particularly "good" at failing, we can't allow our kids to learn to do so, and to learn to celebrate their failures together with their successes. We are, after all, at choice about the input we give our kids, so that they can trust themselves to create and seize opportunities we might not even have imagined. It means being curious and non-judgmental about their interests and efforts, knowing that whatever they undertake will lead them, by however circuitous a route, to where they are going. In all of this process, discipline is a gift that, when instilled from a young age, often – surprisingly – does not require a heavy hand at all.

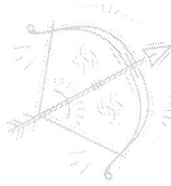

CHAPTER 7

The Plant Needs a Bigger Pot

From an early age, children are avid learners who love challenges. As they grow, constantly setting their sights on what is next for them, they imitate older children and emulate their parents, often in amusing ways. Small children play house, or play doctor, and long to be on the same sports team as their older siblings.

Even very small tots will demonstrate their budding independence. Instead of holding mommy's hand, our little one wants to run ahead on her own. Who is not familiar with the sight of a toddler exercising her newfound ability to walk, trotting gleefully off in the opposite direction as her mother sprints to catch up with her?

For children, part of growing up is also about pushing the limits that we set for them. It can be disconcerting to find oneself faced with a defiant toddler who appears to say "No" to just about everything we would like to get her to do. We all know that this stage is normal in a child's development – those *"terrible twos"* (or threes) that we have all read about – but the vehemence with which our young charges refuse to comply can come as a surprise.

The Art of Compromise

It is at this point that many of us have our first encounter with our children's demand for independence, even as they continue to depend on us for virtually all of their basic needs. Indeed, one of the dilemmas that many of us face as parents is just how intransigent to be in the face of our kids' growing independence and desire for autonomy.

What may be fairly straightforward to us when our children are two or three years old becomes less so as they grow and continue to seek new ways of asserting their growing desire for emancipation. Clearly, we will not hand a two-year-old a knife and fork, but at what point can our child be entrusted with setting the table, including placing knives and forks for the adults, first under our watchful eye and then alone? Often children resist being shepherded in their efforts to try new things, pushing away the parental hand that attempts to guide them as they proudly perform tasks that they are allowed to do on their own for the first time.

Children absolutely know when we don't want them to do something that we feel is tricky or hazardous for them, and inevitably, that is precisely what they want to do. They want to bring the sharp knives to the table together with the forks, and are not happy to be assigned only part of the task.

The art of compromise works well with children, as long as we set the limits. An obvious example of striking a compromise in this case would be the parent bringing the knife to the table, and then allowing the child to carefully set it on the placemat or tablecloth where it belongs. Compromise may call for some creativity and the willingness to be flexible on our part, but it garners good results in terms of children's self-esteem and their perception of their own ability to stretch themselves and do things that are beyond the limits initially set for them.

Once the Newness Fades: Shifting Perspectives

We know that with many of the things that our children are initially eager to learn and be allowed to do, once the newness fades the "thing" itself becomes old hat and their interest wanes. Our children are delighted to be allowed to carry items to the table, individually or on a tray, while we are still cautious about letting them do so. However, once they have been given the opportunity to exercise their skills and become good at setting the table – or whatever other task we have assigned them – they will frequently start to balk or procrastinate when we ask them to do it as a matter of course.

This propensity is not limited to childhood. The teenager who is learning to drive will happily chauffeur his parents anywhere while the experience is still new and exciting. Once the newness wears off, however, the same experience becomes a bothersome chore.

In fact, if we take this apparently trivial example and apply it to our own lives, there can hardly be a better illustration of how what we consider to be Reality is actually no more than the reflection of our *feelings* about that situation. The same circumstances that appear to us to be favorable from one perspective can seem annoying or unfortunate from another.

If we extrapolate the above example to another context, such as getting hired to a new position, we can see how our initial reaction of: *Wow, I've got a new job, I'm so lucky!* can eventually turn into: *I'm so bored in this job; I already know it backward and forward; I need new challenges.* The job is the same, but our perspective has changed. What was initially new and interesting has become humdrum and predictable.

As parents, we know that making things seem new and exciting for our children is not always possible, not the least because we may not always be in the mood to do so or have access at that particular moment to the creativity or bright idea that will inspire us. However, we inherently know that when infants get fussy, or when we take away from them something that they want and they burst into tears, distracting them with something new can often be enough to make them forget what it was that got them upset. We instinctively find something that will change their perspective from one of frustration to one of curiosity.

Happily, what works for them also works for us: as adults, this shift in perspective is something we can consciously choose to do for ourselves, changing the way we experience the situation we are in by simply deciding to see it in a new light. In fact, our perspective not just toward a specific situation, but toward life as a whole, is something we can consciously choose.

Responsibility and Choice

Children not only like things that are new; they love having responsibilities that stretch them and make them feel grown-up and capable. Such responsibilities, given progressively, can make our kids feel more engaged as members of their family and ultimately, as members of their community. Instead of finding ourselves, when our children are already teenagers, with the question of how to instill in them a sense of responsibility, we can begin when they are small, giving them simple tasks and chores that let them know we trust and believe in them. It builds their self-esteem and their sense of accountability.

As mentioned earlier in this book, as we give our children responsibilities, we can teach them about choice. Again, I am not referring to the right to choose whether or not they will take on the responsibilities we ask of them. As parents, we are going to be asking our children to undertake different tasks, whether it be walking the dog or washing the dishes. Some tasks may be fun; others more of a chore; and as I have already stated, many things that begin as fun may at some point turn into drudgery.

Here, when I speak of choice, it is more about choosing "how we want to be" with what it is we have to do. Most of us were never taught that *we get to choose how we feel about our circumstances;* mostly we just react based on our learned expectations. For example: we can do a chore feeling we are "put upon" because we would rather be doing something else, or we can choose to do a chore feeling proud to be part of a team in which everyone plays a part.

Some time ago, a coaching client of mine asked me what she could do to get her two teenagers to be more responsible without scaring them by telling them about the "tough economic realities" and the possibility that it would not be easy for them to get ahead in life. Having evidently blurred the distinction between *responsibility* and *hardship,* she had been keeping her children in a kind of Neverland of innocence and immaturity that she felt would somehow shelter them from the tough world that awaited them outside when they became adults.

It's useful to remember that, for our children and for ourselves, *assuming responsibility* entails quite the opposite: *it is actually about freedom and the ability to choose what we want to do with our circumstances in life.* As we give our young children the opportunity to take on more responsibilities, we are not only showing them that we trust and rely on them, but we are actually instilling in them a sense of what responsibility means in the broadest sense of the word; i.e., consciously deciding how they will lead their lives as they pass through adolescence and into adulthood.

Again, for them it means mindfully choosing not only what they want to do, but how they want to be with the circumstances they encounter, and even with the circumstances they want to create for themselves in their lives. Certainly it is a radically different perspective from the one put forward to me by the concerned mother, above, whose children had never had the opportunity to develop the creativity and resourcefulness that would enable them to overcome difficult circumstances when they arose.

Responsibility from this standpoint goes hand in hand with choice and opportunity. As our children take on responsibility in the household – little by little and in accordance with their age and ability to take on new tasks – we can show them how they can do the same for themselves as individuals, taking on responsibility for what they do and what they feel, consciously choosing what to do with the circumstances they encounter. It is an empowering vision; one that without a doubt constitutes a prophylaxis against pessimism and the victimhood that is so prevalent in our society.

In fact, pessimism and depression are often the result of a perceived inability to change or influence what happens to us. Victimhood is the perception that we are impotent and vulnerable in an inherently difficult world, and that we have little or no control over our circumstances.

The World English Dictionary defines "responsibility" as: *the ability or authority to act or decide on one's own, without supervision.* There is no reference to hardship or tribulations. The same capacity that our children employ in taking on new tasks, and acquiring autonomy in doing them, is used by them to decide on their own *how they want to be in this world.*

It is not something that happens overnight, and indeed, one may only be aware that this process of choice and decision-making has taken hold after many years of repetition and encouragement. In my son's case, I would say it wasn't until he had reached his early teens that the message had been assimilated and he was actually aware of his ability and responsibility in choosing not only his actions, but his feelings and emotions as well.

Building Emotional Intelligence

It may sound odd at first to imagine choosing one's emotions, and of course, many of our emotions will remain spontaneous. But when we decide to feel good about something, our entire perspective changes, and this ability is something we can apply to any area of our lives.

An awareness of and ability to connect with our emotions is also the first building block of *emotional intelligence*, a concept associated with success and happiness in life. When we help our children hone their ability to identify and manage – rather than suppress – their feelings, we are doing them a great favor that will stand them in good stead as they grow.

It's curious that we want our children to be responsible when they grow up, yet often fail to see how the foundation for responsibility and discipline is laid when they are very young.

In our own household we had conversations about a variety of subjects, often around the dinner table or in the living room, and my child, from the time he was old enough to have an opinion, was typically included. We discovered, to our surprise, that even as a youngster his comments were often quite astute.

Family discussions were something I myself grew up with, and I remember my mother once telling me that in her youth she and her sister had always been invited to express their views in family conversations, so I suppose in our case the tradition goes back a long way: in my son's case, at least as far as his great-grandparents. I am also sure that one can decide to begin this tradition in any household, at any time.

Here I would take a moment to make a plea for family time. Even after my separation, when my son and I became the entirety of our downsized family "unit", I made a point of having as many meals together as we could. Meals were a chance to catch up on what was going on in each other's day and to celebrate achievements, big and small. Celebrations included getting a great grade on a tough exam, or having a difficult conversation with someone and seeing it go well…

or not so well, but learning what went wrong and what could be done better next time. We always celebrate discovery – of where we stand or what is next for us, or sometimes, just getting clear on what we don't want in our lives – when doing so represents a step forward. Celebration also includes gratitude for what we have.

On days when we do not specifically celebrate an achievement or learning, we share what is going on in our lives. I have learned as a parent that being open, supportive, and in particular, nonjudgmental, has in some way given my son the freedom to be more candid and forthcoming about his own wants and desires, as well as his concerns.

Parents often express to me their desire to experience such confidence and closeness with their own children. What is important, as I see it, is the groundwork that underpins that confidence. Ideally, the building blocks of that groundwork would be laid in early childhood, although I also believe it is never too late to start.

If someone had asked me, way back when, whether I thought my son would eventually share his thoughts and feelings with me, I would have said that it would be great if he did but that I had no expectations around creating such trust and closeness, particularly because my son was more of the *"run around and do it"* type than the *"let's sit and snuggle and talk about it"* type when he was very young.

As a result, such closeness was never a particular objective for me when my child was small, and in fact, I didn't know if it would ultimately happen; I just let him be who he was, allowing him to have his dreams and tell me about them if he wanted, never at any stage introducing my own preconceived notions of what he should do. As he grew older, I would hear him out even when I wasn't sure how he was going to achieve his objectives. I also – and this caveat is important – let him know when I disagreed.

I never gave him *carte blanche* for everything he wanted to do when he was growing up because, like most youngsters, he often wanted to bite off more than he could chew, and I was very clear that his activities had to be age-appropriate. He was allowed to express an opinion, but we as his parents always had the last word.

Ultimately, as I stress elsewhere in this book, consideration and regard for others were consistently the most important principles in our household – something on which his father and I were never prepared to compromise – and that eventually sank in. The same consideration was extended to him, meaning that his right to privacy was acknowledged. At no time did I pry or attempt to glean information from him that he did not want to share. Of course I would ask him about his day when he came home from school, and most of the time my question: *"How did school go?"* was met with a perfunctory, *"Okay",* as he busied himself with something far more interesting to him than recounting to me that day's experience with his classmates or teachers.

I would usually ask for more particulars, but when he didn't provide them, I didn't insist either. At the same time – again, mostly at the dinner table or in the car, when I was chauffeuring him somewhere and he was a captive audience – I began asking him other questions, and also telling him about some of the things that I myself had encountered at work or elsewhere. In other words, the desire to converse and share did not emerge spontaneously, but was nurtured and gradually materialized over time.

A Safe Space

Some might be tempted to conclude that the initial failure of my attempts to get my child to talk more about his day had to do with the fact that he was a boy, less given to expanding in detail upon his activities than he might have had he been a girl. Such gender differences do frequently appear in young children. He was definitely more interested in doing whatever activity was at hand than in spending time talking, a situation that continued for many years.

When I was traveling for work and phoned home, I could almost hear the haste in his voice as he answered my questions in monosyllables, rushing to get to the part: *"I love you too"*, after which he could return his attention to whatever activity of his I had interrupted with my call. Actually, instead of seeing it as an unwillingness to communicate I saw it as a proof of the trust and safety that was built into our relationship, because he was fine without me and knew I would be back when my trip was done.

Again, I am convinced that much of that trust originated in my firmness with him on certain principles on which I refused to budge because they were the bedrock of my beliefs around how he was to be raised. As said earlier, in general we know that setting limits is an important part of child-rearing, but what is often not stressed is the importance of the parent's own conviction that the limits being imposed are fundamental and non-negotiable.

When we show by our words and actions that we are impeccable and uncompromising with our deepest values – in my case, as stressed earlier, the key value was respect – our children not only learn to honor the value, but learn to trust and appreciate us for it as well. In other words, parental firmness, judiciously applied, creates a foundation of safety and trust in which our relationship with our children can expand.

Part of the trust was also based on my willingness to hear my son out when he did talk about his experiences and his interests. Further still, there was trust when I disagreed with what he said, because my disagreement was always expressed in a way that contained no judgment of him for what he felt, though I always retained the position of authority that gave me the final say.

There are many examples of the way we build trust, and I have included an entire chapter on the subject in this book. As I have already mentioned, it is built by modeling, ourselves, the behaviors and attitudes that we wish to instill in our children; indeed, by treating our children with the same consideration that we ourselves would wish to be given. My child was exposed to hearing adult perceptions and moods talked about well before he himself actually began opening up, yet no pressure was ever put on him to share his own feelings – although he was invited to do so.

Getting beyond the mere *"what I did at school and at soccer practice"* to *"how I feel about girls and dating"* actually took some time. As mentioned earlier, I had no expectations in terms of the content of what he would share. I kind of assumed there would be many things he would want to keep to himself, and I respected that too.

As a result, it turned out to be a pleasant surprise to share my son's thoughts and feelings, as well as his dreams. At some point – in fact, beginning when he was a teenager – conversations began to expand beyond the usual superficial remarks about school grades and soccer scores, to touch on aspects of human emotion and behavior that many individuals much older than he might find difficult to articulate. It was certainly not the stereotypical picture of what our adolescents are expected to look like: moody, aloof, intractable... the image of that "difficult" age group that abounds.

In fact, if we consider that the ability to perceive and understand one's feelings and emotions is something innately human, just as emotions themselves are an innately human experience, we can understand the importance of creating fertile ground for this ability to develop and blossom.

In our household, emotions have always been freely expressed. My son is a product of this experience; I am convinced that, together with the potential that was his all along, it has helped him be and express himself as the person he is today. He has emerged as a bearer of peace and optimism, a person who feels deeply and knows how powerful his feelings, added to his intelligence, are, in creating his future in an intentional way. I am also convinced that he will be a better partner and parent himself in the future because his ability to connect with who he is fully – not just limited to mind and body, but including heart and soul as well – has allowed him to tap into his potential in a way that is free and unconstrained.

Positive Expectations

As kids grow, their perspectives naturally shift. As parents, not only can we be attuned to the changes that appear; in many instances we can actually create the expectation in our youngsters of what such changes will be. Of course, to some extent we already do this naturally when we tell our children that there are things they can't do because they're too little, thus implying that as they grow older they will acquire the right and privilege of doing them.

In my son's case, I discovered the value of generating positive expectations with regard to some things that he didn't initially like. The simple example below is easily extrapolated to other areas of life where generating a positive expectation will facilitate our child-rearing efforts and build our child's self-esteem:

At home I made an effort to make meals varied, in an attempt to get my son used to a range of different foods, including a number of vegetables, of course, and a variety of cheeses. My child liked most cheeses, but decided he didn't like goat cheese (one of my own personal favorites). My response to his initial reaction was, *"Don't worry. When you grow up you'll probably learn to like it."* I used the same line for other foods that he wasn't wild about, such as broccoli and garbanzos. Every now and then, when I prepared a meal that included one of his un-favorite foods, I would ask him to try a small portion to decide whether he finally liked it.

If he said he didn't like it, I simply replied, *"That's okay. You can still get to like it when you grow up."* There was no pressure put on him to like those foods, but at the same time there was a kind of expectation created that he would end up liking them. In fact, my son now loves goat cheese and broccoli, and does eat garbanzos... although they are still not his favorite! I figure that's okay... Having never managed to like Brussels sprouts myself, I understand that there are some foods one may just not love!

The point is, when we treat our children the way we would like to see them be; i.e., creating an expectation of positive behavior before they have yet displayed it, we are predisposing them to act that way. When all of our emphasis is on correcting negative behavior, it is their negative behavior – or our anticipation of their negative behavior – that is getting all of our attention. Under such circumstances our children's behavior is influenced primarily by the prospect of correction or punishment if they don't behave, or by their need to win our approval when they do.

Since discipline is in fact important, I feel a distinction needs to be made here. Naturally, we want to correct negative behavior, and also to show children what we expect of them. The difference lies in the *underlying premise* for our actions.

Our positive expectations reflect a *belief* about our children: that they are good, capable, willing, and can do well. A simple example such as the one just given – above and beyond the issue of food choices – is actually a statement of trust in my child.

Small achievements such as this one lay the groundwork for the expectations that our children themselves will have as they grow, and the way they see the world. In this regard, positive expectations and discipline go hand in hand, and are fundamental to enabling our children to embrace the world and their lives in it. Even when we need to intervene to correct our youngsters' behavior, the underlying premise is one of supporting them rather than holding them back.

I mention, elsewhere in this book, that the correction, discipline and approval we give our children are like the training wheels that help them navigate on their bicycle while they are still learning to ride. We are supporting them until they become independent, and are able to stay in balance for themselves.

My own father, who taught his three children how to ride their bikes, always said that his success – his kids learned much quicker than most – was due to the fact that after taking the training wheels off he would run alongside us as we pedaled, holding a gentle hand close, ready to support us when we tipped, but never actually holding on to the bike. That way his children were actually able to get a feel for their bike, learning how to control it themselves, finding their balance their own way.

Thinking back to those times I find this image is a great metaphor for the way we support our kids as they grow. The bike is their life, and they learn to handle it on their own as they graduate, bit by bit, from using training wheels, to getting our support as they need it, to complete mastery, when riding it is as natural to them as walking or running.

When the *underlying premise* for the way we treat our children is that they are perfect from birth, with their own path to follow and their own way of being in this world, we are actually there to guide them and give them the "toolkit" of useful learning in their early years that will enable them to become independent and self-motivated. That is, in fact, our role as parents.

Setting Limits

Of course children will require discipline and limits too… but what exactly are those limits supposed to be? For some parents, setting limits means solicitously steering their kids down a safe and narrow path that is meant to take them to a successful future with the fewest upsets possible. Other parents fret about what limits to set, and *when*. In fact, the limits themselves can be very simple and designed to gradually allow children considerable freedom as time goes by.

There are limits having to do with manners, which means anything from learning how to say *please* and *thank you* to knowing that it is not okay for our infant to play with her food or throw her spoon when she gets upset. Many limits are about what is age-appropriate: for example, the age at which children can go out on their own. Most such limits appear to be basic common sense to us when children are small, although after a certain age, parents' decisions will primarily be determined by whether their attitude toward child-raising is stricter or more "laissez-faire".

There will be some tension between what kids want to do – often emulating their friends, or inspired by perceived advantages in other families, where more laxity is the rule – and what parents decide is right for their children. However, these limits are not in contradiction with the basic *underlying premise,* which is the way we perceive our children, holding them to be complete and resourceful from day one. We guide them, but do not change them.

We create a safe container in which they grow, like a small flower pot for a seedling that will eventually need to be transplanted into something bigger to make room for its growing roots. When the plant outgrows its pot it cannot flourish as it does when the pot is spacious. Yet from the time when it is still a seed to when it reaches maturity, the plant is perfect, containing within it the capacity to burgeon and thrive.

Discipline Furthers their Potential

Some might argue that the need for discipline is proof that our children need to be molded and shaped. If our children were indeed perfect from day one, the objection might go, certainly discipline would not be necessary.

However, seen from the standpoint of their innate perfection, discipline is actually a learning process that allows our children to be at their most brilliant, a bit like the cutting and polishing of the facets of a diamond whose beauty was in it all along.

I personally like the following dictionary definition of "discipline": *activity, exercise, or a regimen that develops or improves a skill; training.* Or again: *the ability to control one's own behavior.*

When I say our children are perfect, it's because they contain within them the potential to lead a fulfilling life, following the path or purpose that they desire. They will need to equip themselves with the tools to do so, just as we do when we seek to learn something new, or perfect what we already know.

Discipline is just another form of training that hones certain skills. When youngsters are small it serves, initially, to give them a sense of security as we show our love for them by modeling for them what is acceptable behavior. They are taught manners, and certain social skills that will vary depending on our culture – and on our family!

Discipline provides a structure in which to feel safe. It's like playing any game: if we know the rules we can concentrate on just playing, but if the rules are unclear, or there are no rules, the game becomes chaotic and confusing. When our attention is on the confusion we perform less well, and our creativity has no space to expand. In fact, in any sport experienced players can "forget" the rules because they are so internalized. The rules become the foundation on which their own talent and proficiency can grow.

So the message here is: some rules are necessary, because they create the structure enabling our kids to be on their best game, but once those rules are learned and the structure is in place, considerable freedom is possible. As our children grow, discipline is a skill that they themselves can apply: learning self-restraint and the ability to focus is an important part of the toolkit that they will need in achieving self-mastery, freeing up more energy for self-motivation as well.

At the same time, while self-motivation is most apparent when children do what they love, if we instill in them the knowledge that they can choose their perspective, this ability, together with self-discipline, can enable them to find motivation even in tackling things that are not initially appealing.

In essence, I see discipline as the antithesis of punishment. I like to think of it as a learning process: together with self-motivation, discipline is a cornerstone of personal growth. It is a positive exercise rather than a negative one: an opportunity to reinforce the good habits that will increase self-restraint and control and actually enhance self-motivation.

It is for this reason that discipline is most effective when it's based on the expectation that our children will behave well, rather than the presumption that they won't. A great example of this underlying belief is McGregor's Theory X and Theory Y, developed for management settings, but actually applicable to human beings in general.

Both theories are based on an underlying belief: Theory X is the underlying assumption in which we hold that most people, left to their own devices, are irresponsible, indifferent and unmotivated. Theory Y is the underlying assumption that people are self-motivated, naturally seek self-fulfillment and will willingly commit to objectives that respond to this inner desire. Guess which group of people, based on the assumption held by their managers, performs better?

In like fashion, our children will respond naturally to the way we hold them, whether we consider them to be lazy and unreliable, or resourceful and responsible. In fact, the way we see them is not only the first big step toward setting the stage for how they will grow; the way we see them is actually a choice we make; the way we *have chosen* to see them. The choice may be made consciously or unconsciously, but it will have an impact on how our kids see themselves, and on the beliefs about themselves that they will carry around with them into adulthood.

When we see children from birth as containing their full potential within, it is like holding an intention for them: one that will enhance the qualities they possess innately.

I feel it is worth spending a moment to glance at the antithesis of this outlook on child-rearing. As mentioned earlier, when the premise for correction and discipline is a belief that children, like clay, have to be molded and shaped into what we want them to be, the only motivation that our children have for doing what we ask of them is *to please us*.

I am not referring here to the efforts made by small children to get their parents to admire and applaud their first accomplishments, be it riding a bike or drawing a picture. As mentioned earlier, knowing that

for children, being "grown up" is a big incentive, parents tend naturally to lavish praise upon their fledgling endeavors; such praise actually
fosters self-esteem, and it is with this intention that it is given.

Such praise is quite different from parental approval that is *"earned"*
– the implication of course being that it can also be *withheld* – thereby turning it into both an objective and, eventually… a limitation,
guiding our efforts and conditioning us to follow whatever path that is
deemed by others to be correct.

Circumventing our Limiting Beliefs

The belief that children have to be shaped into something usually
emerges from a fear on our part that if our children are allowed to
naturally follow their inclinations, they will somehow escape our control … with unpredictable consequences. There is a belief that we are
responsible for making them into well-adjusted, competent members
of society.

The problem is that we believe we know ahead of time what will
be best for them based on our own experience of the world, without
actually allowing them to find it out for themselves. Our kids are told
that they have to behave a certain way to *win approval/be successful/get
ahead,* and their self-esteem reposes essentially on the external approval they earn by conforming to others' idea – held first by parents, and
then by society – of who they should be.

In fact, the idea held by many parents that our children have to be
molded into something actually derives from the underlying fear that
our kids may intrinsically not be good enough just the way they are.

If this statement appears impossible or contradictory to parents who love their children *more than anything else in the world,* it is useful to consider just why we place so much emphasis on having them *do better.* Or *be* better. Do we ask ourselves: Better than what? To what end? Do we stop to think about the implications of urging our children to be achievers separate from a consideration of who they are as human beings, and in what way achievement – academic, physical or artistic – will help bring out the best in them, whatever they feel that may be?

Again, the widespread notion that our children need to be shaped into *something* stems from a belief that they would somehow be better if they would just behave or appear differently in some way. And because our intentions are good, we may be unaware that what we are unwittingly doing is attempting to dissimulate or compensate for what we perceive about our children as being "not good enough". Instead of seeing our children as innately whole and unique, we see what doesn't tally with what we believe to be meritorious or requisite in our society, and feel it is our parental responsibility to change whatever that might be.

In this way, we project our own limitations or limiting beliefs onto our kids. What worked for us will work for them. And interestingly, what didn't work for us is *also* often still brandished as a goal to be achieved. In this case, our children are often seen as a chance to vicariously redeem ourselves for our own unsuccessful efforts to squeeze into a mold that didn't fit. Or we think that where we failed, our children, if sufficiently exhorted to do so, will succeed. It's interesting to see how often parents, rather than discarding the mold that didn't fit, will try to extrude their own children through that very same mold.

Acceptance

Indeed, more than parental approval, what is at stake is *acceptance*. When parental acceptance is conditional – i.e., *granted* when children conform to our expectations; *withheld* when they do not – the compass that guides them and the only gauge of their results is the degree to which they can "earn" this acceptance. (I use the two words, "earn" and "acceptance" together advisedly, because as I see them, in this context they are actually inherently contradictory).

The problem with this sort of motivation is that there is no real self-motivation. Not to mention the fact that basing our actions on winning someone else's approval or acceptance may appear normal to us when it applies to children, but what about when we are adults? Who says that our children, who felt compelled to do things to win our approval, will not continue to seek approval from other sources for what they do throughout their lives? Isn't it something we often discover ourselves doing? The little voice in the back of our head telling us, as adults, that we shouldn't take risks, that we will fail, look stupid, or risk incurring someone else's disapproval, comes from the original need to conform to someone else's idea of who we are.

Children whose parents value them for who they are value themselves. When raising children becomes a process of discovery and delight – complete with the occasional tribulations along the way – children flourish and learn to delight in life on their own. Being valued for who we are is a gift. We can offer this gift to our kids, even if we never really benefited from it ourselves. It's a gift that enables our children to connect with who they are; from this place of connection they will discover what it is that they want to do on this planet and the unique contribution that is theirs to make. It may look nothing like what we imagine for them, but it will give them a foothold in our changing world where they can grow and thrive, experiencing happiness and fulfillment in the process. It doesn't get any better than that.

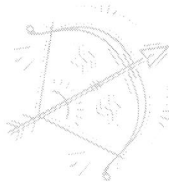

CHAPTER 8

The Myth of the Perfect Parent

*H*ow many parents, and parents-to-be, struggle with the belief that if they did not have particularly skillful parents themselves, they will never be capable of raising happy, well-balanced children?

The idea that we inherit our parents' shortcomings and idiosyncrasies is widespread. This belief is due, in large part, to the fact that there is a natural tendency to perpetuate what we learn in our home environment.

Parenting as a Creative Act

The result is that a number of prospective parents worry a good deal about whether they will be up to the task of raising children if their own childhood was less than ideal. Those who had a wonderful childhood and gifted parents may feel utterly confident at the prospect of raising kids, while those who didn't may fret over not having a model to follow.

Yet, Parenting *is a Creative Act.*

There's good news … We all have the ability to be great parents if we so choose! We aren't limited clones, pinched off the original like a piece of sourdough taken to make the starter for a new batch. We can decide how we want to be as parents, and we can raise children who are well-adjusted, regardless of their personality traits and temperament.

Without the benefit of a strong, positive relationship with their own parents, some new parents tread a more cautious path in raising their offspring. Others may be overly indulgent. Yet parenting is more than a sum total of rules that we pass on. It's about who we are, what we have to give and, not less importantly, what we're prepared to learn from our children.

For some of us, the stretch lies in allowing ourselves to be more permissive; for others, it means being stricter. If there were things one grew up with that are worth keeping, it makes sense do so. But we can always find ways to improve upon what we received from our parents, because times change, children change, and society itself evolves.

Stepping out of Their Way

Children born today are far more alert and receive more external stimuli than was once the case, and a globalized world offers them many more opportunities to become who they want to be. As a result, the potential for them to dream up a totally amazing life for themselves exists; we can allow them to tap into their imagination and go for what they really want if we can just step out of their way.

Regardless of the parenting we ourselves received, there can be a great temptation to think not only that we must be role models, but that we have the duty to set our kids off on the right path to their future as well. It may indeed be our idea of what good parents do. In doing so, however, we may unconsciously transfer to our children the same limitations that we were taught by our own well-meaning parents.

If we imagine an empty stage on which children are given a few props and costumes, and each is asked to create a sketch, we know that our child's performance will be different from another child's. Our children are the actors; the performance is the product of their individual imagination and creativity. It should come as a relief to know that being a good parent does not involve being playwright and director as well! All we need to do is build the stage; we don't have to mastermind the results.

Curiously, even siblings may create completely different scenarios using the same props, something parents may point to in perplexity as individual differences become apparent. It is this uniqueness that is the external expression of the fundamental creativity of each human being, and the reason why we can't second-guess what lies within our children, waiting to emerge. In fact, our attempts to steer our child toward a particular pursuit might be totally off the mark.

Our Preconceptions: The Perfect Child

For many of us, the ultimate validation that we are Perfect Parents is having a Perfect Child *(see the difference between this notion and the concept of* "perfection" *referred to in the Glossary of this book).*

It may be very clear to us what perfection means, since it is based on our own expectations, yet the concept itself is intrinsically subjective, and in each household probably means something different. It is natural to arrive at conclusions about our children and how they meet our expectations, so as parents we need to be able to cultivate the ability to revise our assumptions, staying open to what may yet emerge.

The quest for perfection is something to which I allude elsewhere in this book. The Perfect Child might be the one with the best grades, or the best behavior, or the one who has been elected class leader or won the community poetry prize. It might be the talented athlete, or the child who is admired and emulated by friends and classmates.

What constitutes perfect for some parents is very different for others. Some parents may applaud originality; others, brilliance or studiousness. There is a natural tendency to *read into* our children's accomplishments, seeing them as harbingers of success. On the lookout, we are eager to seize upon any sign that could presage future excellence.

I used to watch my son play tennis, racing around the court to return all the balls, his determination reducing us to laughter, and wonder whether he might go far as a tennis player. He didn't appear to enjoy swimming much, but when he changed schools for a year he ended up taking swimming lessons with his class at a nearby sports club and – much to my surprise – came home one day with a letter that, based on his performance, offered him a scholarship to go and train with their team. He became an avid swimmer, participating in competitive events by the time he was 9, thereby upending my initial conclusion that he would never take to the sport.

Although he seemed to do well at most sports, my child seemed to have his heart set on playing soccer, or "football" as it is called here. Like most youngsters his age, he grew up with an admiration for soccer players, and *Barça,* Barcelona's soccer team, is prestigious around the world for its accomplishments.

I confess I never could see him becoming a great soccer player in a sport that is so popular and competitive that only a handful of players ever reach notoriety or manage to make a living from it, but I never discouraged him. Today, he still swims (non-competitively) for exercise, and is a passably good soccer player, although matches are local team events, and the team members tend to be university friends and acquaintances.

Another example of a misconception on my part concerned language. Since my son was already learning Spanish and Catalan in school and was speaking English at home with me (or more accurately, I would speak to him in English and he mostly answered me in Spanish), I thought it would be a good idea to teach him to read English phonetically, as I had learned to do from my own mother. His school was also teaching English, but applied the system of rote learning rather than teaching phonics.

Unfortunately for me, in my attempts to help him learn to read and spell, reading phonetically in English is quite different from reading phonetically in Spanish, and a simple word such as *"my"* in English, became *"m-a-i",* when my child (who had learned Spanish phonics at school) was asked to spell it. This difficulty, combined with the fact that I could never seem to get him to read, brought me to the conclusion that language might never be one of his strongest suits and that he would probably never be very good at spelling, an ability considered by my own family to be of paramount importance throughout my youth.

I eventually shifted from feeling that I had failed as a parent, to accepting the fact that my son might never be a reader, keeping in mind that even if his English spelling was not perfect, his spoken English was quite good. Had I insisted on *making* him read, he might have reacted by refusing to pick up another book that was not required reading at school.

However, not making *my* priority *his* priority produced surprising results. Ultimately, although at the time of this writing he is not drawn by fiction, he is an avid reader of books and articles on a range of subjects that appeal to him. In his late teens he began purchasing and reading tomes in English on different areas of interest, chief among them being the music business; his legal vocabulary in this field far outstrips my own.

The Reality of Perfect Parenthood: Our Mistakes, Our Failings

For the purpose of this book I take the stand that as parents, we want to do the best job we can of raising our children. Yet we often find hanging over our heads an unspoken expectation; a kind of ideal standard to which we must aspire: the status of *Perfect Parent*.

How many of us have experienced apprehension – either from time to time or as a persistent background hum – over whether our parenting decisions qualify (or disqualify) us as good parents?

I suspect most of us have had the experience of being assailed by doubt at some time or another as we wonder whether our parenting approach is the best for our child. Looking for a recipe that will turn out a happy, well-adjusted youngster, when there are so many versions of the recipe and the ingredients are so diverse, is a challenge that can be daunting at times.

Striving to be a Perfect Parent has its pitfalls. The need to have everything go smoothly can lure us into believing that we always need to be right; that our authority must go unquestioned; that acknowledging our mistakes is a sign of weakness that could jeopardize that authority; and that if we veer an *nth* of a degree off the course of what we imagine is expected of us as Perfect Parents, our parental ship will end up in uncharted territory, or worse still, founder completely.

Yet children are remarkably elastic creatures, with a high tolerance for the mistakes their parents are bound to make. As role models we seek to convey certain moral principles and instill the learning that we feel our children need to be able to function in society ... yet we are fallible.

So here's a news flash: we can admit it! Contrary to what we might think, being honest about our imperfections creates trust; finding a parenting balance that works is in large part about relinquishing the need to make it perfect.

I certainly wasn't a Perfect Parent... (I confess: I didn't try to be!). Being able to laugh at myself was helpful. My confession that I had never liked studying grammar myself was my response, at one point, to my child's difficulty in applying himself to learning grammar. My confession was totally honest. To this day I do not know the parts of speech, although proper *use* of English was considered fundamental in my home growing up. We just never dwelled on whether what we were using was a gerund or a phrasal verb. However I did add that, since it was one of his subjects, it would be good if he tried to learn it as well as he could, and then later decide what to do with it.

Embarrassing our Kids is Part of the Process!

And how do we know we are a Perfect Parent anyway?

We're told that, as modern parents, we must be considerate of our children and aware of their concerns. For sure, listening to our kids is good policy. Being attuned to their needs and desires helps us build and foster communication with them, and gives them the freedom to express themselves.

Yet one of the ideas that has come hand in hand with the *new wave* of Perfect Parenthood is the notion that we have to protect our children's feelings at all costs. The underlying message is that when we occasionally fail to be attentive to their emotions, or we do something that embarrasses them in front of their peers, we're somehow at fault. The tables are turned: *we as parents* have to be on our best behavior.

Now, just to be frank:

I disagree that we have to put our needs – and indeed, our personality – on the back burner, in order to be good parents. I balk at both the idea that we have to be absolutely faultless in tending to our children's feelings, and the implicit message that if, despite being considerate of them, we somehow wound their pride or allow them to feel slighted, we have fallen down on the job.

In fact, admonitions to parents to be responsive to their kids has turned parenting into such serious business that in many cases it has generated a kind of fundamentalist, follow-the-rules approach to child-rearing.

As in all fundamentalist movements, perverse effects appear. One of these effects is seen in well-meaning parents who lavish attention on their kids as a way to prove to themselves that they qualify for Perfect Parenthood. Such parents may come across as politically correct and smug, or alternatively, as sentimental and solicitous. In either case the need to be perfect, regardless of how that notion is interpreted, colors their parental focus. The result is parenting that not only doesn't feel natural, but doesn't look particularly enjoyable.

Indeed, taken to the extreme, we could find ourselves tiptoeing around our children's egos in an effort to ensure that they grow up without the experience of having been put on the spot by something we, their parents, have done.

But hey, we're human too! We get to be real. I actually think it's great learning for kids to be able to deal with their very *human* parents and our foibles (P.S. it will also make for great conversation with their siblings and friends later on…). I've come to the conclusion that being mortified by your parents is one of the rites of passage into adulthood.

One such example from an experience with my own child comes to mind. He must have been about 8 years old at the time. He and I were walking up the street when we encountered a woman trying to figure out which button to press on the parking meter for the particular zone in which she had left her car. I stopped to help her out, and then got into an animated conversation with her about – I don't know what… the weather, the car industry, politics… I can't remember! My son stood there and fidgeted while we carried on, and when we finally went on our way, turned to me and said, *"Mom, I hate it when you talk like that with people you don't know"*.

I replied, matter-of-factly, *"You know what, Serge? My mom used to do the same thing. She would strike up a conversation with the cashiers at the supermarket, or the teller at the bank, or the mechanic at the garage... Not even the mechanic who was working on her car; just another one who just happened to be nearby... It used to be so embarrassing."*

Upon hearing this confession, he earnestly retorted, *"Well, then.. you should respect me as a child!"* (He did, indeed, have logic on his side).

With equal conviction, I replied, *"Honey, you know what? Children have to be embarrassed by their parents. It's part of growing up."*

I don't know where that reply came from, though it felt true at the moment I said it. He appeared to ponder it briefly, but it must have made sense because he didn't argue.

Thinking about it, the things our own parents did that we found most exasperating often evolve over the years into a shared family memory that constitutes a bond of intimacy held by siblings, close friends and relations. When you consider it, it also expands our tolerance for what we can expect from others... and curiously, the same behavior we hated in our parents is often forgiven when displayed by some other, unrelated individual.

What is Really Important?

It seems to me that part of being a parent is understanding that neither will we always do things one hundred percent right, nor will we get a one hundred percent response from our child. I built in my own notion of elasticity around this idea, because I stopped worrying about the small stuff.

Of course, I confess to experiencing the occasional pang of inadequacy, at least initially, upon seeing other children react to their mother's admonitions with an alacrity that contrasted with my own son's casual attitude.

On our frequent trips to the playground, my young son was pretty much oblivious to my calls telling him it was time to leave. I watched other mothers get their children's attention, telling them it was dinnertime, or that so-and-so was waiting for them, or presenting some other apparently compelling argument, because their little ones would drop the ball and trot complacently over, ready to depart.

Not my child. Try as I might, I was never able to produce the same reaction in him that other mothers managed to get in their offspring. I would have liked to see some sign of willingness; of cheerful *obedience*. Well, let me just say obedience.

I even resorted to the cheap tactic of counting down. *"Honey, you have five minutes left before we go."* And then, *"Honey, only three minutes left…"* By that time, a total of about ten minutes had actually gone by. When I finally announced that the time was up, he would say, *"Just five minutes more"* (or something like that). We were routinely the last ones off the playground.

That's my confession. So have I failed as a parent?

As time has gone by I've become aware that there is a part of me that does not see time as important, and that is precisely what I conveyed to my son.

Parenting is about the whole picture: what we give our children, what we expect from them, what is important, or very important, and what is secondary or unimportant. Children quickly learn that each parent can have very different expectations, and like chameleons, they adapt to what is demanded of them. The rest is something to be haggled over, or occasionally won by attrition. In some cases a kind of a *modus vivendi* or compromise may be devised.

The way I see it, I was relaxed about some rules, but there were other rules that formed the bedrock of my child's upbringing: I have already mentioned such things as respect for others, courtesy and certain social graces, on which I refused to budge, and which he learned early on were not negotiable. Just as my tolerance for his insouciance in circumstances that were not particularly important to me – like getting him to leave in the middle of an exciting soccer game at the playground (they were all exciting) to get home at a particular time – was perceived by him as a license to stretch the remaining time as much as possible, my refusal to relinquish principles that I felt were fundamental to grow up with was also perceived and never really contested.

That is a reflection of my values, as a parent and as a person. I'm relaxed about time (I fit perfectly into a Latin culture!); however, I insist upon being on *time* – and extend that to my son – when it affects others, because that is about courtesy, and for me, regard for others is the underpinning of every relationship.

So it's important to know where we can be flexible, and where we want to stand our ground. Children pull on the elasticity that exists, but learn to toe the line when it is carved in stone. It seems to me that as parents we have to know what's important to us and where we're not prepared to give in, and then stand by our convictions. If we make every interaction with our kids a tug-of-war of principles, the effect is to dilute the whole. However, on those matters that are important to us, if we cave in we not only lose credibility, but our authority is undermined… a consideration that brings me to yet another of the challenges of parenthood.

Authority and the Perfect Parent

One of the expectations that parents contend with has to do with *authority*: the litmus test of the Perfect Parent.

For many parents the issue of authority is an ongoing source of angst. Interestingly, there are some widespread beliefs around authority that I have found to be untrue.

One such belief is that authority has to be imposed at all costs. Indeed, being in a position to tell one's child what to do (or not do) is commonly perceived as proof of parental authority. In other words, as long as we can still order our kids around, we are in control. This approach works with infants and toddlers, and to some degree, with children and preadolescents, but in a demonstration of emotional intelligence on their part that evokes the adage *"where there's a law there's a loophole"*, youngsters are quick to discover how much we mean what we say, and often work out ways to circumvent the rules imposed.

Authority is tricky business. When parents wield their authority by "laying down the law", with no cogent explanation or justification given, their authority loses substance and begins to erode. At the same time, we are admonished that we need to set limits for our children for their own good. It's no wonder so many parents agonize over how much freedom to give their children, and where to say no.

In an effort to keep the upper hand, some parents acquire the knee-jerk reaction of saying no to everything: a blanket disapproval of anything that suggests a departure from the rules. Others appear to take a more insouciant approach to asserting authority, basically tuning out to avoid noticing their youngster's annoying antics until it becomes unbearable (at which point they may hit the roof).

There are also parents who say no, only to cave in immediately thereafter. When their child misbehaves they venture a halfhearted reprimand (which may or may not be heeded), ostensibly more to convince themselves and any possible onlookers of their authority than to produce a real result.

In fact, the generally accepted notion that parents must exercise authority over their children has given rise to all kinds of misconceptions about how kids should be raised, and the way in which Perfect Parents assume this responsibility. That parents so often struggle with *when* – and *how* – to say no, is a reflection of the confusion that reigns in a matter that continues to be one of the central themes of child-rearing.

But authority doesn't stand alone. It goes hand in hand with responsibility, respect, and honesty. *Authority is the means, not the end,* a valuable skill in ushering our children through their formative years and into adulthood. Our authority is the vehicle for the many things we want our children to learn.

But it's a two-way street. Our exercise of parental authority cannot be at the expense of allowing our children to learn and exercise responsibility themselves. Responsibility looks different at different ages: it can be anything from picking up toys and putting them away, to walking the dog, clearing the table, turning school projects in on time, learning how to handle money, or being back home at an agreed-upon time.

Sustainable Authority

When we respect our children as individuals, we earn respect from them as well… and the authority to demand that they respect others. We earn moral authority and credibility. When I say *earn*, I refer to the axiom frequently mentioned in business circles, but not so often in families, that *"authority is earned, not imposed"*. This wisdom, perhaps more evident in a corporate setting among adults than in the relationship between parents and children, speaks to the essence of authority, which is not merely being able to tell others what to do, but commanding the respect – and willingness to be influenced – of the person under that authority.

Our authority also comes from honesty. Being able to say we don't know, when we have no answer; being able to admit our mistakes (by the way, our kids are aware of them anyway); and being able to say we are sorry, and mean it, all enhance our authority.

More than an occasion to establish our credentials as Perfect Parents, the exercise of authority is an opportunity to be a role model for our children. Do we like it when others pontificate? …Then why do we do it with our children? Do we like to be ordered around? Do we like to be told *"No"*, with no reasons given?

Telling our child, *"Don't do that because you'll hurt yourself"*, or

"Don't do that because it's rude" is very different from, *"Don't do that because I said so, and I'm the one who gives the orders around here"!* When the requests we make of our children are accompanied by "please" and "thank you", we are also modeling behavior that will serve them well.

While these examples may seem statements of the obvious, it's surprising to see how many parents default to giving orders to get their children to respond.

Giving our children a chance to understand why we want them to act a certain way, or why we are upset with them, hones their emotional intelligence and gives them an opportunity to become more secure, perceptive individuals themselves. If we can relinquish the need to assert our authority at all costs, our authority is actually reinforced, and will be much more authentic and *sustainable*.

The need to build *sustainable authority* may not be so obvious when children are small, but as time goes by they may not be as willing to accept what their parents tell them at face value, and orders may meet with skepticism and resistance. Of course, resistance may occur anyway, because *sustainable authority* also involves an element of negotiation under certain circumstances.

Wielding their Influence

While it is true that there are some questions that are non-negotiable (again, in my world that includes honesty and regard for others...), there are also negotiations that can allow children to use their intelligence and creativity and understand that they, too, have power to influence people in a position of authority.

Some resistance to our demands will occur, as is natural in children who may be engrossed in an activity that is far more exciting than the prospect of setting the table or taking out the trash. Also, older children who are beginning to go out on their own may try to push the limits to see how late a curfew they can negotiate.

I remember my own son, in his early teens, insisting he needed to be out with his friends until 1 a.m. I adamantly refused, and said he had to be back by 11 p.m. (bearing in mind that Spain is a country where people often sit down to dinner at 10 p.m.). We finally struck a compromise – midnight – which satisfied him, and which I had initially decided would be acceptable to me. However, he was held accountable for being home at the stipulated time, with no excuses.

There were times, too, when he managed to convince me of something that was important to him, despite the fact that I had initially refused. The topic would certainly not have been one of those bedrock principles that for me are non-negotiable. It was something where I could acquiesce without major consequences by finding an alternative solution that we worked out together. Perhaps it was a case of him wanting to spend the night at a friend's house when I had other plans for our family that conflicted. Certainly not a life-or-death matter, but one in which I had the final say.

Underlying my initial *No* was the awareness that the *No* was there not solely to make a point, but because there was a valid reason for it. When we found an alternative solution, it became possible to change the *No* to a *Yes*. Such cases turned out to be an opportunity for him to learn to defend his point and encounter alternative solutions, as well as to exercise his own particular charm and charisma.

Seen in retrospect, and given the growing realization in our society of the importance of social skills and emotional intelligence, which involve not only perceiving and controlling one's own emotions but being able to influence others, it is of great value for children to become aware of the impact they can have on others, including their own parents.

I'm not talking about endless arguing where parent and child dig in their heels and refuse to budge because there is something more at stake than just the issue at hand. Children may engage in an argument with their parents in an effort to sway them, or as a way of expressing their growing independence. As parents we can still use the same approach: give a *No* where we think it is needed, and on occasion, when warranted, allow the *No* to become a *Yes*.

In some families, the battle over the *Nos* becomes entrenched; indeed, it may become a way of life. It's interesting to see how some of these contentious scenarios persist into adulthood, with parents and their adult children bickering over details that any casual onlooker would deem paltry. A sense of humor is a great antidote to the temptation to get caught up in a spiral of words in which neither side can be the winner. And sometimes, striking a bargain in which something else is allowed – because it is reasonable from the parent's standpoint – avoids a standoff and allows the child a tangential victory that is important to them.

Authority is not a Zero-Sum Game

What is important is that it is not about ensuring that we win the battle and they lose. Parent-child disagreements are not a zero-sum game in which we can only demonstrate our authority if none of our child's demands are met. For example, if the demand is to stay out late with friends and we feel it is unreasonable for our child's age, we can refuse to allow a late night, but occasionally allow our youngster to negotiate staying over at a friend's house instead of having to come home early.

The rule would be, there are no rules. If we, as parents, know what is important for us - letting our children know and telling them why – we gain our children's respect, because they are being treated as intelligent individuals and are made to understand that there are reasons for our decisions as well as consequences to their actions.

And hey, there are times when we will tell our kids: *"Do it because I told you so!"* Or: *"You know why, so just do it!"* No one wants to spend hours explaining something over and over again, trying to persuade a child who persists in arguing back in the hope of winning by attrition. Once children know that it is their responsibility to keep their room neat, we are not going to allow ourselves to get dragged into a daily debate about whether they should be making their bed!

I see it as a bank account in which parents have made deposits of tolerance and trust. In times of disagreement or conflict, when parents tell their kids *"Do it because I told you so"*, that order is effective because it draws on a reserve of goodwill, understanding and respect that is already in place (*see Glossary for* Goodwill Reserve). When we skip the niceties it's like making a withdrawal from the account; it works because there is leeway in a flexible parent-child relationship for parents to be unyielding, when they so choose, in laying down the law.

If it sounds as though parents' authority might be jeopardized by allowing children to have a say in what they are asked to do, that is because the basis of this parent-child relationship is very different from an authoritarian approach and variations thereof. It is based on the underlying notion that *we are all part of our family unit, pitching in together to make it work.* As parent I do my share, and I also ask things of my children, enlisting their input into our partnership. I continue to "be in charge" because I am the parent, but the way I wield authority is different. We are working together to make our family unit a success. I am not asking for strict obedience for the sake of my position in command, but as a contribution to our family, helping it to thrive.

Success of the family unit itself will look different depending on each family, but regardless of whether the approach is stricter and more systematic, or looser and more creative, children's participation as an essential part of the family "system" is fundamental to making *sustainable authority* work.

Lest anyone think that this parent-child dialogue begins when children are adolescents, I would remind them that we naturally negotiate with infants, even before they can speak. When children make a beeline for an object that happens to be breakable or hazardous, and we put it out of their reach, the usual response is for them to begin to fuss, or even burst into tears. As mentioned earlier, we distract them by drawing their attention to something else and making it attractive to them, taking their mind off the initial object that had caught their interest.

Slightly older children can actively make choices. A mother I know, after getting a call from the kindergarten teacher saying that her five-year old had been obstreperous in the classroom, negotiated with him how he was going to behave at school. She calmly told her son that he had been behaving like a two year-old, adding that if he wanted to be treated like a two year-old, that was fine. He would wear diapers again, be spoon-fed, ride on the baby rides at the park, and sit and watch the older children play.

Not unsurprisingly, her son refused to go back to being a two year-old, so she reminded him that if he wanted to be treated like a five year-old he had to behave like one. He thought about that prospect for a moment, then asserted that he wanted to be a five year-old.

Some days later this mother received a call from the teacher who reported, with pleasure, that her child was now behaving himself, and he was no longer acting up in class.

This approach is an example of what I call *sustainable authority*. Children are made to understand that their actions have consequences, and are given the opportunity to exercise responsibility, even at a young age. It makes children active participants, rather than passive recipients, in the learning that they are meant to receive.

Children who are engrossed in a game may be allowed to decide that they get to play for another half hour before doing their homework, or watch their favorite TV show before taking out the trash. The onus is then on them to uphold their end of the bargain, or face the consequences of not doing so. However, allowing them to decide within reason how they want to organize their time gives them a chance to exercise responsibility and, to a certain degree, influence, over the person in authority.

Sustainable Authority Includes our Imperfections

So what is *sustainable authority*?

Sustainable authority is the term I use to refer to an ongoing relationship of credibility and influence that depends not on physical strength or fear, but rather, on trust in the motives and conduct of the person in authority.

Authority without respect is lacking in content; the equivalent of an empty box. Eventually, when we get past the wrapping to what is inside the box, we know whether there is anything in it. When it is empty, what at first glance appears to be something of substance turns out to be just… air.

What happens next is interesting. Children who realize their parents are asserting their authority only to ensure they have the upper hand, without the benefit of credibility, frequently do one of two things. One might be to rebel, contesting what their parents say. The other might be to tiptoe around the parental figure in such a way as not to offend them or point out that their authority is a sham, thereby becoming complicit in an effort to sustain that parent's image of themselves.

It brings to mind the tale of *The Emperor's New Clothes,* the Hans Christian Andersen story of an Emperor's determination to keep up appearances despite the lack of any substance – in this case, clothes – by imagining himself dressed in exquisite finery while parading, with nothing on, through throngs of people who saw no clothes but colluded in upholding his pretense of authority.

Similarly, when faced with a masquerade of parental authority, our children see us as we really are but engage in the artifice of allowing us to imagine that we actually exert authority over them. They may do as we say, but they see who we are.

Once again, at the core of authority is the matter of respect. If we attempt to assert our authority without knowing why we are doing it, we are just going through the motions. Authority exerted together with consideration for our children, and a clear stand for having them show courtesy toward us and others, is extremely compelling. In fact, one way to distinguish between a mere imposition of our will and genuine authority is to look at the learning component: what is the usefulness of what we want our children to know?

By being discerning in our authority, we model for our children a way to be in this world. For those who might be tempted to try to be a model of the Perfect Parent, in fact, modeling imperfection is probably more important, ultimately, than attempting to be perfect. Instead of perfection, we model caring, love, trust, honesty and fallibility, as well as a willingness to stand up for and insist on having respected what is important to us – be that honesty, graciousness, teamwork, or any of the many values we hold dear.

By respecting our children and instilling in them respect for us as their parents – as well as regard for their peers, for their elders, for nature, and for our planet – we invite our children to step into a place of power and humility. They are shown consideration, yet this recognition is given with the understanding that they are no better than others. They are quite simply unique.

CHAPTER 9

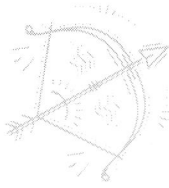

They are Already Perfect

As parents, it's natural for us to want to give our children the best: those things that we feel will help them in life and prepare them for the future. The ways in which we do so are as varied as our parenting styles, yet there is a common thread that is often present in our child rearing efforts: the need to have our children be good at something, and for them to have a shot at success.

I'm quite sure that if someone had a toolkit of contrivances that could be used to ensure children's success, it would be an off-the-charts best seller. In fact, there are many formulas and methods on the market that claim to improve youngsters' performance, virtually from birth up until their late teens, adding to the advice and recommendations of authorities on how children ought to be raised.

Not being an expert in child or adolescent psychology, I will not talk about facts backed up by tomes of research. I will assert, however, that our children have what they need when they are born. If we look, we can recognize this innate perfection, just as we can look around ourselves and perceive the timeless beauty of nature that appears so manifestly to have been created by a higher intelligence. In our children's case, I am not talking about physical beauty or a bright mind.

What children are born with is the stuff that they need in order to thrive, and to grasp whatever learning they are to obtain on this planet. What they have to learn in their lifetime is as individual as each child, and each child is perfectly equipped for that learning to happen, whatever that may look like in their instance. If we look at our lifetime as a learning experience, it is satisfying to recognize that the building blocks for our learning are already present. Our life experiences help move us toward self-awareness and personal growth, but everything we need in order to do so is already within us.

Creating the Right Conditions: Allowing Them to Dream

As I emphasize throughout this book, when I say that children have what they need when they are born, I am by no any means stating that they do not need to be taught or guided. Indeed, there are many skills that they can and do learn from us. Most of all, we are in the best position to provide the fertile ground where they can blossom.

As we know, a seed will grow into a hardy plant given the right conditions, yet all of the properties that will enable the plant to emerge and thrive are already contained within that seed. This evidence is actually more important than it might at first seem. We would not expect to get an oak tree from a tomato seed, or a tomato plant from an acorn. Yet curiously, we often insist on how our children should turn out, instead of finding out from them what they want, and allowing them to grow into their dreams.

If you ask a five year-old what he wants to be, he might say: a fireman. Some will actually become firemen, though most will not. For the most part we indulge small children, allowing them to play-act the roles they dream up for themselves. Importance is not attached to wanting to be a fireman, or a prince, or a dragon-slayer when a child is still young, because we assume it is only play.

Dreams change as children grow, but dreams themselves are the way children exercise their creativity, and are a way for them to explore. Yet we often have our own ideas about what our children should (or should not) be when the time comes to get serious about the future.

Acquaintances of ours once told me, in front of their 12 year-old son: "*Billy says he wants to be an astronaut*". It was said with a smile and a gesture that said to everyone – child included – that his parents had no expectation of his ever becoming an astronaut, as his mother added, with a shake of the head: "*… but he spends all his time daydreaming*".

A little while later I had a brief conversation with Billy, in which I asked him what it would be like to be an astronaut. Shyly at first, he began sharing with me the excitement and wonder that he experienced when he dreamed about outer space. We talked about space walking and launch pads, about distant planets and living without gravity. Finally, I said to him, "*If you want to be an astronaut, go for it. There are lots of things you'll need to know to be an astronaut, but you can learn them!*"

Now you might say: how likely is this boy to become an astronaut, particularly considering he doesn't really apply himself to his studies?

My answer would be: does it matter? Even if Billy decided to buckle down and work hard, it is indeed possible that he could change his mind along the way, or discover that he didn't really want to be an astronaut. He might be happy in some related area: for example, working in the control room, or being involved in building the space shuttle. Or he could do something totally different if that's where his dream took him, as he got clearer about what he wanted. The key message here is: *it's not about settling for less; it's about being able to pinpoint what one really desires.*

I ask: is it worse to dream of being an astronaut and to discover one day that it's not for you, or to be told from an early age that you can't, that it's impossible for you to achieve such a dream, and pointless to imagine doing so? The corollary of the "no you can't" message is, of course, that there are a number of respectable, *practical* jobs that you can aspire to and have a chance of getting if you study hard, attend a good university, and go down a sensible career path.

Their Calling

Let's take a look, for a moment, at college or university students. How many are still hesitant about what they ultimately want to do, essentially because they haven't felt the "tug" that would pull them toward a particular profession? Many of these young people share a common experience: they have never been allowed to *want their dreams.* Such "trivial pursuits" were deleted from their vocabulary (and sometimes even from their consciousness) long before they reached the age to choose a course of study.

What would happen if such youths were encouraged from an early age to find out what they were really passionate about, and to use their talents to make a contribution to society that would also be fulfilling to them? When individuals live their potential to the fullest, finding what they have to bring to the world in their own unique way, what they are actually achieving is fulfillment of a gift of the highest order.

Parents who sign their children up to learn to play the piano or take ballet lessons frequently do so with the idea of giving them a well-rounded education. Yet if those children decide at some point that they want to pursue the arts professionally, their parents may attempt to steer them in another direction or ensure that they get a university degree in some "serious" subject so they have something to fall back on. What might at first glance appear to be a sensible idea — or conversely, an instance of parental hypocrisy, depending upon one's view — is actually an expression of an underlying fear: fear that our children, without some kind of "marketable" skills, will not be able to make their way in a materialistic society that is itself driven by fear.

Do we know what our children want? Do we actually want to know? We are the ones with the experience, after all... It may be hard for us to reexamine our parental role as "guides" to our children as they grow, as we seek to turn them into happy, accomplished adults.

I would revisit this notion by saying that we do have many things to teach our children: things like learning to share, staying away from a hot stove, showing consideration for others (including other forms of life), and being conscientious about one's responsibilities, among others. That is the foundation upon which our children's lives will take shape. But just like the seed that will grow to be a particular type of plant (again, we won't expect a geranium seed to become a eucalyptus tree!) each child has a calling, the need to express something within that is waiting for the right moment to flourish. This calling is present in the child when he or she is born, as potential waiting to be revealed and nurtured.

Discovering our calling has been a long road for many of us, often made longer by the fact that, chances are, no one ever encouraged us to find out what it really was. What if we were to give our own children the gift of allowing them, as they grow, to continue to be who they are and discover what they love to do? It's something children do naturally and spontaneously when they are young: as we all know, there is nothing more authentic than a small child!

Encouraging our children's creativity in every sense (including dreaming!) and giving permission for them to engage freely in the process of exploration and discovery is one of the greatest gifts we can give them. Like everything else in the human experience, finding out what it is that will fulfill us is often a product of trial and error. It is a process experienced as much by children and adolescents as it is by the adults who accompany them on this edifying journey.

Feelings and Emotions: Tuning In

So yes, it's important to start listening to what our children long for. The catch is, when we show interest, when we ask children what they want, we have to actually mean it. We have to really listen. Children who are listened to are encouraged not only to keep exploring, but to share with us their steps forward. Those who only hear a perfunctory:

"that's nice", or "good girl/boy", with no particular interest taken, will end up realizing at some point that they might just as well keep their opinions to themselves.

Feelings are as much a part of who they are as their thoughts and dreams, and the key to understanding our children is to connect – and allow *them* to connect – with what they feel. Ultimately, kids who know that they are listened to and that what they think and feel is important and worthwhile become more attuned to their own feelings as a result.

It's not by chance that our society began emphasizing the importance of feelings and emotions when it "discovered" their importance in good decision-making. This preoccupation spread to organizations, where leaders' emotional intelligence became considered a harbinger of their effectiveness.

Emotion, once considered the "poor relation" of the intellect, is now widely considered to be essential to good decision-making, and to thriving in one's life as a whole. The term "emotional intelligence" is not just a buzzword of New Age thinking; it is at the very quick of our being, necessary to our survival, and a notion that has finally been given legitimacy by quantum physicists who tell us about our "feeling world".

How great to be able to give our children an advantage as they grow, by helping them tune in to what they feel! Exploring their feelings with them can be as simple as sharing a happy moment or empathizing with them when they feel sad. It's not about dwelling on sadness, but about letting it be expressed. In this way, they come to recognize the feelings experienced by themselves and others, an awareness that will help them function more effectively – and intuitively – as adults.

I have already mentioned family conversations. When my son was still a youngster it was common for us to talk about feelings and emotions, and what motivated people to do the things they did: it was just normal table conversation in our household. As a result, he grew up with an understanding of what prompted people to act in certain ways.

Perhaps as a result of this practice, by the time he was 11 or 12 he was already making surprisingly insightful observations about certain behaviors he perceived. His ability to "get to the heart" of an emotional issue, I am convinced, arose from his ease and familiarity with feelings, starting with his own.

In fact, growing up, there was nothing my son loved better than having a conversation about what made people act or react the way they did in certain situations. It wasn't gossip or criticism; it was a genuine effort to understand what prompted people to do the things they did. Sitting around and talking about behavior was as enticing to him as playing Monopoly or a game of cards. It seemed at the time like a game or exercise, but in retrospect, I realized that feeding his natural curiosity about what made people tick was a way of honing his emotional intelligence. There was no conscious effort put into it; it was merely something that his young, inquiring mind enjoyed exploring.

His ability to understand his own and others' feelings has stood him in good stead. It undoubtedly contributed to his self-confidence and equanimity as a youngster in handling conversations with adults, and enabled him to react in a level-headed way when difficult circumstances arose.

Our Influence

Perfection is, in itself, an intriguing concept. For the purposes of this book, perfection would best be described as a completeness, or wholeness, that characterizes us as individuals when we are born; one that includes our gifts and also our *imperfections*: some call it our divine nature *(see Glossary for more on this notion)*. Interestingly, our quest for perfection frequently involves making changes to the things we see as being not quite perfect enough; something that often includes our own children.

Even those parents who would assert that they aren't seeking "perfection" in their children are likely trying to get their children to get better at the things they do. No problem there. The question is, above and beyond helping our kids to expand their range by studying and learning things that might not initially appear to be their strongest suit, who gets to decide what pursuits are right for each child? Our tendency to have a bias is actually a reminder that what is "desirable" is a very individual matter.

Yet perfection is immediately visible to us when we look for it – and that goes beyond physical appearance or IQ. The perfection of nature is often breathtaking. Each infant is a perfect creation, its essence shared by everything around it. There is a reason why our children are here, and we can help them discover it by creating a safe space for them to grow with love, discipline and encouragement... and sometimes, just standing back and enjoying who they are.

In our desire for our children to grow up to be happy, upstanding (successful?) members of society, we often intervene more than we need to in some areas, and less than we should in others. We may, rather than rooting for them and encouraging them, tend to steer them in the direction we think will best serve them.

As parents it's natural to try to influence how our children will grow up by attempting to maximize or minimize the influence played by their environment. Undoubtedly that is why many parents not only try to equip themselves with information on how best to raise their kids, but also try to shape or control the environment in which their kids will grow up: "environment" being not only a geographical location and physical surroundings, but schoolmates, friends, and childhood experiences as well. Parents seek out the best school, encourage their kids to make certain friends and not others, and involve them in experiences that are intended to build character, or develop their sensibilities (soccer matches, theater classes, music lessons, etc.)

Those parents who do not have the means to choose the best school for their child or pay for expensive sports equipment or music lessons are often left without any means of influencing the external environment except through admonitions and example-setting. These parents often influence their children through their own commitment to overcoming their circumstances, ensuring that their children's basic needs are met, and providing a decent upbringing. They may even become powerful role models for their children, by virtue of the qualities of perseverance and fortitude in the face of adversity that they represent.

Celebrating their Uniqueness

Interestingly, some children seem to do well in spite of their origins and circumstances. Sometimes the challenging circumstances are not financial; many highly dysfunctional families live very comfortably from a monetary standpoint. What is it that sets these particular individuals apart from the rest of their family members? It appears clear that, apart from their inherited parental traits, children have something that is theirs alone when they are born, and whatever that something is, it is what makes them unique.

Without entering into a discussion around survivors, or overcoming adversity, or how a musical genius is born into a family that has never demonstrated any particular interest or talent in that domain, I do believe that what is missing in a lot of child-rearing theories is not only acknowledging, but placing attention, precisely on that part of the child that is uniquely their own, and that is neither the result of parental input, nor the result of the circumstances into which they have been born and raised.

An obvious example of this uniqueness – one I mention elsewhere in this book – is the case of siblings who appear to be like night and day. In fact, some children appear to be so totally unlike their siblings, or even their parents, that mom or dad will jokingly say that they appear to have "come from a different family".

As said earlier, knowing that such differences exist, many parents are on the lookout for some sign that their child will excel, even if it is in an area in which they themselves were never particularly proficient. At first glance, this parental interest would appear to be an acknowledgment of that child's uniqueness: of course we understand that our child may not follow the same path we did.

Once our child's apparent gifts or talents are discovered, much time, energy and encouragement – often money as well – may then be poured into cultivating them and turning them into something exceptional. Many individuals who are successful in their field of work have their parents' dedication and belief in them to thank for it.

Nevertheless, there is a flip side to the coin of parental dedication and, often, sacrifice. In focusing on our child's talents, we can lose sight of their desires, their dreams, and what they long to do with their lives as they grow into who they are. Often we can see so clearly where their gifts lie that we build up a dream for them that may or may not coincide with what they really want to do… because their talents and their dreams may diverge.

In the case of children who have many aptitudes, we as parents may encourage the entire range of aptitudes, but actually favor those that coincide with our notion of what will work for them, attempting to steer our kids toward a course of study or a career that – based on our experience – will provide them with a reliable income, or professional prestige. Or we may try to get them to employ their aptitudes in a way that we feel is a better use of their talents. It's hard for us to resist the temptation to imagine and want for our children a successful future, whatever that may represent in our mind.

Yet there is a caveat.

The risk lies in focusing more on the ability than on the dream. Our children may be multitalented, but ultimately, who gets to decide what it is that they will do with their particular aptitudes?

I refer here not to those parents who order by decree that their child will study medicine to follow the family tradition of becoming doctors, or who push their kids to study engineering because it is what worked for them. I have in mind, as I write, many of the open-mind-ed, "progressive" parents who in fact want to foster their child's unique talents, regardless of whether that path diverges from their own.

I say this, first, to give credit to those parents for their genuine in-terest in encouraging and allowing their children's talents to blossom, but also because, contrary to what one might expect, many young peo-ple brought up by caring parents who invest time and money to help them express their gifts continue to flounder, or have misgivings about the course of study, or even the profession, that they eventually choose.

While it's true that individuals mature differently, and we may genu-inely not know what we want to do at the age (somewhere in our teens) when we are asked to decide what we want our future to look like, there are other aspects that I have discovered also come into play. Certainly, one of those may be: not wanting to disappoint one's parents.

It is something that has appeared frequently in my years of working as a coach with people who realize they find no meaning in what they do professionally, and don't know where to start searching for some-thing else. Many of these people have a secret dream: something that they would have loved to do. But it wasn't "practical" or "possible", and so it was abandoned in favor of something that met with their parents' seal of approval, back when that mattered. Often, it still does.

As parents, therefore, we might ask ourselves: *What does our chil-dren's success say about them? What does it say about us?*

There is a reason why I raise these questions, and it has to do with the way we look at our children's future. Ultimately, when we become invested in a particular outcome, we do a disservice to our child.

As parents it may be tempting to hover over our children as they grow, alert for incipient signs of talent, on the lookout for any har-binger of our child's singularity. Of course the singularity is there, al-though it may not assume the shape or form that we imagine. It's normal to want our children to succeed, and yet... pouncing upon a budding interest or the fledgling signs of a particular strength as por-tentous of future success can mislead us into encouraging one aptitude at the expense of another that has yet to emerge.

The danger is not so much in encouraging a particular ability as it is in clinging to it: as parents, deciding that we know our children's path better than they do. It is a more insidious type of control that parents wield, because to all intents and purposes we are actually supporting our child in what they do well. We are not telling our child to study law because dad was a lawyer — we understand that our child is more of a creative type – yet we do insist that she go on and use her creativity in some serious line of work that will ensure her a decent living... and perhaps give her a shot at professional prestige as well.

Accepting their Path

What happens when she decides she wants to teach art at an inner-city school where the gratification is not in the income, but in seeing dis-advantaged kids get to use their talents and blossom? Or perhaps, to work in a non-profit organization earning a small salary, because that work is the way she has chosen to make a difference, rather than study-ing advertising? How do we react? Where will we find the trust within us to accept that our child is following her own path?

I will cite an example with my son to illustrate this point:

As a hands-on parent I was naturally curious to know what interests my son might like to pursue as he grew to adulthood. In this sense, like any other parent, I was keen to discover what particular gifts or talents he might have and want to develop. He enjoyed math, developed a distaste for history and social studies, and loved gym and virtually any kind of physical activity. Although a drawing of his was selected to be the school Christmas card one year when he was about 6 years old, drawing was not something he appeared to wish to pursue, and by the time he was an adolescent he had actually become convinced that he wasn't particularly good at it.

Nevertheless, through the art program at his school, in the 10th grade he was introduced to drafting and design. He became totally enthused, embarking on drafting projects that were considerably more challenging than the ones assigned as homework. He announced that he would like to become an architect. In the next two years of high school he began taking the preparatory courses that would help equip him with some of the basic knowledge that he would need at university, doing well at them and enjoying his studies.

When he applied to, and was accepted at the Polytechnic University in Barcelona, he became immersed in his architecture studies. It appeared that he had found his calling.

Three years later – including an interlude of 5 months taken from his studies to work on a cruise ship (during which he also learned Italian and discovered an interest in foreign languages) – he made the decision to drop out of architecture school to pursue music full time.

Now, it wasn't as though he hadn't been interested in music before. He had learned to play the piano when he was a youngster, and took drum lessons for a while in addition to teaching himself to play the guitar. For a time, even after he began serious music studies at the jazz conservatory in Barcelona, he continued to study architecture, combining the two. He composed music, actually applying the same talent for spatial visualization that was required for architecture, only now he was using it to create musical scores.

Then one day he informed me that he didn't see music only as a hobby, and couldn't envisage dividing his attention between architecture and music. In other words, he felt he had to make a choice.

His rationale was simple. "*I don't want to be the architect who graduated at the bottom of his class, and music and architecture both require a lot of time and dedication; it's hard to divide time between the two. And I don't see myself starting to study music and playing with a band after I graduate from architecture school. By then it will be too late.*"

Leaving aside the fact that there are architects who are also musicians and have indeed managed to do both, I tried to understand what was behind his decision. His music was also attached to a bigger project; in some way, it felt as though he was intuiting a path for himself that required his full attention and dedication.

I have to say I was not completely surprised by his announcement. We talked about it and I agreed that if it was what he really wanted to do, then he should go for it. He assured me that he planned to continue studies at his music school. What did surprise me, however, was when he told me that he wanted his voice to be the instrument he majored in at school.

To be clear, I should point out that while my son enjoyed singing, up until that point his singing voice had been what I would call "average". Being his mother, I could easily inflate his credentials, saying he had always had a gift for singing. But that wouldn't be true. And while I did see he had musical talent as a whole – he had a very good ear, and had done quite a bit of composing already at that point – I was a bit concerned that he might be getting onto the wrong track. After all, he could have studied more piano, or any other instrument, while continuing to master music theory.

But I didn't tell him that. He was determined to sing, so I gave him my support, and inside myself, hoped for the best. I also trusted him, although I didn't really see where he would go with his dream of becoming a singer. I should add that, in this regard, I did take into account the amount of time and energy that I saw him devoting to his voice and music studies. Had he done nothing but lie around on the couch dreaming about being a musician, I would have stepped in to suggest that he might want to reconsider his future. But he devoted long hours to studying and becoming more skilled at music theory. He continued to work on his voice, although for some time his progress was slow.

During that period I continued to wonder whether he would be able to achieve his dream of being a singer, because his voice didn't appear to be on a par with his other musical talents. It's hard as parents to watch our children throw themselves wholeheartedly into some activity for which we see no future. Sometimes they seem determined to pursue a course of work or study for which, as far as we can tell, they have no outstanding aptitudes, choosing that path over another for which we are convinced that they have greater talent or abilities.

Inventing our Lives: Freedom to Experiment

I make this observation pointedly, inviting parents to see their children's dreams as the blossoms yet to appear on the branches of a plant that may already appear perfect. Our children are on a path that will take them wherever they need to go. Often, in pursuing an interest, they learn at some point that this interest is not going to be their life's path. Yet by exploring it they get closer to where they do want to go, as they are led to other areas that they decide to investigate. What they eventually do may be quite different from what they aimed for at the start.

We need to remember that whatever they do will take them, eventually, to wherever they need to be, if they trust and follow their instinct. When our child has the dream of becoming a famous basketball player, or football player, who are we to tell them no? They may or may not actually do so. Yet by going out and actually engaging in that sport, something else may emerge that will take them closer to what they want.

In my son's case, he has turned his voice into the instrument he wanted it to be, something achieved through dedication and time spent achieving mastery. It has been the result not only of his own conviction that music was an area he wanted to pursue, but that he has found his path to something that he wants to create in this world.

I said before: the ability is not to be confused with the dream. Now I say: *The dream itself is not to be confused with the way in which it materializes.* By allowing our children to have all of their dreams – the full range; not only those that will take them somewhere that to us appears to make sense – something gets created that will serve them in their path to becoming fulfilled adults.

When what they initially dream of doesn't "work out", instead of telling them that they have failed and using this argument to prove that dreams aren't to be relied on, we can ask them what they have learned, and encourage them – should they need it, because they may not – toward their new, or different dream (which could perfectly well be a different version of the same dream).

Great inventors make hundreds of attempts – sometimes many more – before their creations emerge, perfect for all to see. We are the inventors of our lives, and trial and error is the way we discover what really works. Just as is the case in much scientific investigation, where researchers seeking a cure for a disease come upon a miracle molecule … *for a different disease!* … we don't know, until we try, where our experiments will take us.

It is this freedom to experiment, and experience what happens when we do, that children engage in naturally; it is a natural learning process that we sometimes stifle in our attempts to help them "get it right". When we insist that they attempt to move forward in their lives along the safest path with as few mistakes as possible we actually do them a disservice, depriving them of a great learning experience and the possibility to discover much earlier on what it is that will make them happy and fulfilled.

They are the seed, containing within itself all of its potential… but because – unlike a plant – human beings have a higher purpose that has to do with gaining awareness of who they are and why they are here on this earth, they do not immediately emerge with this knowledge in their consciousness. It is a process of discovery, unique to human beings, and that is why human beings, unlike other creatures, are equipped with the ability to dream.

Authenticity and Purpose

In sum, when I affirm that "children are already perfect", I am asserting that they have within them everything they need. It is when they connect with their own authenticity that they can make the decisions that will enable them to forge a path that is uniquely their own. Sometimes there are things they must learn along the way that we can't understand because they aren't part of our own experience. It's something that's often hard for parents to grapple with, since we can't see how they will get where they want to go.

Most of all, if we start telling our children that they can't do things that to us appear impossible or totally irrelevant to where we think they need or want to go, at some point they will stop confiding in us. Their dreams may remain their private domain, or they may actually forget how to dream, losing touch with their innate ability to imagine far beyond what already is.

Many inspirational speakers incite us to have faith and to trust the unknown. It's something that children do naturally, if so allowed. We can suggest, encourage, inquire and, all in all, try to offer the optimum conditions within our means to enable them to experiment and discover what it is they want to do. We can use our criteria to help our children make sound choices. But when their passion leads them elsewhere… it's important to listen!

In my son's case, as he grew into a teenager, above and beyond his love of music, a new sense of purpose began to emerge: his role as a leader. He discovered an interest in business and management, seeking out reading materials that reinforced his instinctive business sense, which was undoubtedly driven as much by his emotional intelligence as it was by his love of numbers.

He began doing volunteer work as a leader in a youth organization, discovering and developing his ability to inspire and galvanize young people by reconnecting them with their own innate ability to dream. Interestingly, the planning, organizational and people skills required for youth leaders, particularly for the 14 to 16 year-old age group that he was working with, are very similar to those required in a business environment. For him, it was an opportunity to put his skills to the test, reinforcing his conviction that the process of trusting, creating and believing were as effective for others as they were for him.

The rest of his story is still to be written. At this point, he has connected *who he is* with *what he wants to do* in this world. At the "tender" age of 19 or 20 he already knew that his purpose on this planet was to serve others. As I write this book I can say: what that will look like is yet to be seen.

Most of all, I can say that I trust that he is on the path that will take him where he needs to go. His connection with what is important to him has enabled him to understand that the way he will make a difference in the world will probably be different from the path others will pursue.

Indeed, there is a way that we are all somehow the same, and yet diverse. When we believe in our children and support them, they will find a way to express their authenticity. They will understand that the singular gifts that are theirs to bring forth do not make them superior to others, but are the way that they, like others around them, can manifest their creativity and assume their own rightful place in this world.

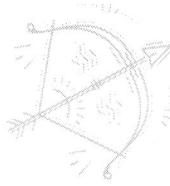

CHAPTER 10

Break the Mold – Change the Paradigms

*T*he concept of child-rearing has changed over the years. A wealth of information now exists, often provided by experts in the field, offering guidance in bringing up our children. Still, for many parents, uncertainty as to how to go about this important mission has continued to persist.

What was once considered to be a stage in life – parenting – is now commonly understood to be an enormous responsibility with far-reaching consequences. We have learned that what we do as parents can have a lasting impact on our child.

There have always been "good" parents and "bad" parents, but once upon a time the distinction was pretty clear. Now, "good" parents do not merely get their kids through school; they provide them with the best education possible. They make sure their kids have the clothes and engage in activities that will make them socially accepted. These social trappings are often provided like a prophylactic administered to ward off the dreaded disease of peer pressure, or worse: bullying.

Alongside our efforts to smooth the way for our children to reach maturity unscathed we may feel they are growing up far faster than they should, pulled irresistibly toward adulthood as if by a magnet. We want to provide them with what they need to ensure that on the journey to becoming their adult selves they do not succumb to the difficulties they encounter along the way.

Most parents strive to meet their children's needs, devoting time and money to the endeavor, often at great personal sacrifice. Yet these parents are also frequently beset by doubts: the old way of doing things no longer appears to be effective, and neither child-rearing nor, indeed, life itself, appears to be as simple and straightforward as it once seemed.

Children of Now and the Future

It may already be apparent to us that our children are somehow different from the way we were, or the way our parents were. They are also born into a different, rapidly changing environment.

In our modern, "technified" society, many parents may find that the benefits of immediate communication and access to information (and often, instant gratification) come with a tradeoff: the perils of too much information; indeed, way too much of everything. Often there is the concern that a kind of desensitization may occur. Instant gratification, frequently a blessing, can be a double-edged sword, as it diminishes our tolerance for delays. Patience is at a premium in a society where results are obtained at the click of a button.

Sometimes this glut of information and possibilities can seem overwhelming. Is it possible that our children are actually equipped not only to deal with, but also to make use of, the tremendous opportunities available to them, learning from the pitfalls as well? How do we prepare them to receive the best, while fending off the dangers that dwell in the profusion of social, scientific and technological changes that materialize at dizzying speed?

Yet perhaps what is dizzying to us is *exhilarating* to them. We are like beginners on skis, cautiously picking our way down a particularly steep incline, startled by the youngsters who speed past us, caught up in the adrenaline rush that comes from flowing and being at one with the very force that propels them. Do we ask them to slow down and focus their attention on the abrupt terrain and the possibility of falling, or do we celebrate their natural mastery, while making sure that they end up with some technique to accompany it?

Our children are the children of now and the future. There is little use trying to insist on fitting them into a straightjacket of rules carried over from an earlier time when children themselves were different. Society was different. Our options were different.

We may have become aware of these differences, many of which were spawned by scientific and spiritual discoveries that have called upon us to revise the way we think, and the way we perceive life itself. Whether we struggle to adapt - or naturally embrace - a universe in which we are all meant to shine, our experience of life shifts as we move from seeing it as a series of limitations to be overcome, to seeing it as a source of endless possibility.

While it is true that the "old way" of doing things often seems ineffectual when it comes to raising our kids, I would see it as proof that our children are indeed in many ways unlike earlier generations of young people. They are born more alert, rapidly assimilating all kinds of technological information, and they have an astounding ability to take in inputs from many different sources at once. It is as though there has been an evolution in these young beings, who will also be faced with different challenges from those that confronted their parents.

What this change implies is that we may have to reconsider some of the things we have always believed to be true. Breaking a mold when it no longer serves its purpose is an intelligent move, as well as, often, a radical act. As we raise our children in our changing society, we may be called upon to revisit things that our own parents took for granted. In so doing we can keep what is useful, while being open to new ways of doing things.

The changes of paradigm I have summed up below encapsulate the key concepts considered in this book. They require a shift in our mindset as parents and adults, because they run counter to many commonly accepted ways of thinking and doing things. Incorporating this new way of thinking will not only enable us to raise children who are confident and in touch with their own deepest desires and potential, but will act as a catalyst for our own growth and personal development. The same changes of paradigm that we exercise in raising our children will be beneficial to us in all of our relationships, including those with our friends, partners and colleagues.

Change of Paradigm 1 – Earning our Authority

If there is one question that continues to constitute a challenge for many parents, it is: How do I assert my authority?

The fear of losing control and finding one's authority challenged is a daunting prospect for many parents. Difficult teens are considered by many to be a fact of life. What if teenagers didn't have a need to rebel?

I have given much thought to this paradigm. As mentioned earlier, I found it intriguing that parents who took delight in their toddler's antics would frequently express dread at the thought of what would happen when that child became an adolescent. As we know, mere mention of the fact that one has a teenager will frequently be met with knowing looks and sympathetic nods, in implicit recognition of a common condition experienced by all parents.

In an earlier chapter, I refer to my conclusion that with children, as with adults, genuine authority is earned rather than imposed. While children are still young it may be sufficient to speak or act forcefully to get them to do as we say, but there comes a point when we have to be convincing as well. They are keenly aware of how congruent we are in terms of what we do and say. The old adage, *"practice what you preach"*, suddenly acquires relevance: here, we are modeling good behavior, not just talking about it. Our authority grows as we model honesty, integrity, and yes, fallibility.

More than trying to "impose" our authority, as parents we "earn" our authority: we gain respect and credibility by being true to who we are. That includes knowing our values and standing by them, while showing a willingness to be "real", understanding, compassionate and

– when need be – flexible as well. It includes the ability to say we're sorry when we aren't up to the task, as may sometimes be the case.

Our authority will grow, even during our kids' teen years, if in raising our kids we are loving (always), firm (when needed), have a sense of humor (where we can muster it!) and convey a sense that we are "all in this together". We run the family and decide on priorities, practical matters and turning our kids into polite, well-behaved young people, yet when it comes to *who they are becoming,* we focus on playing a supporting role in getting them to where they want to go. In this regard, discipline is designed to provide long-term learning that will benefit them, as it prepares them to strike out and create a future of their own.

Genuine authority is *sustainable,* meaning that it can survive the pressures that will inevitably be placed on it in the course of our child's passage from infancy to adulthood (see *Goodwill Reserve* and *Sustainable Authority* in the Glossary at the end of this book). Our authority is effective because our kids understand that we are giving the best of ourselves, and that this package also comes with imperfections. When we listen to them, create a structure for them within which they can grow, and most of all, model what we want them to learn from us, our authority grows. In the process, children and parents can enjoy each other's company from a place of mutual consideration and respect.

Change of paradigm 2 – Respect is for children too

As readers of this book will have had ample opportunity to observe, one of the cornerstones – perhaps THE cornerstone of child-rearing in my world – is respect. Interestingly, and perhaps disconcertingly to some, that means respect for children as well. So another change of paradigm I want to put forward is that children, regardless of their age, are not somehow lesser beings who acquire the status of "person" as they mature, but are actually "small people", worthy of respect from the moment they are born.

They require a vocabulary that is age-appropriate, and while they are young it's important to use clear, simple concepts with them, but they absolutely deserve the same consideration that they would be given if they were adults. We have the privilege and responsibility of ushering them into adulthood. That does not include exercise of our power in ways that are abusive, or skewed by our perception of our superior physical size or experience.

Increasingly – and fortunately – there is a trend in our society toward respecting and empathizing with other human beings. I am speaking of Western society, where such niceties have traditionally taken a back seat to the acquisition of hard knowledge, and where individual accomplishment is typically extolled. Other societies, many of which are considered less "developed" than our own, place great store in the acknowledgment of others, and even the ritual of greeting someone – a friend, neighbor or even a stranger – is considered essential etiquette before carrying out any other business with that person.

Nevertheless, such consideration and acknowledgment are rarely extended to children. Children are often seen as an unfinished version of an adult; occasionally, as virtually a different species! However, while we as adults have both the right and the obligation to make many decisions for our children, they can and want to have a say in matters that concern them. Actually, if we are attuned to their needs from the moment they are born, we will find that they are already actively interacting with us. We don't always need words to communicate with them; just the willingness to engage.

Similarly, when children misbehave because they are spoiled, it is because we as parents have opted to disengage from productive communication with them. Seen in this light, spoiling a child is not only a breakdown in communication, but a breakdown of *respect on our part* as parents *toward our children,* because giving in to immediate gratification is a short-sighted, inadequate replacement for instilling the behaviors that will serve them throughout their lives: things such as patience, tolerance, regard for others, sociability and self-control.

In fact, respect for our children is the ideal starting point for a great relationship with them that will carry over into adulthood. If we show them consideration and trust them as people, they will respond in kind. We are laying the groundwork for them to become the best they can be. By treating them as whole and complete human beings we open up possibilities for them because we implicitly consider them to be filled with the potential to do whatever they desire.

Change of paradigm 3 – Redefining success – Redefining Failure

Another place where a change of paradigm is needed: *What are our children going to do with their lives?? Will they be successful as adults?*

So often we imagine our children excelling at school or in sports, turning into accomplished professionals, holding down a well-paid job, having a family… and we tend to steer them toward whatever route we think will take them there. Underlying our insistence that they do well at school is our dream for them of the future we hope they will have.

At the same time, schools on the whole have failed to adapt to the needs of our children. In our exam-based academic system where evaluations are the norm, children tend to be compared to a statistical average, and individual children who have a particular quality or gift but fail to meet other criteria that would qualify them as academically "successful" often get left by the wayside. Others who do well academically may have further talents that, if developed, would bring them great satisfaction and personal success.

Yet parents and society as a whole tend to use academic achievement as a yardstick to measure our children's potential. What if our dream for them were not the right one? What if we were to consider that even those children who appear to adapt perfectly to our expectations might be happier and more successful in the long run if they blazed a trail of their own?

Given that "success" is a word open to many interpretations, I suggest, in the context of this book, that it be considered more like an outcome of the three inalienable rights set forth by the U.S. founding fathers: namely, the right to life, liberty and the pursuit of happiness. If we take this hallowed notion and fast-forward to our current times, success would be defined more by personal fulfillment than by social or professional achievement.

What is better, then, or worse? That our children have a dream for themselves of what they long to do, one that we as parents cannot see or imagine? Or that we have a dream for them, and they neither see it nor relate to it unless we convince them of it? Who will have to follow through and persevere, nose to the grindstone, to achieve that dream? Isn't achieving someone else's dream a kind of Pyrrhic victory, even if that dream is your parents'?

There may come a time in our children's lives when our dream for them takes over; our children do not contest what we want for them for fear of disappointing us. In the name of *"wanting the best for our children"* and making use of the authority of our experience, we pass off our dream as a truth, tantamount to success. The corollary of this process, as we gradually replace our children's dream with our own, is that their dream becomes devalued, in our eyes and their own.

How many adults are reluctant to voice their dreams because they learned as children that those dreams were not worthwhile according to the version of success that they were taught? And nowadays, in an era in which we are expected to be able to "go for it", how much money is spent on coaches and mentors who focus essentially on … getting their clients to dream? Often a childhood dream, discounted as "unrealistic" or "impossible" is taken up later in life. What if that dream had been allowed to blossom in childhood? What kind of energy and creativity might it have engendered?

The other side of that coin is *failure*, which has quite unfairly gotten itself a bad name. Failure is actually an essential part of learning. The willingness to fail gives us the freedom to try new things and expand our range much further than we do when we are constrained by the need to get things right the first time around. So failure is actually valuable and important. From this perspective we can see failure as proof that we are actually swinging out and giving something our best shot. Celebrating failure is a great way to acknowledge that we have stretched ourselves, often beyond what is comfortable and familiar, as we get closer to where we want to go. And of course, the same holds for our children too.

Change of Paradigm 4 –
How we Feel is a Choice we Make

Another ramification of the principle of allowing our children to decide for themselves has to do with having them learn to take responsibility not only for their actions, but for their feelings. How we feel is not someone else's fault, but a choice we make. The question they can learn to respond to is: what do you want to do with your circumstances? Instead of blaming others, children can learn how to look at situations differently and choose what to do with upsetting circumstances in a way that is far more empowering than just complaining about them.

True, the idea that other people are responsible for making us happy, or unhappy, is widespread. In fact, if this idea didn't exist it would do away with most of the love songs that ever hit the top of the charts! However, making others responsible for our happiness means relinquishing our own power to create happiness for ourselves. Ultimately, and contrary to what all the songs say, giving away our power does not make us happier in the long run.

As parents we can model for our children the ability to take responsibility for their own lives and what they want. The more we take charge of our own lives, indeed, the more satisfaction we obtain!

While the prevailing idea is that others are to blame for our emotional state and the way we feel, it runs counter to the reality, which is that we can decide how we want to be with whatever circumstances we have. For our children to be able to access their creativity to the full – finding the resources within that will enable them to carve out for themselves the life that they want – it is important for them to know that they hold the reins of their lives. No one who ever changed their own life, or changed the world, did so by sitting back and playing victim.

In believing that we can't achieve what we want, we implicitly give our power away… which is why, when we think that we can't make changes in our lives… we actually can't. Our belief is repeatedly confirmed to us as a kind of self-fulfilling prophecy, at least until such time as we decide to change our thought process and feelings, and begin to realign with what we really want.

Deciding to choose what we want to feel is a simple and very powerful way to take charge of our own lives, and an antidote to despondency in those difficult moments that are bound to arise. It also sets the stage for taking responsibility for our own life, rather than pointing a finger at others (family, co-workers, the government, the economy) as time goes by, and making external circumstances responsible for our personal happiness or dissatisfaction.

In this regard, children who are taught or led to believe that they are somehow "better" than others also lose this freedom to choose. A belief in one's own superiority needs subsequently to be justified: when things don't go well there is a temptation to find fault with others, rather than looking at where we ourselves may have erred. Indeed, some adults go to great lengths to justify themselves to avoid acknowledging their "fallibility", because it would undermine the structure of perceived superiority that they assimilated at some point in their childhood.

In reality, the "superiority complex" that some people display has its origin in a hidden fear of being found worthless if they should actually fail. That fear, in turn, is based on the belief that *I am valued for my achievements* and *not for who I am.*

Change of Paradigm 5 – Who We Are vs. What We Do

Our children will grow up believing what they are told about themselves, just as we did. Sometimes it is not so much what is said as what is implied by our parents and the people around us, and as we grow older, by society as well.

In our efforts to encourage our youngsters to be the best they can be, their "best" is often measured in accomplishments, rather than being an invitation to them to put their best foot forward and simply be themselves, whoever that may be.

In Western society there is much greater emphasis on *doing* than on *being. What we do* is the yardstick of our worth; to such an extent, in fact, that many adults confuse their professional roles with their notion of who they really are. Their professional successes and failures become a measure of their self-worth. Indeed, overly identifying with one's professional achievements can become a way of offsetting feelings of personal inadequacy whose seeds were planted at an early age.

The problem is, doing so is like decorating the facade of a building whose foundations are on unstable ground. From the outside it looks grand, but on the inside it feels unsafe. There is a part of us that may believe the external appearances we offer, but another part knows the "truth" that we have come to believe: that we are never good enough.

This confusion initially begins in childhood, when youngsters learn that they are valued and "liked" to the extent that they meet certain expectations. In our current world this experience is repeated and reinforced by social media, if youngsters are not taught otherwise.

Children are bidden to get good grades, to behave, and to excel at any one of a number of things. Praise may be lavished on them when they do so, or alternatively – because such achievements are expected of them – they may not be praised for what they have achieved, but rather, chided, punished, ostracized, or otherwise made to feel inadequate when they don't meet the expectations placed upon them, first by family, and later, by society.

Considering our children's actions, successes, and "failures" separately from *who they are* gives them the confidence to try new things and persevere, going beyond their comfort zone, because "failure" is just another part of the process of discovery. Conversely, when *who they are* is equated with *what they do*, fear of failure may loom so large that they may never venture outside of the tiny comfort zone of what they know how to "do well" to explore what lies beyond.

We may have seen it in ourselves at some point: the sense of being valued for one's achievements and not for oneself is responsible for our feeling aggrieved when we receive negative feedback. If our sense of self-worth hinges on how we perform, it's natural that feedback that is critical of something we have done will feel like an unfair swipe at our self-esteem. When feedback or criticism is taken personally, the tendency is to shut down and feel hurt or angry when these remarks are received, regardless of the intention behind them.

In my experience, mastery at receiving feedback is achieved when, regardless of the intention of the person offering the observation, one can take from it whatever is useful and constructive, be grateful for it, and leave the rest.

Adults who are critical of themselves and find it hard to accept praise often come from backgrounds where nothing was considered good enough to warrant praise, or where they were commended for doing things that were never really what they wanted themselves. Praise was conditional on *acting* a certain way (as the *good* boy/girl) or *doing* certain things. No one ever told those children that they were intrinsically wonderful, just the way they were.

Change of Paradigm 6 — Our Children are Already Perfect

There is another change of paradigm that I am convinced is the underpinning for all of the above. It is a change in our belief about our children. If we start by seeing our children from birth as *creative and whole,* this premise becomes the bedrock upon which child-rearing will be solidly founded. (*for more* about Perfection, *see* Glossary)

Complaining that our children are lazy, stupid, incompetent or rebellious is a sure way to plant the seed of laziness, incompetence and resentment. It is like having a drain that is clogged, and throwing in more debris in the hope that somehow the pipe will come unplugged.

The pipe is our line of communication with our children, and while there are parents who are natural communicators with their youngsters, others manage to get by while their children are small but find it increasingly difficult to communicate with them as they grow. The reason for this diminishing communication is that the latter has essentially been unidirectional, *from parent to child.* When we fail to listen to our children, they understand that at some level we do not value them for who they are, and the connection becomes more superficial; less substantive and meaningful.

Valuing our children for who they are means there is no need to "fix" them to have them meet our expectations. Rules and discipline are important, yet our children come into this world with exactly what they need to live their lives and discover whatever it is they are meant to do while they are here, because they, as beings, are an extension of the universe itself.

What a change it would be if instead of focusing on what doesn't work with our children we were to shine a light on the positive qualities we see in them; on what we *believe* them to be: clever, capable, determined, creative, spirited...... there is a long list that is specific to each child! The change of paradigm lies in focusing not on what we don't want, but on the qualities that are already there and that we hope to foster in our children.

In the process – and this statement should come as a pleasant surprise for many – we can also be who we are! True, we want to set an example for our kids, but we don't need to expend energy on trying to "be perfect" ourselves; just being honest with our children is enough. Besides, as they progress through childhood toward adolescence, they will begin to figure out for themselves that we are far from flawless ourselves…

Change of Paradigm 7 – We Can be Fallible

This paradigm asserts our right as parents to be fallible, and to allow our children to know it.

How much energy is futilely expended trying to demonstrate to our children that we are right, or that we can handle whatever comes up with aplomb? If we are honest with our children – occasionally making fun of ourselves when the situation warrants – and are willing to reveal our foibles, they will rise to the occasion. Children love this kind of honesty from their parents, so it saves a lot of useless pretense and builds our bargaining power with them if we come clean.

As I discuss elsewhere in this book, our relationship with our kids is like a bank account into which we make deposits of trust, honesty and positive feedback, amassing a reserve of goodwill that stands us in good stead when we are "less than perfect", or lose our cool, as parents.

I myself often dipped into the reserve of authority that had been built up through trust, part of which was the result of my being willing to tell on myself when I made a mistake. I also became aware that, in comparison with other families, our parent-child relationship was more collegial than most, based on the certainty of support and understanding from me, and a sense of humor, for the most part, to turn things around. Even blowing my stack, when it did happen, didn't damage our relationship, because so much understanding and tolerance had been built into it.

Of course, it's not about endlessly apologizing to our children, or bemoaning how we've screwed up. But there's no doubt that having a sense of humor and being willing to own up to our shortcomings has a salubrious effect on our relationship with them.

Again, in our interactions with children, when we emphasize the positive: giving love and understanding, showing a genuine interest in them, emphasizing respect, and setting limits, the store of trust and benevolence that is created can act as a cushion when we when we lose our cool and yell, or simply have to admit that we don't know.

I didn't worry if I had exactly the right words to tell my child that I was annoyed with him, or that I expected more from him on certain occasions. Sometimes, losing my cool was exactly what was needed. Because I rarely lost my composure, when I did, it meant that something important had happened, and he paid attention.

Change of Paradigm 8 — A Way of Their Own

This paradigm is about being open to learning from our children; in particular, learning what they need from us. If we truly listen to them we can enrich their experiences while helping them find their own way. Listening skills have never been as important. Proactively listening to our children helps us learn what makes them tick, and understand where they need more support from us.

We can also convey to them the values that are important to us: those that are specifically ours, and those that are a reflection of social and cultural standards.

Do children themselves have innate values? They respond positively to love and respect, and negatively to hostility and disrespect, so they are obviously programmed before birth to favor certain values. Nevertheless, as they grow older these values are expressed in different ways, and children acquire others that are uniquely theirs.

Indeed, part of this paradigm would be: teaching children values also includes being open to *their* values.

Our own values are a starting point, but they are not a blueprint for our children's lives. Things like respect, honesty, and having a sense of humor are universal values that will stand them in good stead. At some point they may develop an interest in travel or nature, learning or community; personal preferences that become part of their own particular set of values *(for more about* Values, *see* Glossary).

This reality, together with the realization as parents that our children have individual gifts and abilities that characterize them, is an invitation to explore further just what it is that makes each child so unique. It is an opportunity to watch and discover who they are as they blossom into their most authentic selves.

Children often have a particular flair for learning things that may have been a stumbling block for their parents. What technologically-challenged parent has not watched in awe as their tot confidently navigates the computer, intuitively knowing what comes next? It's clear that children have a way of their own of doing things and being in this world that does not necessarily come from us. If we give them the freedom to explore instead of trying to straightjacket them into our way of doing things – tried and true perhaps, but *our way* nonetheless – they will find their own path.

There are thousands of books on how to raise children. I would agree with most of them that seeking to understand what our children need, correcting them when they misbehave, and having them understand the consequences of what they do, will help us raise gracious, thinking (and feeling) adults, who show consideration toward others and can themselves be fine, upstanding citizens.

What is important to note is that by raising them in this way *we actually free them to be creative,* by providing them with a structure that gives them security by setting limits on behaviors that are not acceptable. It is an upbringing that gives them the confidence to find a way of their own and pursue it, despite the obstacles they will surely encounter on their path.

For those who might find a statement linking freedom and structure to be a contradiction, I would liken it to our own experience when we learn something new as adults. We take a course in, say, ballroom dancing. When we begin, we probably already like the music, but we don't know any of the steps. We may, if not corrected, actually acquire bad habits that keep us from learning the right steps. But once we have learned, we can stop thinking about the steps and – just dance!

Change of Paradigm 9 – The Power of Trust

We can create a new paradigm by having a relationship with our child that is based on trust.

Being attentive to our children has this effect on them: as infants they learn to get our attention by crying or smiling, and when we respond to them it instills in them the confidence that they have the ability to influence their environment. Understanding that this demand for attention is legitimate can allay the concerns of parents apprehensive of giving their children any power, often for fear of spoiling them. Children who are ignored feel powerless to influence their world, and will often resort to other tactics – such as drawing attention to themselves in undesirable ways – to compensate.

By the same token, youngsters who learn how to influence their environment and the people in it will trust their ability as they grow to create the life they want, and to make things happen in their world. They will have the confidence to pursue their dreams because, ultimately, they trust that they will find the path that will take them there.

Being able to influence one's environment takes different forms, but it begins with trust in oneself, something that infants and children acquire when they are given parental support where needed and the freedom to be themselves, with some rules and limits placed judiciously, like training wheels, to help them get to where they need to go.

We need to interfere a lot less than we tend to think we do. In fact, if there were one key message it would be: *children need to have the freedom to explore what the world has to offer, and find out about it for themselves. We need to resist warning them about our "bad" experiences, or admonishing them to "watch out" for perils that for them may simply not exist.*

Restraint in imparting to our children the results of our hard-earned experience requires a considerable shift in mindset, not the least because it turns a lot of what we have come to believe about parenting on its head. As adults it is natural to assume that the store of knowledge we have acquired can be used to create a safe space for our children to grow, free of the stumbling blocks that we ourselves have encountered in our lives and have – or possibly *have not* – overcome.

The risk is that, being innately biased by our own experiences which become the lens through which we see the world, we may end up simply transferring our acquired fears and doubts to them. It takes courage and curiosity to withhold our advice and allow our children to imagine and discover for themselves how they will do whatever it is they dream to do.

This challenge is not an insignificant one. We may have some particularly strong ideas about what will or will not work for our kids, and about our parental duty to instill that knowledge in them. Because of the widespread belief that an essential part of parenting involves counseling one's children, when this apparently fundamental task is taken away, parents may be left wondering what their role should actually be. Yet it is important that we believe in our children's ability to successfully embark on and negotiate whatever road they choose, finding their own way to surmount the obstacles that appear along that path. We also need to trust that valuable learning will be gained from the setbacks they experience along the way.

Ultimately, we need to trust in our children themselves. Indeed, if we allow ourselves to stand back and watch, we will begin to perceive in them the outward manifestation of their innate gifts, something that is theirs to bring to the world in their own way and that, like a seed, requires very little more than fertile ground (and water – and sunshine!) to thrive. It is almost shockingly simple, considering how enigmatic and laborious parenthood is often considered to be.

Allowing them to do so will enable them to create a trusting, intuitive relationship with the universe as they use their innate creativity to shape for themselves the life that they really want.

Change of Paradigm 10 — The Path of our Dreams Lies Within

It has become clear to me that we need to adopt a new way of thinking.

I don't know how many times my son said he wanted to do something and a part of me thought: that's impossible. There are too many obstacles. His talents don't lie in that direction. There is too much competition... (The list is long...)

Undoubtedly, the difference between many other parents and myself was simply that I refrained from speaking aloud the doubts that his dreams raised in my mind. There was a part of me that teetered on that edge of uncertainty: I didn't see how it could possibly be achieved, but what if.... he could actually find a way to do so?

There was an inner debate in which I engaged when my son was a youngster, and which I have – in retrospect – learned to appreciate. It is the tug-of-war between what we have learned and what our authentic self knows to be true.

If we were able to access our essence, divested of all of the social and educational pollutants that have come to diminish its luster, we would know that our mission is to follow our dreams. We were each created, unique individuals that we are, to follow a path that is ours alone. No one else will do exactly the same thing in precisely the same way as we will.

Our essence is like a magic lamp, whose genie is our creativity and potential. What frequently appears to us as a rusty, dusty piece of junk is who we are, full of dreams and possibility. Curiously, we have somehow come to believe that our wishes are granted by some external force. To the extent that we are one with the universe, and understand that we are actually a part of that force, that is certainly true. However, it is as we realize our creativity and potential in this creative universe that our dreams begin to take shape.

A corruption of the *three wishes* notion is the idea that finding the lamp is about as likely as winning the lottery, and that the success bestowed upon the lucky few is a confirmation that good fortune smiles only upon a tiny minority who have been favored by chance.

In an attempt to achieve that same success, we may be tempted to imitate what others have done to achieve happiness or notoriety, and encourage our children to emulate the individuals who personify accomplishment in our eyes. Yet to do so is to do a disservice to our youngsters. Looking outward to find the key to our happiness can lead us upon a long and frustrating search that takes us nowhere.

What applies to our children also applies to us. Looking inward to know what we really want is key to finding the path that will bring us lasting happiness and satisfaction in our lives.

A Modern Parable

A fascinating example of the wisdom within is contained in the book "The Wizard of Oz", from the Frank L. Baum series. In the story, Dorothy, who is transported by a tornado to the Land of Oz, goes on a kind of surreal odyssey, in the company of a tin woodman, a scarecrow and a cowardly lion, with the sole purpose of finding her way back to Kansas. Together they overcome misadventures and challenges – including contending with an army of flying monkeys and an evil witch – to achieve their dreams.

Upon reaching the Emerald City where the Wizard resides, they are ordered by the Wizard to find, and bring back, the broom of the wicked Witch of the West in order for their wishes to be granted. The four valiantly set off and are faced with a series of predicaments, until Dorothy finally succeeds in disposing of the Witch by dousing her with a bucket of water.

When they return to see the Wizard, the broom of the Wicked Witch in hand as proof of her demise, the Wizard is exposed as a fake, unable to grant them what they most desire. In a curious display of the power of conviction, the inspired charlatan grants the Tin Woodman a heart, the Scarecrow a diploma, and the Lion, a medal with the word *"Courage"* upon it. Dorothy's three companions are transformed by believing that they have acquired the properties conveyed by the objects given them, which in reality are a structure designed to call forth the qualities they already possess.

Dorothy, however, is dismayed to learn that the Wizard has nothing for her.

He finally offers to take her back to Kansas himself, and a hot-air balloon is prepared for this purpose amidst much pomp and excitement; however, when she clambers out at the last minute to retrieve her dog, Toto, who has escaped, the balloon takes off without her.

Her last opportunity lost, Dorothy despairs of ever returning to

Kansas. As she dissolves in tears, Glinda the good Witch appears to point the way. "Use the magic slippers," she instructs her. "You have always had the power within you to go home. Just click your heels together three times and say 'There's no place like home.'"

Doing so transports Dorothy back to Kansas, where she had longed to be. It is the parable of a heroine intent on pursuing her goal in the face of countless obstacles and setbacks, only to find that the answer has been within her all along. *"There's no place like home"* is a keen reminder that the source of our power and creativity lies within ourselves, and that our attempt to fulfill our longing by embarking on a quest outside of ourselves is bound to be futile. Indeed, there is a simplicity in the answer that springs from within: it requires no battles, no conflicts, no wild-goose chase in pursuit of an evanescent outcome.

Everyone loves success stories in which the protagonist overcomes adversity to achieve a dream, and they abound. Such stories of accomplishment are extremely seductive, but they invite us to contemplate success from the standpoint of the achievement at the end of the story, looking with the eyes of success back at the path that led there. It is easy for us to dismiss the incipient dreams of our child, which can seem paltry and insubstantial in comparison, because they have not yet coalesced into something more tangible. Yet they contain the seed of who our children are wanting to become.

Interestingly, when our children are allowed to move toward their dream, it may shift and actually look different. It is at this point that an onlooker might point to their initial desire and conclude that they have failed. After all, they have ostensibly abandoned what they originally set out to do and reset their sights on something else. However, the process of exploring and deepening their perception of what they want opens other doors that will allow them to fine-tune their intentions and get clear on what they really desire. It is only by moving toward the original dream arising from their essence that they start the process of transforming it into reality.

I suppose it was an inkling of that essence – something that, without really comprehending it, I willed myself to trust – that kept me from voicing out loud the doubts that my mind conjured up, as a parent to my young son. It was only later that I understood that any qualms I had were the product of my own experiences and outlook on life, and that imposing them on my son's life and ambitions could have skewed his perspective of what was possible for him to achieve, denying him the opportunity to find his own way empirically.

Understanding that dreams transform and flow, and that we may be moving toward something without being entirely clear where we are headed – that is, of course, until we have advanced far enough to enjoy the lucidity of hindsight – has led me to the conclusion that *whatever we do will take us wherever we're going.* It means sometimes not knowing – just intuiting – where we are going, with the only certainty being that when we get where we are going and turn to look back, we will know that the path we took to get there makes sense.

It's important for us to know, and to convey to our children, that irrespective of the path they take, they will end up where they are supposed to be, in a process that is ongoing. It's a learning process, and along the way they will acquire the experience and understanding that they need to grow and find their own singular path to happiness and fulfillment as human beings.

An Informal Glossary of Terms used in This Book

· ·

ADVICE OVERLOAD: The result produced when opinions, suggestions and admonitions are so liberally dispensed that the intended recipient simply tunes out. Such advice is frequently given unsolicited. We can perhaps think of someone who does the same to us. Creating advice overload is an unproductive use of our influence, since such advice usually ends up being ignored anyway. It is the opposite of advice-giving on a "need-to-know" basis. (See: *JIT advice-giving*).

An **antidote** to advice overload is to ration our advice, be honest that the advice we are offering is an opinion based on *our* experience, and invite the intended recipient to view it as another option for consideration.

CHOICE: A decision that we make each time we consciously undertake to do something, or to *feel, think or be* a certain way. It is important to note that *doing nothing* is also a choice that we make. In the context of this book, choice is considered to be as essential for our children's development as it is for us, because it emphasizes the importance of our free will and the power to take charge of our lives. Choice brings freedom; it also implies responsibility, because it means not blaming others for how we feel. It is an **antidote** to victimhood: we get to decide how we want to be with our circumstances.

DREAMS: In this book, "dreaming" refers to the *conscious visualization* of what we want, a creative image that we can intentionally expand and develop in our mind's eye, as opposed to the largely unconscious dreaming associated with sleep, although such dreaming is also a source of information to us. All human beings dream, and the ability to dream and creatively imagine what we want is essential to our development and fulfillment as human beings.

The Archer's Bow posits that we were given the capacity to dream in order to go beyond what already is, to create what we want in a way that is uniquely our own. Dreams, if we heed them, are the nudge that sets us on the path of greatest fulfillment. Our dreams, containing the essence of what we desire, are the raw material from which we create our future. At the same time, ***dreaming also helps create that future energetically***, by putting us on a vibrational level in consonance with what we want, enabling us to attract it to ourselves, or create it in our lives. So it is at once the *source* of what we create and the *means* to achieving it.

COMMUNICATION: In the context of this book, communication is understood to be bi-directional, or as we might say informally, *"a two-way street"*, meaning that it includes a listening component as well. It includes both verbal and non-verbal expression of thoughts and feelings. Productive communication initiated with our children when they are small sets the stage for productive conversations with them throughout their childhood, and into adolescence and adulthood.

DISCIPLINE: Discipline is understood as a potentiator: a structure guiding and supporting our creativity toward its materialization. Looking at discipline merely as a way to correct negative behavior is misleading. The underlying premise for instilling discipline is that, ultimately, it gives our children the structure, confidence, dedication, and willingness to invest the time and energy that they will need to go for what they really want.

The 10,000 hour rule, a concept popularized by author Malcolm Gladwell, referring to the time and dedication needed to achieve expertise in any given field, is a great reminder of the importance of discipline in our lives.

FAILURE: A simple definition of failure would be: *"Not achieving what one has set out to do"*, or *"not attaining an expected standard in doing so"*. We experience failure when we try something and it doesn't work out as we'd hoped, or alternatively, when our *fear of failure* keeps us from trying it in the first place.

The difference between the two: *"failing in motion"* versus *"failing in your head",* in Sergi's words, is that the former is characterized by forward movement; the latter, by paralysis that leads nowhere.

Failure is part and parcel of the learning process: an essential step toward achieving mastery. As such, failure is *something to be celebrated,* as a sign of progress on the path toward achieving what we want.

GOODWILL RESERVE: A reserve of goodwill is like an imaginary bank account in which the positive messages, tolerance, and trust practiced by parents are "deposited". When we as parents lose our cool, fall down on the job, blow our top or resort to barking orders because we're simply at a loss as to what to do, it's like making a withdrawal from that account: being able to dip into this reserve of trust and affection means that even at times when we aren't being our most skillful selves, the relationship doesn't break down.

A hefty "bank account" of love and understanding will offset many of our parental failings. The same concept can be applied to the reserve of trust created in any relationship between two or more people. For more on the reserve of goodwill, see the book "The Seven Principles for Making Marriage Work" (Gottman, Silver), where the importance of including such positivity in our relationships is discussed.

INALIENABLE RIGHTS: These rights are: *Life, liberty and the pursuit of happiness,* just as spelled out by the U.S. founding fathers in the Declaration of Independence. In The Archer's Bow, "success" is not measured in professional or economic terms, but as our experience of those three inalienable rights, which are our personal roadmap to fulfillment (*see* Success, *in this glossary).*

JIT ADVICE GIVING: This concept is borrowed from the business context, where JIT refers to *just-in-time* production aimed at improving quality and efficiency, and reducing waste in the production process. Applied to learning, it is seen as the opportunity for learners to choose a desired content on a need-to-know basis. In the context of *advice-giving,* JIT stands for: Judicious, Impartial and Timely. **Judicious**, because advice is best administered in small doses; **Impartial**, because the best advice is judgment-free, and **Timely**, because it is most effective when dispensed opportunely. The same concept of reduced waste and greater efficiency applies.

NAG-OMETER: In our relationships, it is easy for our helpful reminders, advice, and gentle prodding to turn into something more persistent and far less productive, commonly known as *nagging*. What I call the "Nag-ometer" is actually our very own internal measuring system for gauging the impact we have on others when we nag.

The importance of monitoring the quantity and quality of our unsolicited comments comes from their tendency to lose effectiveness with time. If we want to be effective in our communication, it's important to calibrate how our admonitions are being dispensed (and received). That's where the "Nag-ometer" comes in. It signals to us when we have exceeded the dose of information that the other person will actually assimilate before tuning us out. We actually (intuitively) know whether we are having our intended impact. Our Nag-ometer is there for us: we just have to tune in to it to know when we have become heavy-handed and communication ceases to be productive.

PARENTAL FOOTPRINT: One of the outcomes of parenting is to imprint a system of beliefs and values that then becomes our children's view of Reality. As parents, and even simply as human beings, our assumptions around "what is right" have been shaped by our culture, our experiences, and the parental footprint we ourselves received during our upbringing. When we pass on these assumptions to our children, we are passing on our own parental footprint to them. It is important to be aware that our assumptions may well include some of our own limiting beliefs.

PERFECTION: Our perfection, in the context of this book, includes the beauty of the natural flaws that make us who we are. It has an essence quality to it. Some would call it our divine nature. When children are born they are perfect because they are as they are meant to be, regardless of how that is. Another very different thing is the effort to "be perfect", or "do perfect", which is essentially our response to the learned behavior that we are not good enough just as we are.

RED-FLAG MOMENT: A red-flag moment is a situation in which we are tempted to sacrifice a deeper conviction – such as the belief that our children should go for what makes them happy – in favor of something that satisfies our own need, as parents, to feel good. Dictating what will be best for our children even when it diverges from what they themselves want is often done because it mitigates our feelings of apprehension and discomfort at not knowing where our children's dreams will take them.

The risk is that, rather than supporting our children in what they want to go for, we let our own fears, judgments, or outside pressure, override that deeper belief. Our attempt to make our own experience better by having our children do what will make us feel good is often justified with arguments based on our assumptions of what is "best" for them.

REALITY: What we call Reality is in fact our *perspective* of the experiences and situations that appear in our lives. It is different from Circumstances, which are objectively the same for us all: losing a race; winning the lottery; getting a new job; having a baby. Our view of Reality as being easy or difficult will be determined by *how we see* those situations. Some people have a positive take on Reality despite challenging circumstances, whereas for others, challenging circumstances bring feelings of resentment or trepidation, and the sense that Reality is hard.

Because our view of Reality is so often colored by the sum total of our experiences, in *The Archer's Bow* parents are encouraged to exercise caution when telling their children what will work and what will not, based on their *own experience of Reality,* which may be very different from what their children will find when they set out on their own to achieve something.

RESPECT: According to one definition, it is *"esteem for or a sense of the worth or excellence of a person, a personal quality or ability, or something considered as a manifestation of a personal quality or ability".* In the Archer's Bow, Respect – for both adults and children – is seen as consideration for *the being within,* separate from the acquired skills and knowledge that come with experience. Respect for our children can be practiced while ensuring that social etiquette, limits and discipline are acquired as well.

RESPONSIBILITY: One dictionary definition of the word "responsible" is: *"able to be trusted to do what is right or to do the things that are expected or required"*. In this book, Responsibility has this notion of "reliability" and "trustworthiness", yet goes beyond, to include an *empowering, proactive intention*: taking responsibility for using the gifts we are given, taking responsibility for how we feel, and most importantly, taking responsibility for choosing what we want to do with our circumstances. These aspects apply to adults and children alike.

SUCCESS: Success is understood to be the attainment of something that we consider to be a favorable outcome; something beneficial to us. It will not necessarily coincide with what others consider to be beneficial to us, and indeed, we may at times find ourselves being judged by individuals whose notion of success is quite different from our own. In the Archer's Bow, success is measured more in terms of personal fulfillment than social or professional achievement, although those aspects may indeed deepen one's sense of personal fulfillment.

The change of paradigm here is that success is defined on our own terms. In this book, success is measured from the standpoint of the three inalienable rights set forth by the U.S. founding fathers: namely, the right to life, liberty and the pursuit of happiness (*see* Inalienable Rights *in this glossary*).

SUSPENSION OF DISBELIEF: "Suspension of disbelief" refers to a willingness on our part to "not know", and instead just be curious about what our children really want. It's easy to discount their dreams as fantasy, particularly when we feel we know what is best for them. The "disbelief" we want to set aside is the assumption that our children's dreams are simple illusions that will lead them on a futile search for something that is unattainable, or a waste of time.

Our experiences color the way we see the world. It's easy to dismiss our children's ability to see it differently, as they begin to create their own experiences. Suspending disbelief enables us to set aside our doubts and choose to be open to what we don't know, prompting questions from a place of curiosity that actually feeds our children's creativity.

SUSTAINABLE AUTHORITY: *Sustainable authority* is the term I use to refer to an ongoing relationship of credibility and influence that depends not on physical strength or fear, but rather, on trust in the motives and conduct of the person wielding authority. "Earned" rather than imposed, it is attained when the person in authority inspires the respect – and willingness to be influenced – of the person under that authority

Sustainable authority is generated when we model honesty, respect, credibility, a sense of humor and the willingness to admit our mistakes. Keeping in mind that authority is a means, not an end, letting go of the need to assert our authority at all costs actually reinforces our authority, making it more authentic and *sustainable.*

VALUES: Throughout this book, the term "value" is used to refer to a principle - or underlying belief about something - that we cherish or hold dear. There are many traditionally widely accepted values, such as Honesty, Integrity, Hard work, Friendship, Compassion, Loyalty and Discipline, to name only a few.

Beyond these time-honored, universal values, there are others we can come up with that have meaning for us, and describe the way we see the world: Beauty, Travel, Having fun, Nature, Cooking, Fitness, Adventure, Family, Curiosity, Thriftiness, Service to others, Tradition, Love, Freedom, Discovery, Playfulness, Generosity, and Learning are just some of the many values we could think of.

Values are important because of what they say about us. It's important to recognize that while some of our children's values will be similar to our own – especially such universally held values as honesty, loyalty and friendship, for example – others may be completely different. Indeed, when we dig deeper to find out what someone else's values really mean to them, we may find differences in the meaning of values that on the surface appear to be the same. An example: one person might equate **Freedom** with having a high paying job that provides them with the financial means to do whatever they like; for someone else, **Freedom** might signify having no commitments at all, and never having any more money than whatever they need to live from day to day.

Such distinctions are worth exploring when we consider the values that anyone else, including our children, choose to embrace.

Author Note

. . . .

*A*s you may imagine, if you have read this far, for me, writing this book was a labor of love. My own doubts about dipping into something so personal – the fragments taken from my own story with my son – were ultimately offset by the conviction that our children have a story that needs to be told.

My dream is that we can raise healthy, wholesome youngsters who can take their future into their own hands; find fulfilment by following their own "nudge"; and know how to bestow compassion, love, respect and generosity on others because they themselves have benefited from it.

Whether we are young or old, it's never too late to start exploring what we can do differently or better. I hope that reading this book has offered an opportunity to reconsider some thoughts and ideas that may have been there by default: certainly, for me, writing the book has been a revelatory experience.

If you enjoyed this book, I would also love for you to review it! Doing so will encourage others to benefit from the learning and insight that will come from revisiting their parenting efforts - and their own childhood experiences - from a new perspective.

Thank you!

The Author

. . . .

Virginia Skrobisch, MA CPCC PCC, has led a rich, varied life as a cultural explorer, language lover and inspired parent. Although her work as a professional conference interpreter and translator fulfilled her passion for words and for bridging cultures for over 25 years, it was not until her decision to train and work as a life coach in 2006 that she found her calling as an agent for conscious change.

An ever-inquisitive learner and inveterate "askoholic", her higher studies began at Mount Holyoke college, where she graduated longer ago than she would like to remember. Most of her life since then has taken place in Europe.

Originally from New York, she currently lives and works as a writer and professional coach in Barcelona, the vibrant Mediterranean city known for its Modernist architecture and vanguard cuisine. It is here where she raised her son and discovered a passion for working with people to bring about meaningful change in their lives.

You can learn more at www.virginiaskrobisch-author.com, where she will be posting her thoughts, probably quite randomly, on subjects designed to be of genuine interest to her readers. You are also invited to connect with her at facebook.com/VirginiaSkrobischWriter, where she will share insights and ideas on parenting and other things that in one way or another have an impact on our lives.

Printed in Great Britain
by Amazon

PRAISE FOR KATE GRENVILLE'S
AWARD-WINNING NOVEL
A ROOM MADE OF LEAVES

'Almost flawless…Deep in research and beautifully realised.'
HEATHER ROSE

'Fabulous…[It will] make you think deeply about home and
belonging and our hidden and brutal colonial past.'
MELANIE CHENG

'Beautifully observed…A superb piece of work.'
LEIGH SALES

'Vividly rendered, warmly sympathetic, daring in speculative
breadth: a full-length portrait in oils of a woman known
to most of us only in profile miniature.'
AUSTRALIAN

'[A] stunning literary achievement.'
GUARDIAN AUSTRALIA

'Grenville's prose is elegant and meticulously crafted…
Despite the trappings of history…her achievement here is not a
historical one. *A Room Made of Leaves* questions, rhetorically,
how to live ethically with a history that is unfair.'
SATURDAY PAPER

'[Gives] voice to the countless generations of women who
were prevented from telling their true stories…Compelling.'
HERALD SUN

'Grenville offers a potentially myth-busting version
of a turbulent time.'
BOOKLIST (STARRED REVIEW)

'Elizabeth—passionate, clever and endlessly
resilient—is brilliantly conjured.'
THE TIMES (UK)

ELIZABETH MACARTHUR'S LETTERS

KATE GRENVILLE is one of Australia's most celebrated writers. Her international bestseller *The Secret River* was awarded local and overseas prizes, has been adapted for the stage and as an acclaimed television miniseries, and is now a much-loved classic. Grenville's other novels include *Sarah Thornhill*, *The Lieutenant*, *Dark Places* and the Orange Prize winner *The Idea of Perfection*. Her most recent books are two works of non-fiction, *One Life: My Mother's Story* and *The Case Against Fragrance*, and the bestselling novel *A Room Made of Leaves*. She has also written three books about the writing process. In 2017 Grenville was awarded the Australia Council Award for Lifetime Achievement in Literature.

kategrenville.com.au

ELIZABETH MACARTHUR'S LETTERS

EDITED BY
KATE GRENVILLE

t

TEXT PUBLISHING MELBOURNE AUSTRALIA

The Text Publishing Company acknowledges the Traditional Owners of the country on which we work, the Wurundjeri people of the Kulin Nation, and pays respect to their Elders past and present.

textpublishing.com.au

The Text Publishing Company
Wurundjeri Country, Level 6, Royal Bank Chambers, 287 Collins Street,
Melbourne Victoria 3000 Australia

Published by The Text Publishing Company, 2022

Book design by Imogen Stubbs
Jacket painting: unknown artist, portrait reputedly of Elizabeth Macarthur, undated, oil on canvas, 90 x 70.5 cm, DG 221, State Library of NSW
Endpapers: adapted from a cross-written letter by Elizabeth Macarthur, courtesy State Library of NSW; photo by Kate Grenville
Typeset by J&M Typesetting

Printed and bound in Australia by Griffin Press, part of Ovato, an accredited ISO/NZS 14001:2004 Environmental Management System printer.

ISBN: 9781922458582 (hardback)
ISBN: 9781922459749 (ebook)

A catalogue record for this book is available from the National Library of Australia

CONTENTS

ELIZABETH MACARTHUR SPEAKS FOR HERSELF

Twenty years ago, doing background research into early Sydney for a project that became my novel *The Secret River*, I came across an extract from the letters of Elizabeth Macarthur. She wasn't of direct relevance to my project, and what I'd learned about the Macarthurs at school hadn't interested me much. John Macarthur was 'the father of the wool industry' and Elizabeth was his devoted wife. Hardly stuff to set the pulse racing. It was only because the letter referred to Lieutenant William Dawes, about whom I was planning to write, that I even read it. Dawes was the colony's first astronomer, and his story is a fascinating one. As I read what Elizabeth Macarthur had to say about him, I felt that flash of excitement that every writer waits for, hopes for.

> Mr Dawes we do not see so frequently. He is so much engaged with the stars that to mortal eyes he is not always visible. I had the presumption to become his pupil and meant to learn a little of astronomy. It is true I have had many pleasant walks to his house (something less than half a mile from Sydney), having given him much trouble in making orreries, and explaining to me the general principles of the heavenly bodies, but I soon found I had mistaken my abilities and blush at my error.

Those five words 'I blush at my error' seemed to blaze off the page. I'd read enough late-eighteenth-century letters to know how startling it was for a woman to express—especially in relation to a man not her husband—such a physical, hot-blooded moment. After all, why do we blush? When we're in the grip of some strong emotion—shame or embarrassment… or desire.

It took two decades (and five intervening books) for me to get to that story, which became the novel *A Room Made of Leaves*. To start, I read more of Elizabeth Macarthur's letters, hoping for a few more moments like the blush. At first I was disappointed. There are times when you get a vivid sense of a living person. But many of the letters are surprisingly bland, considering the context in which they were written.

How could this be, I wondered. Elizabeth Macarthur's life had been lived among the tumult, brutality and Machiavellian scheming of a remote penal colony. Her husband was a man who comes across, in the record he left, as arrogant, ruthless, hot-tempered: a man who boasted of destroying anyone who dared to stand between him and his ambition.

It's true that a woman of Elizabeth Macarthur's time wasn't expected to involve herself in the affairs of the world. She was supposed to be content to sit at home, looking after her children and doing embroidery. But I didn't think Elizabeth Macarthur was that kind of woman. When the mask of demure formality drops in the letters, we hear the voice of a very different woman: shrewd, informed, wryly witty.

Reading on, wondering at the disconnect between the letters and the life, I began to think that Elizabeth Macarthur's letters could be seen as a wonderful piece of fiction, sustained over sixty years. The fiction depicted a devoted, devout, obedient wife, unfailingly happy and cheerful, married to a man who was loving, admirable and, mystifyingly, disliked by almost everyone he encountered. I pictured Elizabeth Macarthur smiling to herself as she wrote sentence after sentence of this fiction, relishing the delicious ironies of saying exactly the opposite of what she really thought.

There aren't many examples of women of that time kicking against the bars they were forced to live behind, but there are enough to make it clear that they didn't all accept their lot. In the novels of Jane Austen—a near-contemporary of Elizabeth Macarthur and from a similar social background—there's no mistaking the author's frustration and sense of injustice at the narrow choices her heroines had. Of course, she didn't write directly about any of that—not many women of the time could leave any such scandalous thoughts on paper. Instead, she exploited one of the very few weapons a woman had: irony.

In my reading of Elizabeth Macarthur, that's the weapon she was using too. She might say, in relation to the return of her husband from a long absence: 'you may imagine how great was my joy on the arrival of McArthur', constructing a beautifully double-faced sentence. Yes, the friend to whom she was writing probably could imagine exactly how great was her joy: none whatsoever.

I began to glimpse a novel about doubleness, about false stories obscuring true ones, of layers of concealment peeling back one after the other. If Elizabeth Macarthur had written

3

a kind of fiction in the letters—telling the story of a sunny life without shadows—I set myself the task of inventing the story she hadn't told, one that included the darknesses I thought her life must have had. My fiction would take the form of a memoir—Elizabeth Macarthur speaking frankly about her life and feelings—that had been lost for two hundred years and that now, incredibly, had come into my hands.

꙳

So, were these thoughts about Elizabeth Macarthur right? Maybe, maybe not. In fact, as I put this book of correspondence together, I began to doubt my earlier thoughts about her. Perhaps she really was devoted and devout. Perhaps she really did love her husband. One of the reasons I compiled this sample of her letters is to give readers a chance to decide for themselves: to hear her actual voice—Elizabeth speaking for herself—and to read her own words as they came from her pen.

Whatever the truth about Elizabeth Macarthur, writing a novel that built on my speculations about her was a liberty I was prepared to take. That's because the story I wanted to tell, the theme I wanted to explore, was bigger than one particular woman. It was a story about the way oft-told and oft-believed lies can take on the status of truth. For most of the many drafts of the novel, its working title was 'Do Not Believe Too Quickly'. What was in my mind was: Do not believe too quickly the myths about the women of the past. Do not believe too quickly the stereotype of them being content with their lot. And do not believe too quickly other stories either, even if they've taken on the impenetrable gloss of a national myth. I was thinking, of course, of some of the stories the early settlers in Australia—including Elizabeth Macarthur—told about the Indigenous people. As the saying goes, history is written by the victors. What about the other histories, the ones obscured by the victors' stories?

Elizabeth Veale was born in 1766, in the village of Bridgerule in Devon. She was a farmer's daughter. In 1788 she married John Macarthur. His father was a Plymouth draper and he himself was an army officer of the most junior rank. Seeking better prospects than Britain offered, they journeyed to New South Wales in 1790. The British penal colony there—as far from home as it was possible to travel—was two years old when they arrived: a struggling, hungry place that many thought had no future.

John Macarthur was clever, ruthless and energetic, and within a few years he was one of the richest and most powerful men in the colony. Not content with what he had, he constantly pushed the authorities for more, and resented their efforts to curb his power. He spent two long periods back in England facing legal proceedings—the first time for having shot his commanding officer in a duel, the second for having orchestrated a coup against the governor. During these absences—four years, then a few years later another eight—Elizabeth managed the Macarthur enterprises.

Until recently she languished in the shadow of her husband. John Macarthur may have been known to generations of Australians as 'the father of the wool industry', but he was in England during many of the years of successful sheep-breeding. It must have been his wife—no doubt helped by some now mostly nameless others—who managed the flocks and their breeding during those long absences. The wool industry must actually have had a mother, rather than a father.

John Macarthur led a public, controversial, tumultuous life, and its course can be tracked through the enormous amount of documentation he left behind. By contrast, Elizabeth left very little record of herself. But she was a woman of some education, so we do have one window into her life: a large collection of letters. Apart from an incomplete account of her voyage to New South Wales, they're the only documents she left. Unfortunately and oddly, not a single one of the letters she wrote to her husband in the years of his absence has ever come to light—a great loss, as it's there that we might learn about how she faced the many challenges of her life as the manager of a huge pastoral enterprise. But the letters we do have are of great interest now, when the achievements of women—so often hidden behind their husbands—are being discovered and honoured as they never have been before.

I took enormous liberties in writing the novel inspired by Elizabeth Macarthur. There were already several good books about her and her world (in particular those by Joy Hughes, Hazel King and Lennard Bickel, as well as Malcolm Ellis's book about John Macarthur), and as my novel was in its final drafts, Michelle Scott Tucker's comprehensive biography was published. These books presented a thorough account of what could be established about Elizabeth Macarthur's life and character from the fairly scanty record. My fictional Elizabeth was inspired at every point by what's known of the real woman, and especially by her letters, but *A Room Made of Leaves* is a work of the imagination.

This collection of sixty-five letters is only a glimpse of all that she wrote—she was a prolific correspondent. I've drawn heavily from the most active part of her life, from her first arrival in New South Wales up to the death of her husband. She lived for another sixteen years and wrote many more letters in those years.

I've chosen a representative selection of the letters, mostly to family members. I've included just a few of the ones she wrote to others in her social circle—particularly to John Macarthur's protégé, Captain John Piper.

I've pruned the letters pretty hard. Many of them are made long by extended passages about family comings and goings, and local news and gossip. I've reduced a fair amount of that material, leaving a sample rather than every detail. She also recorded important events told to her by others that she didn't see herself (including the smallpox epidemic, and the kidnapping of the Indigenous men Bennelong and Colebee), and I haven't included those. My rule of thumb was to retain the parts of letters that seemed to express the kind of person she was—her personality, her feelings and thoughts, her attitudes—rather than descriptions of events.

I've regularised most spelling (though I've left Elizabeth's several ways of spelling the name Macarthur, along with some other idiosyncrasies), and added paragraph breaks and punctuation for ease of reading. I also, with misgivings, decided not to show with ellipses where I'd edited out material—the dots made for a very jerky read. My aim was to offer a straightforwardly accessible book for a general audience.

Some of the earlier letters have already been published in *The Journal and Letters of Elizabeth Macarthur 1789–1798* (1984), edited by Joy Hughes, and in *Some Early Records of the Macarthurs of Camden* (1914), edited by Sibella Macarthur Onslow. Barbara Manchester also transcribed some of the letters for the State Library of New South Wales.

The original manuscript letters are in the Macarthur Papers and the Piper Papers, held in the Mitchell Library, State Library of New South Wales. I acknowledge with gratitude the library, and warmly thank the staff for their patient and expert help.

We can only hope that one day some of Elizabeth Macarthur's missing letters—especially the ones to her husband—will turn up. They'll give new insights into her still-mysterious inner life. Perhaps, too, in the future a complete transcription of all the letters might be made, although it would be a mighty volume. In the meantime, this book offers a selection of letters by a woman who was present from the earliest days of the colony for the next sixty years, observing with an often amused, always intelligent eye. This is her voice, speaking directly to her correspondents: the voice of an extraordinary woman who, against the odds, thrived in challenging times.

A BRIEF OUTLINE OF ELIZABETH MACARTHUR'S LIFE

1766   Elizabeth Veale born, daughter of a farmer in
       Bridgerule, Devon

1767   John Macarthur born, son of a draper in Plymouth, Devon

1772   Elizabeth's father dies

1778   Elizabeth's mother marries Edmund Leach, yeoman

1781   Mary Isabella Leach (Elizabeth's half-sister) born

1782   John becomes ensign in Fish's Corps

1783   Fish's Corps disbanded; John on half-pay

1788   John returns to full pay as ensign in 68th Regiment;
       Elizabeth and John marry

1789   Edward born;
       John transferred as lieutenant in New South Wales Corps;
       Elizabeth, John and Edward sail from London

1790   Unnamed daughter born and dies at sea;
       Elizabeth, John and Edward arrive in Sydney

1793   Elizabeth (daughter) born

1794   John (son) born

1795   Mary Isabella (daughter) born

1797   James I born and dies

1798   James II born

1800   William born

1801   John sails to England

1805   John returns to NSW

1808   Emmeline born

1809   John sails to England for second time

1817   John again returns to NSW

1831   John (son) dies

1833   John declared insane

1834   John dies

1850   Elizabeth dies

ELIZABETH MACARTHUR'S CHILDREN AND GRANDCHILDREN

Edward (1789–1872), born Bath, England

Unnamed daughter (1790–1790), born and died at sea

Elizabeth (1793–1842), born NSW

John (1794–1831), born NSW

Mary (1795–1852), born NSW

    —Edward, born 1826

    —James, born 1829

    —William, born 1831

    —Isabella, born 1834

    —Frederic, born 1836

James I (1797–1797), born NSW and died at ten months old

James II (1798–1867), born NSW

    —Elizabeth, born 1840

William (1800–1882), born NSW

Emmeline (1808–1888), born NSW

ELIZABETH MACARTHUR'S LETTERS

8 October 1789, to her mother

In October 1788 Elizabeth Veale, the daughter of a farmer in Devon, married John Macarthur, the son of a draper. Macarthur was an ensign—the most junior rank of officer—in the army. He had little money and few prospects of advancement. He may also have had a debt of some five hundred pounds that he had no way of repaying. So, when there was an opportunity to be promoted into a new regiment, he took it—even though it would mean service on the other side of the world, in the primitive conditions of a struggling penal colony.

When this letter was written, Elizabeth was the mother of Edward, a sickly boy of seven or eight months old. Apart from travelling to Chatham Barracks near London for John to take up his military service, she'd never gone far beyond the little village of Bridgerule where she'd grown up.

This letter—the earliest in the library archive—was a rich source for my exploration of the idea of false stories. Elizabeth describes herself as appearing 'timid and irresolute': could this really be so? Within a year she was throwing herself into a challenging life in New South Wales in a way that was anything but timid, anything but irresolute.

In A Room Made of Leaves *I used, verbatim, several parts of this letter—they were the parts that sounded like someone embroidering an elaborate frill of language to prettify the truth. Elizabeth was trying to reassure her mother, not necessarily to say what she really thought. The crops she describes as 'flourishing in a way nearly incredible' had in fact failed. To my eyes this was a lovely bit of doublespeak that she might have enjoyed devising.*

Yes, the success of those crops was indeed 'incredible'—that is, not to be believed.

8th October 1789
Chatham Barracks

In my last letter I informed you, my dear Mother, of my husband's exchange into a Corps destined for New South Wales, from which we have every reasonable expectation of reaping the most material advantages. You will be surprised that even I, who appear timid and irresolute, should be a warm advocate for this scheme. So it is—and believe me I shall be greatly disappointed if anything happens to impede it.

I foresee how terrific and gloomy this will appear to you—to me at first it had the same appearance, while I suffered myself to be blinded by common and vulgar prejudices. I have not now, nor I trust shall ever have one scruple of regret, but what relates to you.

Do but consider that if we must be distant from each other, it is much the same, whether I am two hundred, or more than as many thousand miles apart from you. The same Providence will watch over and protect us, there as here—the sun that shines on you will also afford me the benefit of his cheering rays, and that too in a country where nature hath been so lavish of her bounties, that flowers luxuriantly abound, in the same manner as with culture fruits will do hereafter.

By the last accounts from Port Jackson—where the new settlement is established—we learn that wheat which had been sown, flourished in a manner nearly incredible, & that the Settlers are making rapid progress in building, so that by the time our Corps arrives everything will be made comfortable for their reception.

The new Settlement is an immediate object with Government, & every effort will be made to promote its success.

Your affectionate daughter,
Elizabeth McArthur.

20 April 1790, to her mother

The Macarthurs sailed in November 1789, as part of the Second Fleet taking convicts to New South Wales. The first part of their voyage was a nightmare—John Macarthur had a falling-out with the captain of the ship and as a result Elizabeth became a prisoner, literally nailed into a cabin. (The nightmare was worse for the convicts on board, at least a quarter of whom died.)

The hostilities between John Macarthur and others on the ship finally blazed so hot that—in the middle of the Atlantic!—the Macarthurs were transferred to another vessel. This letter was written when the fleet later put in at the Cape of Good Hope for supplies.

When you compare the blandness of this account of the voyage with the next document, 'An Account of the Voyage to New South Wales', it's clear just how good a fiction writer Elizabeth was. Of course she didn't want to worry her mother—that explains the omissions and beautiful lies in the letter. But reading these documents one after the other shows that, when it suited her, Elizabeth was prepared to reshape the truth fairly radically.

One of the important omissions in this letter is that when Elizabeth wrote it, she was about six months pregnant. Depending on the speed of their passage, that meant there was a good chance the baby would be born on board—hardly ideal.

Reading Elizabeth's letters, there were times when I found her unattractive—so much that I abandoned the novel more than once. The casual reference to enslaved men and women in this letter was one of those moments. Yes, that attitude was common at the time—but not universal. She could have had a more humane perspective, and I wish she had.

Cape of Good Hope, 20th April, 1790

My dear Mother,

I have the happiness to inform you that we arrived safe, and are anchored in the bay, from when I date this on the 14th of this month, after a fine passage of just twelve weeks and three days, from the time we sailed from Portsmouth.

I wish I could also add that we arrived in perfect health, but my poor little boy is a melancholy proof, at this period, of the contrary. He has been very sickly through the passage, and unless a very speedy change take place I am well convinced he will shortly cease to be an inhabitant of this world. I believe I told you in Devonshire that he had nearly cut one of his teeth—I was, however, exceedingly mistaken, for he hath not yet cut any, although they appear very firm in the gums, and I am in hopes that if once one or two had made their appearance, he might yet recover and get strength. He is not near so large as children generally are at four months old, although he is now upwards of twelve.

He is very sensible, very lively, and affords us much pleasure, but the trouble we have had with so delicate a little creature is indescribable, and I wonder my own health hath not suffered more through the attention I have been obliged to pay him. I may justly say with regard to him 'that God tempers the wind to the shorn lamb'.

Mr McArthur has enjoyed a remarkably good share of health ever since we left England, and I trust will continue to do so. I was sorely tried with the length of the passage before we got into port, and stood in need of refreshment very much, but now with the benefit of fresh meat and plenty of fruits and vegetables, I am quite recovered, and assure my beloved Mother that I never was in better health, and in very good spirits which are only damped by poor Edward's illness.

You will expect some account of my voyage, but I scarcely know where to begin or what to tell you. I mean to write Miss Kingdon those particulars. It will be needless for me to repeat the same in both letters, particularly as I have but little spare time, being busy in seeing all our linen washed and got up, and in laying in stock and refreshment to take with us to Botany Bay. I am also advised by our surgeon to spend as much time as possible on shore, in order to get very strong and prepared for the remainder of the voyage. We are to stay here eight days longer and no more.

Tomorrow I go on shore to board during that time. I am to pay a dollar and a half a day, and live with a genteel private family. Mr McArthur cannot quit the ship entirely, but will visit me on shore every day.

You can have no idea of the extravagant charge of the inhabitants for almost all they sell. As an instance of these impositions I must tell you that they charge the ships for a cabbage 1s 6d each. Their bread is not good, being fermented with leaven. Fruit is to be had in great abundance. The grapes are fine—beyond what I can describe to you—you have no idea to what a pitch of luxuriance they arrive. It is here the season of autumn, and apples, pears and such fruits are now just in perfection. We get wine for about 1s the bottle.

The Dutch live very well at their own tables. I like their houses, they are spacious and airy, and their slaves keep them remarkably clean. A man's riches are here determined by the number of his slaves. If you go to a genteel house you will see a dozen of them attending in the hall. I had the honour to be received by the Governor, when the officers paid their respects to him, and was met by his daughter, who was dressed after our mode, but as she could not speak English, nor I Dutch, we could only exchange dumb civilities.

The face of the country is very romantic. Our prospect is bounded by the mountains, the lowest of which is much higher than any I ever saw before. Such walks as I have taken have been very amusing. In every plant I see something new—these works of nature at the foot of the mountains represent a beautiful shrubbery—where innumerable beautiful flowers and plants delight the eye and regale the senses.

I have not yet seen any of the original inhabitants of this coast—the Hottentots—there are some, I am told, who reside about the mountains. They are a harmless set of beings and hurt no one. I have just given you this short account of the Cape of Good Hope, of which you have heard so much, little thinking that your daughter would ever write to you from thence.

I will now tell you of a few circumstances about our passage. We sailed from England with a fair wind, which carried us to the Bay of Biscay. We were there for the space of two days, and in the night had so heavy a gale of wind that I was most terribly alarmed. They told me however, there was no danger—after this storm we soon got into fine weather and constant fair winds.

I wrote to you from Portsmouth that we had a lady going

out with us, the wife of Captain Trail. She appeared a very agreeable woman, but her husband proved himself a perfect sea-monster—so much so, that I requested Mr McArthur to exchange duties with one of the officers in one of the other ships. It was accordingly so arranged, and when about six degrees from the Equator, on a very warm day, when it was quite calm, Mr McArthur, myself, Edward, and our servants left the *Neptune* and embarked on board the *Scarborough*, commanded by Captain Marshall.

Lieutenant Townsend was taken in the *Neptune* in place of Mr McArthur, and we found on board the *Scarborough* an officer of the Troops, Lieutenant Abbott, who from this time lived with us. This exchange took place on the 19th February, and hath proved in every respect satisfactory to me.

Captain Marshall was one of the Captains who commanded a Transport in the First Fleet that went to the New South Wales, and stayed in the Colony four months. He, therefore, frequently amuses us with accounts of the place, and in what state he left it, and upon the whole they are flattering. He is a very humane man, and I am under the greatest obligation to him for his more than common attention to me and Edward.

If it pleases the Almighty that we arrive in safety at Port Jackson, I shall write you a long letter by Captain Marshall, but that letter you must not expect till next June, as the ship is under a charter to bring tea home from China for the East India Company. She therefore will from Port Jackson go on to China, and from thence return to England, which makes the home passage very long.

Whether I may meet with a vessel that returns by the nearest way from Port Jackson to England is very uncertain, indeed I believe it very improbable, and therefore you must not expect it. I hope you will receive this letter in four months from this date, by which—and long before, I trust—we shall be comfortably settled in our New World. If we have a good passage from hence we hope to be at Port Jackson in seven or eight weeks from this time. You may be sure that I shall write to you by every ship that returns, and I pray that you will punctually write to me.

I have now to desire my particular remembrances to all my friends—and first of all, let me notice my Grandfather—I have in some sort a presentiment that impels me to believe I shall yet see him again. Be that as it may, a man arrived at his years, living regularly, and so perfectly weaned from the things of this world, will meet death as a friend when he shall appear. Tell him, with my love, that I have not forgotten his counsel to have ever present to my mind the duty due by us to our Maker.

Believe me,
Your affectionate daughter,
Elizabeth McArthur

An Account of the Voyage to New South Wales

Apart from her letters, this incomplete account of the voyage to New South Wales is the only piece of writing by Elizabeth Macarthur that's come to light.

Unlike the bland phrases of the preceding letter, this sounds like a real voice. At times you can feel the 'horror' she admits to feeling, and at others ('for the first time I began to be a coward') you can hear the wry wit of understatement and self-deprecation. When I lost faith in my novel, those flashes of an authentic voice encouraged me. I could hear this woman. She was a real, complicated person. She wasn't always one I liked—I recoiled from her lack of empathy towards the women convicts here, as I'd recoiled from her indifference to the enslaved men and women. But this 'account' was clearly written for an audience, and the attitude she expressed was the conventional one of the time. I wondered if perhaps we shouldn't assume too much about her real thoughts from this public-facing narrative.

Elizabeth makes no criticism of her husband's behaviour, but it's pretty clear that he provoked much of what she had to endure. And, of course, she was almost certainly not present to witness the conflicts between her husband and others. Her account of them is most likely to be what he told her.

Friday, 13th November, 1789: I took leave of my friends in London, and accompanied by Mr McArthur, hired a Gravesend Boat from Billingsgate which conveyed us to the *Neptune* at Longreach.

Saturday, 14th: the Ship dropped down to Gravesend, at which place we lay till the Tuesday following, and then sailed from the Downs where we arrived on the Thursday. We remained in the Down Friday, & some part of Saturday, and I was much struck with the formidable and romantic appearance of the Cliffs of Deal and of Dover.

On this day Saturday a disagreeable circumstance occurred. Mr Gilbert, Master of the ship, of whom indeed we had heard but an indifferent character, took an opportunity of manifesting himself in such a light to us as precluded all further communication between him & Mr McArthur. In the afternoon of this day we proceeded down the Channel with a fair wind & at different times had in sight several vessels.

On Monday the 23rd, after laying to all night, supposing the ship to be near Plymouth—our astonishment was very great on discovering that we were so far west as the Lizard Point—I could not help viewing the coast of Cornwall, inhospitable as it appeared, but with sensible regret at the thought that I was about to take a long leave of it.

The wind not being favourable towards our return, it was not till Friday 27th, in the morning, that we found ourselves safely anchored in Plymouth Sound. Here I must pay a tribute to dear Devon; I have ever heard admired the agreeable variety of objects in general to be discovered throughout this county but surely the entrance to Plymouth by sea must surpass every other and I think there cannot be a beholder but what must be delighted in contemplating the variety of beautiful scenes, that on every side surround him.

In the afternoon of the day that we arrived at Plymouth,

Mr Harris, our surgeon, and Mr McArthur went ashore—at their return, which was early in the evening, I gathered from some distant hints that a duel had taken place between Mr Gilbert and Mr McArthur.

To describe my feelings on the occasion would not be a difficult task, though they were by no means so acute as reflection has since rendered them, many disagreeable circumstances then pressing on my mind suffering not one principle to actuate me wholly. I therefore did not so seriously consider what I now think of with trembling, the unhappy consequences that might have arisen from so presumptuous a meeting—nor can I be sufficiently thankful to the Almighty disposer of events, that a more lasting cause does not oblige me to consider it with horror.

On Sunday 29th November, accompanied by Captain M. Moriarty, I took a post chaise & reached Launceston that night, and the next morning, about 11 o'clock, I arrived at my Mother's. My time was so limited by Mr Gilbert's report of the ship's sailing, that I could only allow myself two nights at Bridgerule.

Wednesday morning, I was obliged to take leave of it and return to Plymouth where I arrived between 9 and 10 o'clock at night not much enlivened by the short interview I had with my friends, and considerably depressed with the idea of parting with my only surviving parent, perhaps for ever.

I found Mr McArthur at Plymouth, waiting to take me on board, and late as it was, we were under the necessity of going, as an official message had been sent by Mr Gilbert to inform the officers that the ship would sail at 3 o'clock in the morning.

It was afterwards known that he had not the slightest intention of going, and of course could have no view in reporting what he did but that of harassing us.

Captain Nepean went off to the ship in the same boat with us. We had no sooner arrived on board than a complete scene of uproar and confusion presented itself—Captain Gilbert had insulted a sentinel on his post and struck him—the soldier showed a disposition to defend himself and make Mr Gilbert suffer for his imprudence—this led to a great bustle, and the ship's arms were taken out and loaded and arranged on the stern gallery, and three naval lieutenants in possession of the cabin with blunderbusses lying on the table. In this order we found things on board, and Mr Gilbert had thought fit to take himself quickly on shore instead of preparing for sea.

Captain Nepean dispatched Mr Harris immediately to London with an account of these riotous proceedings to his brother—and about 3 o'clock in the morning I retired to rest after the variety of fatigues and alarms of the preceding day. We did not leave Plymouth until Thursday, 10th December, from whence we proceeded to Portsmouth, and anchored in Stokes Bay.

Sunday, 13th—we found the *Scarborough* and *Surprize*, two transports that were to accompany us, ready for sea. Soon after our arrival here, we learnt that Mr Gilbert's conduct had displeased the owners of the ship, and the truth was soon assured by a Mr Trail being appointed in his room—heartily glad was I when he made his exit—we congratulated ourselves with the thought that such another troublesome man could not be found—& consequently our change must be for the better. Experience, however, soon taught us a very disagreeable truth; Mr Trail's character was of a much blacker dye than was ever in Mr Gilbert's nature to exhibit.

Everything was now disposed in order for sea and we only waited for a fair wind. Captain Hill, Mr Prentice, and Mr Harris, who was the surgeon in the *Surprize*, Mr Townsend, and Mr Abbott in the *Scarborough*, and in the *Neptune* Captain Nepean, Mr McArthur—Mrs Trail was on board with her husband—& Mr Shapcote, the agent for the fleet, but as they all lived together, and Captain Nepean with them, we seldom benefited by their society.

The wind continuing to blow westerly, any attempt towards sailing was not made until Tuesday, 5th January, we then had a few hours' fair wind which first took us to Spithead, where we were again obliged to anchor.

Friday, 8th, we again loosened 'every sail to the breeze' and proceeded to sea. Towards night the wind began to prove faithless, and before the next morning blew directly against us, so as totally to impede our course. The next day (Sunday) and night we continued to beat about, hoping that a favourable change would take place, but on Monday morning appearances were so extremely hazardous that prudence dictated the shortest way back again, and our head was once more turned towards that shore we had so recently quitted with an idea of not seeing it again for some years to come. We passed through the Needles and anchored at the Motherbank on Tuesday at about noon—the evening and succeeding day was so dreadfully tempestuous that we had great reason to be thankful at our being safely in harbour.

We remained at the Motherbank until Sunday, 17th January, when a fine clear easterly wind springing up we soon got under sail and proceeded down the Channel with very fine weather.

On Wednesday, being near the Bay of Biscay, the wind shifted to the south, and it began to be very tempestuous, that night and the succeeding day it blew exceedingly hard, and now, for the first time, I began to be a coward. I could not be persuaded that the ship could possibly long resist the violence of the sea which ran mountains high. On Thursday, towards evening, the wind considerably abated, and the next morning it was a perfect calm, but the sea continued greatly agitated by a swell.

On the 25th January, we were again favoured with a fair wind, and a small vessel was seen at a distance with French colours. About this time my poor little boy was taken very ill, and continued in the most pitiable weak state during our passage to the Cape. Added to this my servant was attacked by a fever that raged among the women convicts, and I had hourly every reason to expect that the infection would be communicated to us, as our apartments were so immediately connected with those of the women—we were, however, fortunate enough to escape from this evil.

I have omitted to observe that when Captain Nepean accepted of accommodation in the upper cabin, he thought himself at liberty to dispose of the part allotted to him in the great cabin as best suited his inclinations, adopting that very generous maxim 'every man for himself'. In consequence of this idea and a request from the owners of the ship, he gave permission for one half the cabin to be partitioned off for the reception of female convicts, leaving the other half to us.

Mr McArthur, who saw the inconvenience that would arise from this arrangement, strove by every means to prevent it. He pointed out to Captain Nepean 'that Government had contracted for a cabin for the mutual benefit of the officers ordered to sail in that ship, and that there was no particular allotment for any officer', that, therefore, if he had the means of obtaining better accommodations, and had no use for those prepared him by Government, it was highly indelicate, if not unjust, to think of introducing a set of people to the possession of what was prepared for him, and to the participation of what was assigned to us.

But in this instance, as in many others, reason unassisted by power proved unavailing. A slight partition was erected, which was thought fully sufficient to separate us from the set of abandoned creatures that were to inhabit the other part, and the only satisfaction or concession that Mr McArthur could obtain for this cruel encroachment upon our rights was a promise and assurance that a passage—which from our quarter gallery communicated with the upper cabin—should always be open for our use and even for our servant.

This assurance, trifling as it may appear, was to us an inestimable advantage, as the division in the cabin had rendered the common passage to the deck totally dark, and added to this, it was always filled with convicts and their constant attendants, filth and vermin.

The altercations and little disputes that the concluding of

this business occasioned created a coldness between Captain Nepean, the master of the ship, and Mr McArthur, and at last terminated in a cessation of every kind of intercourse, except on duty with the one, or on business with the other. Thus, unhappily situated, we determined patiently to submit to the unpleasantness we could not remedy, and cheered ourselves with hope of a speedy voyage, not doubting but that things were at the worst. In this conclusion, however, experience proved we had vainly flattered ourselves.

Many of the soldiers frequently complained that a part of their ration was purloined, and as often as they did, Mr M considered it his duty to report it to Captain Nepean. The first time, Captain N replied, 'Trail does everything to oblige me, and I must give up some points to him.' Subsequent reports on the same subject were answered, 'I will see into it.' It would be an injustice to Captain Nepean to suppose that he did not mention it, as there is every reason to conclude he did, from the monstrous and unprovoked insults that always ensued.

I had made it a practice every fine evening to go up through our quarter gallery to the stern gallery to walk or sit with Mr M, and I also took the same road whenever my inclinations led me to the deck—the common passage, as I have before observed, being rendered impassable.

But of these enjoyments I was suddenly deprived by the door of the gallery being closely nailed up on Saturday, 30th January without their deigning to assign any reason for so doing—we have since been told it was to prevent Mr M from listening—a suggestion infamous and unfounded as it was, I shall ever be persuaded originated in the person, who of all others in the ship ought to have been more forward in suppressing it.

Mr McArthur immediately wrote an official letter to the agent, complaining in the strongest language of the injustice of this transaction—in answer to which he was told verbally (a written answer being refused) 'that he should not quarrel with Trail for any man.' Captain Nepean also said 'that the master of the ship had a right to do as he pleased.'

Without hope of relief, I was fain to content myself within the narrow limits of a wretched cabin, for to add to the horrors of the common passage to the deck, Captain N ordered it to be made a hospital for the sick, the consequence of which was that I never left my cabin till I finally quitted the ship. Thus precluded from the general advantages that even the convicts enjoyed—air and exercise—no language can express, no imagination conceive the misery I experienced.

Approaching near the equator (where the heat in the best of situations is almost insupportable), assailed with noisome stenches—that even in the cold of an English winter, hourly effusions of oil of tar in my cabin could not dispel—two sides of it surrounded with wretches whose dreadful imprecations and shocking discourses ever rang in my distracted ears—a sickly infant claiming constant maternal care, my spirits failing, my health forsaking me—nothing but the speedy change which took place, could have prevented me from falling a helpless victim to the unheard of inhumanity of a set of monsters whose triumph and pleasure seemed to consist in aggravating my distresses.

To a person unacquainted with the innumerable insults

and cruelties I was necessitated to bear with, this may appear the language of passion, resentment, or of a heart desiring revenge, but it will be admitted to be the conclusions of truth and of justice when it is known in addition to the wrongs I have already recited that we were deprived of a part of our little ration, and insultingly told we should have less if they thought proper—that a constant watch was set over our servant when getting our daily allowance of water lest the seaman who had the serving of it (knowing our situation) should be induced by motives of humanity to make some small addition to the scanty pittance, and once (so low were we reduced by the connivance of the only person we could look to for support) that the servant was publicly stopped on the deck, with execrations and abuse, and the water examined, although at this time they were expending fifty gallons a day for their stock, and an unlimited quantity for their own uses, and our whole allowance for every purpose was only five quarts.

But to conclude as ungrateful a subject as ever exercised the patience or wounded the feelings of humanity, I will proceed to the last adventures we were concerned in this detested ship.

Mr M, when his duties called him to visit the soldiers, always crept through the only passage now left us, often endangering a limb by tumbling over boxes and other lumber that this place was made the repository of, and frequently contacting heaps of the vermin with which it was infested.

The immediate cause of our leaving the *Neptune* is now to explain. On the 10th February Mr M had just come on deck when the sergeant complained to him of an attempt made to cheat him of several pounds of the men's allowance of meat, which he had scarcely heard when the chief mate of the ship (who was close by) exclaimed he was a d—d rascal.

Mr M, roused at the insult offered to the man, told the mate with some severity that the sergeant would do well to punish him for his insolence. In return Mr M received every kind of abuse that can be supposed to flow from ignorance and brutality. Angered to an extreme degree, but unable to redress himself, Mr M sent for Captain Nepean and related the whole affair, when, strange to tell, he was highly censured for interfering in the business, and told by Captain N 'that he was sufficient to redress any wrongs offered to the men, without the assistance of any one'.

This fresh insult, the knowledge of what we were hourly suffering, and the contemplation of what we had to expect in future, determined Mr M to apply for a remove on board the *Scarborough*. The request was gladly complied with by Captain Nepean, happy to get rid of a person he thought a troublesome examiner of the iniquitous practices of the people he considered his friends.

On 19th February, a favourable day presented itself, and we moved with all our little baggage, rejoiced at an escape from tyranny, insult and every species of oppression. We were in the latitude of 6 degrees N, when our remove took place, and it being quite a calm day Edward and I suffered greatly from the heat, but this was an inconvenience I thought lightly of after what I had been taught to bear. In the *Scarborough* we shared a small cabin with Mrs Abbott. Marshall, the master of the ship, was a plain, honest man, and disposed to make things as comfortable for me as was in his power.

On 22nd we passed a French Guineaman bound to Martinico with slaves. We crossed the line on 25th with a light wind, and on 14th April, after experiencing a severe gale of wind, anchored safely in False Bay.

False Bay is about 20 miles distant from the Cape Town. At the head of the Bay there is a small town which has a pleasing appearance. The houses are all uniformly white-washed on the outside, and the doors and windows painted green. The inhabitants are all such as make a practice of preying on the shipping—not excepting the Governor himself, who scruples not to supply the wants of any at the moderate profit of about five hundred per cent.

The manners of the people, if I may be allowed to judge, from what I saw, are as unfriendly and rude as the appearance of their coast. The country which presents itself to the sea is extremely mountainous and you see nothing but massy rocks and tremendous precipices—within them, however, the soil is fruitful and well repays the labour of the husbandman.

I one day took a walk to what is called the Company's Garden, a piece of ground totally appropriated to the use of the Dutch East India Company, and stocked with vegetables. It is situated about a mile and a half from the town—the intermediate space is uncultivated and presents Africa in its native dress, every shrub and flower I saw, being new, was interesting. Whether my admiration was excited by novelty or the effect of a long voyage, I cannot determine, but I thought at the time I had never in England seen so charming an assemblage from the most laboured production of art.

I forgot to mention that in our voyage from Portsmouth to the Cape, Mr Prentice was put in arrest by Captain Hill. At False Bay, Captain Hill was put in arrest by Captain Nepean.

A few days before we quitted False Bay, Mr McArthur was attacked with a violent and very alarming fever. It continued to rage till every sense was lost and every faculty but life destroyed, and my little boy at that time was so very ill that I could scarcely expect him to survive a day. Alone, unfriended and in such a situation, what do I not owe to a merciful God for granting me support and assistance in these severe moments of affliction.

I was greatly indebted to the attention and kindness of Captain Reid, who commanded an Imperial East Indiaman that then lay in the Bay with us. He visited Mr M frequently and supplied me with a few little comforts that afterwards were of the greatest service.

[The original manuscript is torn here and parts are missing.]

I was also very much obliged to Captain Marshall for his…behaviour, particularly on this occasion…I do not recollect…officers made me the slightest offer of assistance…For five weeks I was obliged to have one & sometimes two soldiers sit up every night—and all the rest I…took myself was laying my head on a locker—till at length one of the…gave me up his cabin. Our passage to the south…be truly called a tempestuous one, we performed it…and it was not till this time that Mr M…recovered to walk without assistance. It…to feel the heavy hand of sickness.

7 March 1791, to Bridget Kingdon

When this letter was written the Macarthurs had been in New South Wales for around nine months. No ships had arrived from England in that time, so there'd been no mail from home. There'd also been no major replenishment of the colony's stores, and food supplies were uncertain.

Bridget Kingdon, the recipient of this letter, was the daughter of the Reverend John Kingdon, vicar of Bridgerule. She and Elizabeth were much the same age and they'd been friends from childhood. When Elizabeth's widowed mother remarried, Elizabeth seems to have gone to live with the Kingdons.

The Reverend Kingdon was an Oxford graduate, and educated his daughter and her friend at home. He did a good job—both women were able to express themselves fluently and expressively in writing.

Dawes, Tench and Worgan were officers who'd come to New South Wales on the First Fleet, two years before the Macarthurs. Mrs Grose and Mrs Paterson were the wives of two military men expected in the colony. Elizabeth was hoping for their arrival because she had little female company. She was the only officer's wife in the colony, and the only other 'genteel' woman was Mary Johnson, the wife of the clergyman, whose company, she rather scathingly writes here, gave her 'neither profit nor pleasure'. Of course there were many other women in Sydney, but they were either convicts or the wives of ordinary soldiers: not considered suitable companions for the wife of an officer. It wasn't till September 1791—over a year after her arrival—that a few other women of an acceptable social level arrived.

It was an extract from this letter that sparked the idea for A Room Made of Leaves. *It's the paragraph about Mr Dawes and in particular those five words 'I blush at my error'.*

I'd already written about William Dawes—my 2009 novel, The Lieutenant *(in which he's called Daniel Rooke), was inspired by his story. Lieutenant Dawes was an officer with the Marine Corps, but was also knowledgeable about languages (he recorded the language of the Gadigal people) and botany, and had a depth of expertise in astronomy. He was given permission to build a hut and a little observatory away from the settlement, in order to study the unfamiliar southern stars.*

In early drafts of The Lieutenant, *Elizabeth Macarthur had appeared at his hut and flirted with him. However, Mr Rooke was already suited—he had a convict mistress, Mrs Brown. Both Elizabeth and Mrs Brown disappeared from the novel in later drafts—I felt they distracted too much from the central drama, Rooke's friendship with the Indigenous girl I called Tagaran and the moral choices he confronted. It was a delight to fish out those early drafts and give the invented Mrs Brown, and Mr Dawes in his own name, a place in the new novel.*

'Foote's Minuet' is easily found online. Listening to its banal tinklings made me feel very close to Elizabeth.

The account here of Daringa's visit gave me the opportunity to introduce the Indigenous people and set the scene for the later development of one of my main preoccupations in A Room Made of Leaves: *the false stories the colonisers told each other to justify what they were doing.*

Sydney, Port Jackson, N.S. Wales,
March the 7th, 1791

At length we have a prospect of communication once more
with our friends by letter. The *Gorgon*, so long wished for, and
so long expected, is not yet arrived, and by her unaccountable
delay, has involved us all in the most mysterious uncertainty,
and clouded our minds with gloomy apprehensions for her
safety. I hope you will have received my letter, dated August,
1790, which I sent by the *Scarborough* transport, by way of
China. I wrote to my mother by the same ship, and a second
letter to her, dated a few weeks after the first, I sent by the
Neptune, who sailed, I think, some time in August. By those
letters I think you will be informed of every material circumstance relative to our voyage and of what happened to us after
our arrival until the ship sailed.

I told you of the unfortunate loss of the *Sirius*, wrecked
on Norfolk Island. The provisions of the Colony, at that time,
being at a very low ebb, it was deemed necessary to take some
step lest supply might not arrive from England in time to
prevent a threatened famine. Every individual of this colony
was reduced to a very short allowance, and the little brig was
despatched to Batavia under the command of Lieutenant Ball,
there to take up a Dutch ship, and purchase a certain quantity
of provisions for this place. This ship arrived on the 3rd June,
and came timely to prevent very great distress.

On 21st June the *Justinian* arrived, a store ship, and on the
29th our fleet was safely anchored in the Cove. As all those
ships were under contract to return by way of China to take

home tea for the East India Company, and there being at that time no ship stationed here, no way was left to convey a relief to the inhabitants of Norfolk Island, but by ordering some of those ships to touch there on their way to China.

The *Justinian* and *Surprize* received orders, and for that purpose re-embarked a certain proportion of provisions for the island. We had every hope that the supplies might arrive in time to prevent any fatal consequence: yet, as we could have no certainty of that, and till some ship should first arrive here that might be dispatched to know the particulars of their fate, our minds were never perfectly easy on their account.

At that time there was, with the *Sirius*'s company, the Marines, and convicts, near seven hundred persons on the Island, and I can truly say that for upwards of six months I never passed a day without reflecting on them with pain and anxiety. Week after week stole away and month after month with little diversity. Each succeeding sunset produced among us wild and vague conjectures of what could be the cause of the *Gorgon*'s delay, and still we remained unsatisfied—indeed all our surmises have nearly worn themselves out and we are at a loss for new ones—time the great resolver of all events alone can determined this seeming mystery to us.

On the 20th October a general cry prevailed through the Garrison of the flags being hoisted (which is a signal of a ship's appearing off the Harbour). I was preparing myself to receive Mrs Grose and Mrs Paterson, being fully persuaded it was the *Gorgon*, however I was soon undeceived, as it proved to be the *Supply* from Batavia—she had a very quick passage but had experienced a very sickly one—Mr Ball very soon called upon us, and complimented me with many little comforts procured at Batavia, which were truly acceptable.

Believe me, my dear friend, that in writing these faithful traits of the pitiable situation of the inhabitants of Norfolk Island, a chill seems to overpower my faculties—my mind has so truly entered into their distresses that a dread comes over me, which I am unable to describe—but it is succeeded by so firm a reliance on the merciful dispensation of an Almighty, whose hand I think we may here trace without presumption, that I can only admire in silence.

I shall begin my relation now of things more immediately occurring to myself. It will be unnecessary to go over the chit-chat of my last letter, such as the state of our house, the attentions we meet with, etc., etc. We passed our time away many weeks cheerfully if not gaily—gaily indeed it could not be said to be. On my first landing everything was new to me, every bird, every insect, flower, etc.—in short all was novelty around me, and was noticed with a degree of eager curiosity and perturbation that after a while subsided into that calmness I have already described.

In my former letter I gave you the character of Mr Dawes, and also of Captain Tench. Those gentlemen and a few others are the chief among whom we visit. Indeed we are in the habit of such intimacy with Captain Tench that few days pass that we do not spend some part of together.

Mr Dawes we do not see so frequently. He is so much engaged with the stars that to mortal eyes he is not always visible. I had the presumption to become his pupil and meant to learn a little of astronomy. It is true I have had many pleasant walks to his house (something less than half a mile from Sydney), having given him much trouble in making orreries, and explaining to me the general principles of the heavenly bodies, but I soon found I had mistaken my abilities and blush at my error.

Still, I wanted something to fill up a certain vacancy in my time which could neither be done by writing, reading or conversation. To the two first I did not feel myself always inclined, and the latter was not in my power, having no female friend to unbend my mind to, nor a single woman with whom I could converse with any satisfaction to myself, the clergyman's wife being a person in whose society I could reap neither profit nor pleasure.

These considerations made me still anxious to learn some easy science to fill up the vacuum of many a solitary day, and at length under the auspices of Mr Dawes I have made a small progress in Botany. No country can exhibit a more copious field for botanical knowledge than this. I am arrived so far as to be able to class and order all common plants. I have found great pleasure in my study—every walk furnished me with subjects to put in practice that theory I had before gained by reading—but alas, my botanical pursuits were most unwelcomely interrupted by Mr McArthur being attacked by a severe illness. In December he got better, and in January we were removed into a more convenient house.

I shall now introduce another acquaintance, Mr Worgan, to you, a gentleman I have not hitherto named. He was a surgeon to the *Sirius,* and happened to be left at this place when that ship met with her fate at Norfolk. It is not improbable this gentleman may himself deliver this letter to you. He is well known to Doctor Cudlipp. I assure you in losing him a very considerable branch of our society will be lopped off.

I shall now tell you of another resource I have to fill up some of my vacant hours. Our new house is ornamented with a pianoforte of Mr Worgan's, he kindly means to leave it with me, and now, under his direction, I have begun a new study, but I fear without my master I shall not make any great proficiency. I am told, however, that I have done wonders in being able to play off 'God Save the King' and 'Foote's Minuet', besides that of reading the notes with great facility.

In spite of music I have not altogether lost sight of my botanical studies. I have only been precluded from pursuing that study by the intense heat of the weather, which has not permitted me to walk much during the summer. The months of December and January have been hotter than I can describe: indeed insufferably so. The thermometer rising from an hundred to an 112 degrees is, I believe 30 degrees above the hottest day known in England.

The general heat is to be borne, but when we are oppressed by the hot winds we have no other resource but to shut up ourselves in our houses and to endeavour to the utmost of our power to exclude every breath of air. This wind blows from the north, and comes as if from an heated oven. These winds are generally succeeded by a thunderstorm so severe and awful that it is impossible for one who has not been a witness to such a violet concussion of the elements to form any notion of it. I am not yet enough used to it to be quite unmoved— it is so different from the thunder we have in England—I cannot help being a little cowardly—yet no injury has ever been suffered from it except a few sheep being killed which were laying under a tree that was struck by the lightning.

A thunderstorm has always the effect to bring heavy rain which cools the air very considerably. I have seen very little rain since my arrival—indeed I do not think we have had a week's rain in the whole time, the consequence of which is our garden produces nothing, all is burnt up—indeed the soil must be allowed to be most wretched and totally unfit for growing European productions—though you could scarcely believe this, as the face of the ground at this moment, when it is in its native state, is flourishing even to luxuriance, producing fine shrubs, trees and flowers which by their lively tints afford a most agreeable landscape.

Beauty, I have heard from some of my unlettered country-men, is but skin deep. I am sure the remark holds good in New South Wales, where all the beauty is literally on the surface, but I believe I must allow it has symmetry of form also to recommend it, as the ground in all the parts that have been discovered is charmingly turned and diversified by agreeable valleys and gently rising hills—but still, these beauties are all exterior.

Many gentlemen have penetrated far into the country, but they find little difference in the appearance of the soil. Some rivers have been discovered, to one of which the Governor has given the name of the Hawkesbury; it is a very noble one, and empties itself into the sea at a harbour which Captain Cook in his voyage named Broken Bay. Another river has been discovered, which some call the Nepean, another the

Tench and another the Worgan. It is supposed by some that those three are one, and the same river only has been lighted upon by explorers at different distances from its source. If the British Government think fit to continue the colony, those rivers may be of great utility.

I have not yet seen the famous settlement of Rose Hill, but it is very likely my next letter to you may be dated from there. Captain Nepean has an idea that the Governor will remove the remainder of his detachment and men thither, as soon as the barracks are completed, which are already half-finished. We shall be well pleased to remove anywhere with Captain Nepean—he is truly a good-hearted man—and has, I believe, a great friendship for Mr McArthur.

You will observe I have made no excursion of any consequence—perhaps you will wonder how I should make any in a country like this. I will tell you how—the Harbour of Port Jackson is universally allowed to be the finest in the known world, from the mouth of which to Rose Hill they call 16 miles in a straight direction, and it is so beautifully formed that I can conceive of nothing equal to it, branching out into a number of arms and coves, forming little islands and points of land, so agreeable and romantic that the most fanciful imagination must tire, and I think allow itself to be outdone and yield the palm to reality and simple nature.

In a Harbour so formed, and of such extent, a number of pleasant little water parties might be made to some of these islands or bays, and a number I yet promise myself, but, hitherto, from Mr McArthur's long confinement, and since his recovery, from the heat of the weather, I had been enabled

43

to put but one in execution, and that was to a Bay near the harbour's mouth, about six miles from Sydney. We passed the day in walking among the rocks and upon the sands very agreeably. I looked carefully for some shells for you but could find none better than what you get at Bude or Widemouth. Above this bay, about half a mile distance, is a very high hill which commands an extensive view of the wide ocean, on it is placed a flag-staff which can also be seen at Sydney.

Of my walks round Sydney the longest has not extended beyond three miles, and that distance I have, I believe, only ventured upon twice: once to a farm which Captain Nepean has for his company, to which we sent our tea equipage and drank tea on the turf, and once to a hill situated between this and Botany Bay where I could command a prospect of that famous spot. Nor do I think there is any probability of my seeing much of the inland country until it is cleared, as beyond a certain distance round the Colony there is nothing but native paths, very narrow and very incommodious.

The natives are certainly not a very gallant set of people, who take pleasure in escorting their ladies. No—they suffer them humbly to follow Indian file like.

The natives visit us every day, more or less. Men, women and children, they come with great confidence, without spears or any other offensive weapons—a great many have taken up their abode entirely amongst us, and Bennelong and Colby, with their wives, come in frequently.

Mrs Colby, whose name is Daringa, brought in a new-born female infant of hers for me to see, about six weeks since—it was wrapped up in the soft bark of a tree, a specimen

44

of which I have preserved—it is a kind of mantle not much known in England I fancy. I ordered something for the poor woman to eat, and had her taken proper care of for some little while. When she first presented herself to me she appeared feeble and faint—she has since been regular in her visits—the child thrives remarkably well, and I discover a softness and gentleness of manner in Daringa truly interesting.

We do not in general encourage them to come to our houses, as you may conceive there are some <u>offensive</u> circumstances which makes their company by no means desirable, unless it be those who live wholly with us.

A good deal of their language (if it may be so called) is now understood, but we can learn nothing from them respecting the interior part of the country. It seems they are as much unacquainted with it as ourselves. All their knowledge and pursuits are confined to that of procuring for themselves a bare subsistence. They chiefly abide about the sea coast. The women appear to be under <u>very great</u> subjugation. They are employed in the most laborious part of their work. They fish and also make the lines and hooks and indeed seem very little otherways than slaves to their husbands. They weave their lines from the bark of a certain tree, which we call May from the perfume the flower has which strongly resembles the white thorn that blows in that month in England. Their hooks they grind into form from a shell—they perform this with great dexterity upon any rough stone. Their canoes are made of the bark of some of their gum trees, taken off in a particular form for that purpose. These they paddle about the coves and bays very dexterously. The weapons they use are a spear, a wooden sword, a stone adze or axe, and a fish gig—the latter is wholly used in spearing the fish in the water.

The spears which they aim and discharge with wonderful ingenuity at a <u>great</u> distance are some of them most dangerous weapons, having many barbs in them of sharpened shells, but they are still under such terror of our firearms that a single armed man would drive <u>an hundred</u> natives with their spears, and we take care not to venture walking to any distance <u>unarmed</u>, a soldier or two always attending when we make any excursion. I have never yet met a single native in the woods.

I told you in my last letter I thought their dialect pleasing—some of their names I think much so—I will give you a few native names, and begin with the men: Arrabson, Volahoa, Iminwanga, Boldarry, Werong, Watteval, Erroniba. Female names: Milbah, Bood, Barangiroo, Candeniang, Mooningooru, Woriagn, Crewboar.

Mr Dawes, who has studied their language or jargon a good deal, has endeavoured to learn what their notions are of the Deity. It is not discovered that they worship the sun or any of the heavenly bodies, and yet they say all who die go up to the clouds. Mr Dawes thinks they have a tradition of the flood amongst them.

My spirits are at this time low, very low, tomorrow we lose some valuable members of our small society and some very good friends. In so small a society we sensibly feel the loss of every member, more particularly those that are endeared to us by acts of kindness and friendship. From this circumstance and my former letters you may be led to question my happiness, but this much I can with truth add for myself, that since I have had the powers of reason and reflection I never was more <u>sincerely</u> happy <u>than at this time</u>. It is true I have some wishes unaccomplished that I think would add to my comfort, but when I consider this is not a state of <u>perfection</u> I am <u>abundantly content</u>.

Adieu,
E. McArthur

18 March 1791, to her mother

I was struck by the elaborations of syntax at the start of this letter—so far from a natural voice. I also wondered at the jokey inverted commas around 'Old England'—it suggested (at least to a novelist's ear) someone for whom the thought of England was becoming a little remote, a little unreal.

The premature birth and swift death of her daughter isn't dwelled on, but it's hard to imagine anything much sadder or more lonely.

Sydney, Port Jackson, N.S. Wales, March 18th, 1791

At length I sit down to assure my dearest Mother that I am in perfect health, and to add to the pleasure of this circumstance both Mr McArthur and my little Edward are in the full enjoyment of this blessing, and we only want to complete the measure of it, to hear that you are equally happy and well.

I hope you have received all my former letters regularly. The first was written to you from the Cape of Good Hope, the second from this place giving an account of the voyage—of Mr McArthur's dangerous illness and surprising recovery—and of my being in consequence of fatigue and anxiety thrown into premature labour and delivered of a little girl who lived but for an hour.

In the little friendly meetings that we have in Sydney 'The banks of the Tamar' is a general toast. Many of the officers having friends and connections in Devon and Cornwall, the remembrance is pleasing to all. In my last letter I mentioned there being a select number of officers here who had been very attentive to us, and I am happy to say that we still experience the same attentions from them, and however much I may want female society, Mr McArthur can have no reason to complain. The Governor has been in the habit of sending us some little thing or other every day.

Since the *Supply* returned from Batavia I have received from her commander, Mr Ball, many articles at very moderate prices, besides a number of things which he had the goodness to present to me.

We have not attempted anything in the farming way— our neighbours succeed so badly, that we are not encouraged to follow their example. The Government Farm did not this year in grain return three times the seed that had been sown—this great failure is attributable to a very dry season, but it is a general opinion that this country is not well adapted for corn.

The same woman is with me that had charge of Edward when I visited you from Plymouth. He has become very amusing to me—he prattles a little—but is backward with his tongue as he has always been in every other respect.

I hope Mr Pitt has given Mr McArthur promotion— and that by this time he has a company—in which event our thoughts will in some measure turn again towards 'Old England'. I have yet great hopes of seeing my grandfather once more. Tell him so, and that he need be under no apprehension for my religion.

18 November 1791, to her mother

From mid-1791 ships finally began to arrive in Sydney with supplies and new faces, and the extreme isolation of Elizabeth's first year gradually eased.

Rose Hill was the original name of the area later called Parramatta. It was the only place with soil good enough to grow crops, so farming was started in the area, using convict labour. The governor built a second government house on the hill and the area seemed likely to become more important than Sydney as the centre of the colony. To keep the convicts in line, and to protect the crops and the settlement, a garrison of soldiers was permanently stationed there.

That flash of irony (describing her limited society as 'quite brilliant')—how much it told you about the person who wrote it! This was the Elizabeth Macarthur I liked so much.

In June Mr McArthur and myself were removed to Rose Hill with Captain Nepean's company, at which place we remained until about a fortnight since—Mr McArthur was again ordered to Sydney with the command of a detachment of about 60 men.

Rose Hill, now named Parramatta, save only a small piece of rising ground on which the governor has a house, which still retains the name of Rose Hill, is where every exertion is made to carry on cultivation, and where the principal part of the convicts are placed—but as Sydney has the advantage of the cove, and is nearer the sea, it will have the convenience of first communicating with such vessels as may arrive, and it will be the most desirable place for an officer's family for years.

In other respects Parramatta may have advantages, particularly to such as wish to cultivate the land—but officers have so little encouragement in this respect that few will in future attempt it—as evident impediments are thrown in the way to check their undertaking it.

The Governor has said that we shall not again be moved until Major Grose arrives. I hope that may soon take place, as until then we have no prospect of being settled. Captain and Mrs Paterson were with us after their arrival here but a few days, as they were ordered to Norfolk Island.

Lieut-Governor King, who commands that settlement, brought out his lady with him, she was born in Devonshire, her name was Coombe, and she resided many years at Bideford. Her stay here being very short I saw but little of her, and I had reason to believe her possessed of a great share of good nature and frankness, a pleasant consideration should it be my fortune hereafter to visit Norfolk Island. She expects shortly to be confined.

Captain Parker, commander of the *Gorgon*, brought his wife with him—a very amiable, intelligent woman, we have spent many pleasant days together. One of the agents of Transports has also his wife with him, so that our little circle has been of late quite brilliant—we are constantly making little parties in boats up and down the various inlets of the Harbour, taking refreshments with us and dining out under an awning upon some pleasant point of land or in some of the creeks or coves, in which for twenty miles together, these waters abound. There are so many ladies in the Regiment that I am not likely to feel the want of female society as I at first did.

7 December 1791, to her mother

At the end of 1791 the term of service of the Marines ended and most of them were sent back to England. The governor, Arthur Phillip, was ill and exhausted, and was to follow them as soon as his replacement, Major Francis Grose, arrived.

Phillip had steadily refused to grant land to officers, a policy that had outraged John Macarthur. Phillip also opposed an initiative of the officers—led by Macarthur—to charter a ship to buy goods that could be sold at a profit in the colony. The 'unsettled state' that Elizabeth refers to here is a polite way of saying that Macarthur and others schemed and manipulated, attacked and undermined, to pressure Phillip into yielding to their demands.

What sort of mother was Elizabeth? Frankly, the mentions of her son in the letters so far aren't especially warm or loving. But maybe it was a kind of self-protection not to become too attached. In those pre-vaccine, pre-germ-theory times, most mothers lost several children to infections. On the other hand, perhaps her coolness in the letters was just that gushing about your children wasn't considered good manners.

In A Room Made of Leaves *I gave Elizabeth the benefit of the doubt and made her a doting mother.*

Sydney, Port Jackson, New South Wales, Dec 7th, 1791

Edward grows a strong healthy child and from being a great deal of trouble to me ceases to be almost any at all—he prattles everything—& is quite Papa's darling.

We are at present here rather in an unsettled state, which is not very agreeable in any country, and is particularly unpleasant here. I hope when Major Grose arrives we shall not have this evil to complain of.

A company of Marines is to remain here until the remainder of the New South Wales Corps comes out.

Several of the ships that have arrived with convicts are about to engage in a whale fishery. The spermaceti whale abounds on this coast, and the success of those vessels in this fishery will doubtless be the means of establishing a more frequent communication with England.

21 December 1793, to Bridget Kingdon

Once Governor Phillip left, the new governor, Major Grose, gave Macarthur and the other officers everything they wanted: grants of land, convict servants to work it, and unlimited permission to charter ships to bring goods to sell at a profit.

Macarthur was granted one hundred acres at Parramatta and built Elizabeth Farm. He soon extended his holdings by more grants and by purchase. He was promoted, and was also made paymaster to the regiment, giving him control of a large amount of capital to invest in the trade the officers were now busy with. He also created for himself the position of Superintendent of Public Works, which gave him enormous power. After all, in a penal colony, just about everything was a Public Work.

Elizabeth's second surviving child was born in 1793. From then on, pregnancies followed quickly, one after the other. During these years Elizabeth must have been in an almost constant state of pregnancy or recovery.

Her description of the 'brightening-up' of their prospects is written in a formal, matter-of-fact way that robs it of any drama. In fact, behind those words lay a world of scheming, manipulation and ruthless ambition on her husband's part. In that context, this flat account felt to me like a person handling something unsavoury by its corners.

In the novel I made that response by Elizabeth explicit. Still, she's honest. She might dislike what her husband is doing, but she's prepared to recognise with rueful clarity that she's benefiting from it.

My last letter was by the *Atlantic*, the ship which conveyed Governor Phillip from Port Jackson, when I mentioned that our prospects in this country were considerably brightened up, and that Mr McArthur had a handsome addition to his income by having the payment of a company, and transacting the business of Paymaster to the Regiment. Since that period Major Grose has appointed him to inspect or superintend the public works.

What advantage may accrue from this is at present uncertain, but the Major in his despatches to Government has strongly recommended them to confirm the appointment, and to annex to it such a salary as they may conceive equal to the importance of the trust—the Major has also given us a grant of 100 acres of land on the banks of the river close to the town of Parramatta—it is some of the best ground that has been discovered, and ten men are allowed us for the purpose of clearing and cultivating it.

I have one more gift to speak of—it is a very fine cow in calf, of which I am very proud, and for this also we are indebted to Major Grose, and to a family in this country in its present situation it is a gift beyond any value that can be placed upon it.

As Mr McArthur's concerns demand that the greater part of his time should be passed at Parramatta, I think it very probable that in the course of the ensuing winter we may remove our family there.

I have the pleasure to inform you that we enjoy our health uninterruptedly. Edward has grown, and improves even beyond our sanguine expectations, and little Elizabeth is able to walk by one hand, though not 10 months old.

We are in expectation of Captain and Mrs Paterson from Norfolk Island.

EM

22 August 1794, to her mother

When this letter was written Elizabeth had three young children: Edward (five), Elizabeth (nearly two) and John (three months old). This may be at least part of the reason why she copied much of this letter from one of her husband's. But it suggests that husband and wife routinely read each other's letters—something that would make her even more inclined to conceal what she really felt.

Parramatta, New South Wales, 22nd August, 1794

On the 7th of May last I was happily brought to bed of a very fine boy, to whom I have given his Father's name John. He, with the other two, Edward and Elizabeth, are in perfect health, and promise fairly to become everything we could desire.

In November last myself and family all removed to Parramatta, where Mr McArthur had been the greater part of his time since the departure of Governor Phillip, on account of the employment he holds under Government. I write to you now from our own house, a very excellent brick building, 68 feet in length and 18 feet in width, independent of kitchen and servants' apartments. I thank God we enjoy all the comfort we could desire—but to give you a clearer idea of our situation I shall make free to transcribe a paragraph out of the letter of Mr McArthur's addressed to his brother, which is now before me.

'The changes that we have undergone since the departure of Governor Phillip are so great and extraordinary that to recite them all might create some suspicion of their truth. From a state of desponding poverty and threatened famine that this settlement should be raised to its present aspect in so short a time is scarcely credible. As to myself, I have a farm containing nearly 250 acres, of which upwards of 100 are under cultivation, and the greater part of the remainder is cleared of the timber which grows upon it. Of this year's produce I have sold 400 pounds' worth, and I have now remaining in my granaries upwards of 1,800 bushels of corn. I have at this moment twenty acres of fine wheat growing, and eighty acres prepared for Indian corn and potatoes, with which it will be planted in less than a month.

This farm being near the barracks, I can without difficulty attend to the duties of my profession.'

EM

1 September 1798, to Bridget Kingdon

Eight years after the Macarthurs had come to New South Wales, with little money and no certainty of making any, they were among the richest people in the colony. John Macarthur had been astute, foresighted and determined in his plans to make the best of his time in New South Wales. He'd been promoted to captain, had a good income and access to the regiment's funds, and owned hundreds of acres of prime farming land.

The governor who'd now taken over from Major Grose, Captain John Hunter, wanted to limit the power of the officers, as Phillip had. That put him on a collision course with Macarthur.

What a mistress of the bland half-truth Elizabeth is! What she describes as her husband 'declining further interference in the concerns of the government' was in fact a savage falling-out between her husband and the governor. Macarthur's attacks were relentless, ingenious and merciless. They worked—Hunter was recalled.

Moments like this in the letters gave me scope to develop the character of the fictional Elizabeth Macarthur. She saw everything, but recorded almost nothing of her private thoughts. I felt (rightly or wrongly) that I could almost see the tongue planted firmly in her cheek.

Elizabeth had given birth to the Macarthurs' fourth surviving child, Mary, in 1795. In 1797 a fifth, James, was born but died in his first year. A sixth, another James, was born in 1798, and two years later a seventh, William. Their last child, Emmeline, was born in 1808.

In 1796 the Macarthurs' first child, Edward, had been sent to

England to go to school. He was about seven years old. Elizabeth didn't see him again until he was seventeen.

Elizabeth comments blithely that Edward quitted her almost without a tear. But as a mother she'd know that a child of seven wouldn't understand what was happening as he went on board. There'd have been plenty of tears later.

English mothers of a certain class all had to accept separation from their young sons to go to school. They mightn't have recorded their grief at that separation. That doesn't mean they didn't feel it.

The 'sweet boy' James died in 1797. Behind the few words about this 'misfortune' must have been an ocean of sadness.

The last couple of paragraphs of this letter—a strange, unnecessarily complicated tangle of words—struck me as a fascinating invitation to read behind the surface: 'Judge then, my friend, if I ought not to consider myself a happy woman.' How and why has a negative crept in there, when the stated intent of the sentence is to be positive? Elizabeth Macarthur was many things, and one of those things was a subtle and skilled writer. In passages like this I recognised the way syntax, word choice, even punctuation, can let a sentence say one thing, while signalling behind its back to something else altogether: whether deliberately, or just through the unconscious bubbling-up of unacknowledged feelings.

The description of her husband here is pretty much the only time Elizabeth talks in her letters about what kind of person he was. 'Proud', 'haughty', 'instructive'…not exactly anyone's ideal companion. The praise—'beloved', 'universally respected'— sounds to my ears (knowing something of John Macarthur's recorded behaviour to his fellow men) excessive almost to the point of parody. Beloved and universally respected weren't qualities that *most people in Sydney in 1798 would have thought to apply to John Macarthur.*

Many of John Macarthur's letters have survived, so a modern reader can get a feel for the man. He comes across as a complicated and unpredictable person: forceful, witty, clever, impulsive, delighting in ruthless manipulation and powerplays, sometimes full of endearments, at other times cold and reproving: a dominant, contradictory, self-absorbed personality. Life with him wouldn't have been dull, but it couldn't have been easy.

Knowing that Bridget knew her, probably better than anyone else in the world, I like to think that Elizabeth was hoping that her friend would recognise the doubleness of her words.

On the other hand, perhaps John Macarthur was a more agreeable man in private than his letters suggest. After all, an incomplete collection of anyone's correspondence only shows part of who they are. Perhaps Elizabeth really was happy with him, as she so strenuously asserts here.

Parramatta, 1st Sept 1798

Once again, my much loved friend, it is permitted me to sit down under a conviction that the letter I am about to write will be received by you with pleasure. By the capture of a ship off the coast of Brazil we were left without any direct intelligence from Europe for twelve months—we firmly believed that revolution or some national calamity had befallen Great Britain, and we should be left altogether to ourselves, until things at home had resumed some degree of order, and the tempest a little subsided. These fears, however, have by a late arrival proved without foundation.

The country possesses numerous advantages to persons holding appointments under Government. It seems the only part of the globe where quiet is to be expected. We enjoy here one of the finest climates in the world—the necessaries of life are abundant and a fruitful soil affords us many luxuries.

Nothing induces me to wish for a change but the difficulty of educating our children, and were it otherwise, it would be unjust towards them to confine them to so narrow a society. My desire is that they should see a little more of the world, and better learn to appreciate this retirement. Such as it is the little creatures all speak of going home to England with rapture. My dear Edward almost quitted me without a tear. They have early imbibed an idea that England is the seat of happiness and delight—that it contains all that can be gratifying to their senses—and that of course they are there to possess all they desire. It would be difficult to undeceive young people bred up in so secluded a situation, if they had not an opportunity given them of convincing themselves—but hereafter I shall much wonder if some of them make not this place the object of their choice.

By the date of this letter you will see that we still reside on our farm at Parramatta, a native name signifying the head of a river, which it is. The town extends one mile in length from the landing-place, and is terminated by the Government House, which is built on an eminence, named Rose Hill. Our farm, which contains from 400 to 500 acres, is bounded on three sides by water. This is particularly convenient. We have at this time about 120 acres in wheat, all in a promising state. Our gardens, with fruit and vegetables, are extensive and produce abundantly.

The greater part of the country is like an English park, and the trees give it the appearance of a wilderness or shrubbery commonly attached to the habitations of people of fortune, filled with a variety of native plants, placed in a wild irregular manner.

The Hawkesbury River is a noble fresh-water river, taking its rise in a precipitous range of mountains, that it has hitherto been impossible to pass—many attempts have been made, although in vain—I spent an entire day on this river, going in a boat to a beautiful spot, named by the late Governor, 'Richmond Hill'—high and overlooking a great extent of country. On one side are those stupendous barriers to which I have alluded, rising as it were immediately above your head—below, the river itself, still and unruffled—out of sight is heard a waterfall whose distant murmurs add awfulness to the scene. I could have spent more time here, but we were not without apprehension of being interrupted by the natives, as about that time they were very troublesome, and had killed many white people on the banks of the river.

Our stock of cattle is large—we have now fifty head, a dozen horses, and about a thousand sheep—you may conclude from this that we kill mutton, but hitherto we have not been so extravagant. Next year, Mr McArthur tells me, we may begin. I have now a very good dairy, and in general make a sufficiency of butter to supply the family, but it is at present so great an object to rear the calves, that we are careful not to rob them of too much milk. We use our horses both for pleasure and profit—they alternatively run in the chaise or cart.

Mr McArthur once superintended the agricultural concerns of the Government, but since the arrival of Governor Hunter he has declined further interference. By the kindness of the commanding officer of the regiment we are permitted to reside here, and there being a good road, as I have before observed, to Sydney, Mr M is enabled to attend to all his duties at headquarters, although at times upon very short notice. Myself, or one or more of the children, occasionally accompany him. As the distance is convenient, our stay is prolonged as business or pleasure require, or we return the same day, but as our family is large we do not choose to be long absent from home together.

Mr McArthur has frequently in his employment 30 or 40 people, whom we pay weekly for their labour. Eight are employed as stock-keepers, in the garden, stables and house—and five more—besides women servants—these we both feed and clothe, or at least, we furnish them with the means of providing clothes for themselves. We have but two men fed at the expense of the Crown, altho' there are persons who contrive to get twenty or more, which the Governor does not or will not notice.

The officers in the colony, with a few others possessed of money or credit in England, unite together and purchase the cargoes of such vessels as repair to this country from various quarters. Two or more are chosen from the number to bargain for the cargo offered for sale, which is then divided amongst them, in proportion to the amount of their subscriptions.

This arrangement prevents monopoly, and the impositions that would be otherwise practised by masters of ships. These details which may seem prolix are necessary to show you the mode in which we are, in our infant condition, compelled to proceed.

I have had the misfortune to lose a sweet boy of eleven months old, who died very suddenly by an illness occasioned by teething. The other three, Elizabeth, John and Mary, are well. I have lately been made very happy by learning the safe arrival of Edward in England.

How is it, my dearest friend, that you are still single? Are you difficult to please? Or has the war left you so few bachelors from amongst whom to choose? But suffer me to offer you a piece of advice: abate a few of your scruples, and marry. I offer in myself an instance that it is not always, with all our wise foreseeings, those marriages which promise most or least happiness, prove in their result such as our friends may predict. Few of mine, I am certain, when I married thought that either of us had taken a prudent step. I was considered indolent and inactive—Mr McArthur too proud and haughty for our humble fortune or expectations—and yet you see how bountifully Providence has dealt with us.

At this time I can truly say no two people on earth can be happier than we are. In Mr McArthur's society I experience the tenderest affections of a husband, who is instructive and cheerful as a companion. He is an indulgent father, beloved as a master, and universally respected for the integrity of his character. Judge then, my friend, if I ought not to consider myself a happy woman.

I have hitherto in all my letters to my friends forborne to mention Mr McArthur's name, lest it might appear in me too ostentatious. Whenever you marry look out for good sense in a husband. You would never be happy with a person inferior to yourself in point of understanding. So much my early recollection of you and of your character bids me say.

EM

15 September 1799, Bridget Kingdon
to Elizabeth Macarthur

In 1799 Bridget Kingdon was in her thirties but still unmarried. At that age she wouldn't have thought she had much chance of marrying, and she had no other choice than to go on living at home, helping her mother take care of her father and five younger brothers. (In fact, three years later she did marry, but died six months after the wedding.)

When Elizabeth's son Edward was sent to England, he spent some time in Bridgerule with the Kingdons (and in Plymouth with his uncle James Macarthur) and was then put in a boarding school.

This is the only letter I've included in this collection that's to Elizabeth Macarthur rather than from her. I've included it because it tells so much. Bridget's cautiously expressed but (I think) unmistakable dislike of John Macarthur is evident in her picture of him as someone to fear, someone inclined to ridicule less-fortunate others such as an 'old maid'—and someone who might make a good husband, but only if his wife bent to his wishes in suiting him.

This is the first mention of Elizabeth's sister—actually her half-sister—Isabella Leach. She was born a few years after Elizabeth's mother had married a second time, to Edmund Leach. Elizabeth was about fifteen when Isabella was born, and was living with the Kingdons at least part of the time. Why Elizabeth became part of the Kingdons' household, rather than going with her mother into the new marriage, isn't recorded. My characterisation in the novel of Elizabeth as all but an orphan, sidelined by her mother and displaced by her half-sister, evolved as I thought about what the sketchy biographical facts might mean in human terms.

Bridget's remark about Elizabeth's mother showing the correspondence she'd received makes it clear that, as was usual at the time, letters were public documents. If anything candid were to be said, it had to be coded.

Bridgerule, Sept 15th 1799

It is impossible for me to express, my dearest friend, the satisfaction I have received from the perusal of your late letters—a thousand thanks to you for mine. There was but one sentiment in it that I could not approve—and that implies a doubt whether or not I might receive your letters with pleasure, but let me hope, that you could not for a moment be serious on the subject—were we not from childhood brought up together as intimate friends? And whatever attachments may be formed afterwards, it is my opinion they are seldom as lasting or well grounded as those friendships which have continued from early life. Sincerely do I hope that nothing may ever intervene, to lessen a regard, I trust we at present have for each other.

Through you I shall hope for Mr McArthur's friendship, yet I half fear him, for when we are so happy as to see him in your native country, I doubt not that he will laugh at the old maid, it is an odium we must all bear, though I think undeservedly, at least the ridiculers should first point out what these unfortunate females are to do who have not an offer from a person they can approve. But why, my dear friend, do you tax me with being over nice? Let me assure you, you have no reason for it. I honour the marriage state, and had a proper opportunity offered, should not have declined it. What then would you have me do? Not surely to be so eccentric as to reverse the matter, and make an offer (if you would). I have not courage, nor vanity, sufficient to pursue the scheme, unless indeed I had a vast deal of the ready, now so much looked after, indeed so absolutely necessary, but having neither youth, wealth or beauty to recommend me, I shall endeavour to make myself contented with the state I am in—you have my grateful thanks however for your kind advice, though it is not granted me to follow it.

You will I fear think me an egotist—but something it was necessary to say—in answer to that part of your letter—there is not a person in the world to whom I would so soon disclose any sentiments of my heart as yourself—at present I have not a secret lurking there—what has been would afford you no pleasure, and occasion me some regret. Excuse me therefore from writing on a subject that I never allow myself to think on. I look forward to the pleasure of seeing you in England— and then any question you may wish to ask shall be answered with the utmost candour—for there is not a thing respecting myself that I would wish to be a secret to you.

And now my dear Mrs M let me congratulate you on your happier fate, it ever was my opinion that Mr M would make an excellent husband, if he met with a woman whose disposition and accomplishments suited him. In that respect how fortunate, and how fortunate for you, that you met with a man possessed of good sense and sensibility. God grant that your present happiness may be continued to you.

I saw your little Edward after his arrival in England—he is a charming boy—he was allowed to spend but a week with us, and the dear little fellow was so loth to depart, that though we wished for his longer stay we were obliged to join in persuading him to go. He, though so young, would walk with my father the whole morning, in pursuit of a hare, and come in covered with dirt—yet ask if he could not go again tomorrow. He wished to call my father Grandpapa—and said that it was very hard that he could not stay longer—from this Papa and Mama promised he could hope that he will be permitted to spend his Christmas holiday with us. We have desired that Mr Bond who goes to Plymouth this week will solicit leave of Mr McArthur.

Your mother came here last evening to show us the letters she has received from you—and told me that if I meant to write by the ship now going out I must send the letter tomorrow. I was unwilling to let such an opportunity slip—yet have not had a moment's leisure since I received the intelligence, having company in the house. I am obliged to write often at night—you must therefore excuse the unintelligible scrawl I send you—flattering myself that you would rather receive this than none.

You request of me a particular account of your sister—very little have I had an opportunity of seeing or conversing with her—why I know not—but I have an idea that she is rather shy of me—this I know, that she is fonder of my little sister. My brother takes the liberty of advising her as often as she sees him, and that is not always so pleasant to young minds—particularly if they should have an idea that the adviser ought not to interfere with them. Perhaps I also may have been too free of my advice. She sometimes comes here—and from the accounts I hear, she is blessed with a good disposition—and I doubt not but from your and Mr McArthur's kindness to her, she will answer all your expectations. She means to write by the same conveyance whereby I hope this letter will reach you, and I doubt not but she will give a satisfactory account of herself.

When I write to you next I hope to have more time—I am unused to write much by candle. I must bid you adieu with the best wishes of this family. Mind Mr McArthur and yourself fail not to write me by any opportunity. To hear of your welfare is to me the greatest gratification. And now with best respects to Mr McArthur and love to your little ones—tho' unknown—

Believe me my dear friend,
yours sincerely,
B Kingdon.

21 September 1801, to John Piper

John Macarthur was at the heart of many of the tumults and disagreements in the small society of New South Wales, and in 1801 he was at the centre of a bitter dispute between the New South Wales Corps and the governor. His protégé, Captain John Piper, was also embroiled in this dispute.

The climax of the affair was that Macarthur and his commanding officer, Colonel Paterson, fought a duel, and Macarthur shot Paterson through the shoulder. Macarthur was to be sent to England to face an inquiry. Having been Macarthur's second in the duel, Piper also had to appear before a court, but in New South Wales rather than London. Elizabeth Macarthur wrote this note to him a few days after his arrest.

Lieutenant Nicholas Bayly supported John Macarthur in the dispute with the governor.

I've included this and other notes to John Piper partly to show Elizabeth's good sense and cool head, in doing her best to defuse the situation. Her notes to Piper are also interesting because they have quite a different tone and style from her letters home—the prose is clear, full of feeling, authentic and unforced. My guess is that she knew these quick scribbles, unlike her letters home, would probably only be read by their recipient, rather than passed around in the parlour as public documents. She could feel fairly safe in expressing herself with some degree of frankness, and in a forthright way that was probably more like her speech than the elaborations of her formal letters.

Monday Morning

My dear sir,

You may believe me that I am exceedingly concerned to hear of your again being put in arrest—and am equally at a loss to imagine what charge can possibly be preferred against you—may I beg the favour of you to give me some information—I much wish to see Mr Bayly that I might learn every particular. Would to God that I could give you any advice that might be serviceable. Let me beg of you to keep up your spirits and be circumspect & cool in what you do—remember the old adage that when things are at their worst they oft-times mend.

Assure yourself of my best wishes and believe me to be, your sincere friend,
E. McArthur

Pray let me hear from you in the course of the day. I have some <u>particular reasons</u> why I wish to see Mr Bayly.

3 November 1801, to John Piper

Elizabeth wrote this to Piper on the eve of his court martial, at which he was acquitted. He must have followed her excellent advice.

Around the time this note was written, John Macarthur—en route to England to face trial—was also writing to Piper about the various men he saw as his enemies, in a way perfectly calculated to 'add fuel to the fire': 'Let me charge you not to think of laying a hand upon Mackellar. He is my game, and he who interrupts me in the chase will be regardless of the Laws of Friendship...I am now so deeply in, that the game begins to be amusing...Keep up your spirit and show the enemy a good front, for confidence in oneself is the most likely thing that I know to produce dismay in the wretched, unprincipled, pusillanimous wretches we have to contend against. I hope Scarecrow will be sent home—if he be, and I meet with him, either in a war of words or weapons, the Lord have mercy on him, for none will he obtain from me.'

My dear Sir

Believe me that I have great pleasure in congratulating you on the favourable appearance that your trial will terminate according to the very best wishes of your friends. One thing however I cannot, I think, <u>too much insist upon,</u> & that is you will carefully avoid all offensive matter in your defence. It is reckless, my good friend, to add fuel to the fire that has been blazing <u>too long</u> already & to enter into a dry recital of facts in order to convince the minds of your judges is labour thrown away. Your only appeal in my opinion ought to be immediately addressed to their passions—you cannot fail of interesting their feelings on your behalf. Do if possible forward a copy of what you intend to say in the course of tomorrow. Accept of my sincere & best wishes that all may end well.

Your sincere friend
E McArthur
Tuesday afternoon

15 April 1804, to John Piper

John Macarthur left Sydney for London in November 1801. He took with him his children Elizabeth and John—like Edward, they were to go to boarding school in England. Elizabeth was about eight years old, John about seven. The only children left at home were Mary, six; the second James, now three; and one-year-old William.

The main story of A Room Made of Leaves *ends here, with Elizabeth watching the boat sail away. There were a few reasons for doing that. One was that the story had reached a natural pause.*

The more important reason had to do with the theme at the heart of the novel: the necessity of questioning the past, in order to better understand the present.

The early letter of 7 March 1791 describing Daringa's visit has a warmly interested, friendly tone, but later letters are much harsher towards the Indigenous people, especially after several of the Macarthurs' workers were speared to death. That subject—conflict over land—was something I'd already written about in The Secret River. *In this book I wanted to look at another aspect of that conflict: not the conflict itself, but the self-serving stories that the colonists told about it.*

An event that took place a few years before Macarthur left for England—the so-called Battle of Parramatta—gave me a way to dramatise that theme, and bring together the ideas I wanted to embed in the novel. Once that was done, I felt it was best to end it there—though with an epilogue that sketched the later years.

The account of the 'Battle of Parramatta' that Elizabeth would have heard (though she doesn't refer to it in her letters) is still being told. It's one of those places where the past meets the present, and where taking the colonists' stories at face value— believing them too quickly—might be a mistake.

At the time Elizabeth wrote this letter she'd been running the family concerns—great spreads of land, enormous flocks of sheep, and many workers who had to be fed, housed and managed—for nearly three years.

John Piper was now on Norfolk Island.

John Macarthur was still absent. His drawn-out trial had come to nothing, but he'd used the years in London to persuade influential people that there was money to be made from growing fine wool in Australia and that he was the man to do it. When this letter was written his London affairs were wrapped up and he was on his way to Australia, but Elizabeth didn't know when he might arrive and the problems of running the Macarthur enterprises were weighing heavily on her.

The 'serious alarms from the Irishmen' was an uprising of the convicts who tended the government crops. It was quickly and brutally suppressed.

Dear sir,

I have put off writing to you until almost the last moment, in hopes that I should be able to communicate to you some pleasing tidings from England—still am I disappointed, week after week passes on and leaves me a prey to the most anxious and cruel uncertainty. The management of our concerns gets burthensome to me in the extreme and I am perpetually annoyed by some vexation or other.

I was very glad to learn by your letter that your passage over was favourable—I <u>much fear</u> your abode at Norfolk Island will not be so agreeable & satisfactory as I once thought it might have been. Of the disagreeable differences that have arisen, various reports are here circulated, & each party is blamed, just as much as they happen to be liked or disliked by the persons who pass their opinion. These unhappy quarrels are the cause of much inconvenience to those who have no immediate concern in them.

My bargain with Kemp has been attended with much vexation and I have every reason to suppose that the most unfair advantage has been taken of me, without me having the means of redress. Had I known the man before, I should have taken due precautions.

I find myself getting into a detail of complaints, with which, I really beg your pardon for troubling you.

The late serious alarms from the Irishmen you will hear of, from many quarters—we had a fortunate escape. On the Friday that they rose I drank tea with Mary and James at Mr Marsden's not knowing that anything was apprehended. About 5 o'clock when we were sitting at supper our servant burst into the parlour pale and in violent agitation. 'Sir,' says he, looking wildly at Mr Marsden, 'come with me, and you too, madam,' looking at me. Then half shutting the door he told us that the croppies had risen, that they were at my Seven Hills farm and that a number were approaching Parramatta. Mrs Marsden, myself and the children repaired to the barracks. We then learnt that Castle Hill was in flames. The fire was discernible from Parramatta. It was recommended that as many ladies as chose should go to Sydney, as constant intelligence was brought into the barracks of the near approach of the Irishmen who were expected every minute to enter the town—the number reported to be 300. Mrs Williamson, Mrs Abbott, Mrs Marsden, myself and <u>all</u> our children took leave of our few friends and about eleven at night departed for Sydney.

The Irishmen at that moment were at the Park gate making hideous shouts and waiting, as was afterwards found out, only for the signal of two fires in the town to make their descent and destroy or take it. One of those fires was to have been my house or some part of the premises. This, as was afterwards confessed, was artfully contrived to catch the attention of the soldiery. The rebels saw that consideration of my lonely situation and the attachment the soldiers had to my family would induce them, upon seeing the fire, to repair instantly to my relief and the barracks would then be easily secured to themselves. The other fire was to be a thatched hut in the town. Thank God all was happily prevented.

In Parramatta my house was to have been the first attacked—no very flattering distinction, you will say.

We arrived in Sydney about 3 o'clock in the morning. The town was all in arms. The marines from the *Calcutta* disembarked and a great number of the sailors armed. The *Calcutta* was beautifully lighted up. Most of the officers were on shore and kindly received us, poor fugitives, at the wharf. We had determined to take up our abode at Mr Marsden's house, and to this house we and our little <u>frightened sleepy</u> tribe were escorted and civilities were poured in upon us from every quarter.

I began this letter in a very gloomy bad temper but think I have written myself into a better humour and more reasonable way of thinking. God grant me health and patience, for indeed my good friend, I have need of <u>both</u> to keep my mind in tolerable frame. Hourly I am expecting an arrival from England and fain would I indulge the hope of seeing Captain McArthur in the first ship.

After 7 June 1805, to John Piper

John Macarthur returned to New South Wales on 7 June 1805. He brought his daughter Elizabeth back with him, and a governess for her, Miss Lucas. Out of respect for her age, she was later called Mrs Lucas.

John (now eleven years old) and Edward (sixteen) remained in England.

Elizabeth now had most of her brood around her—Elizabeth (twelve), Mary (ten), James (seven) and William (five).

A thread running through Elizabeth's letters is her knowledgeable interest in, and evident love of, horses. Kitty and Jock were two of John Piper's horses, left in the care of friends while he was on Norfolk Island.

While in England, John Macarthur had persuaded Lord Camden to grant him the unheard-of gift of ten thousand acres: five thousand of them immediately, the rest to be given later. And it wasn't just any land—it was the Cowpastures, far and away the best land yet discovered in the colony, and which the first governor had decreed should never be granted away from the Crown.

Macarthur returned full of plans to trade in the fine wool that these acres would produce. During his years in England, he'd established commercial links with the wool trade in London, and when he returned to Sydney he brought with him two men to 'instruct persons in the art of sorting wool'.

With him also came his brother's son Hannibal Macarthur, and Walter Davidson. Davidson was the nephew of the Royal Physician, Sir Walter Farquhar. Farquhar had introduced Macarthur to Lord Camden, and from that introduction had come the eye-wateringly generous land grant to Macarthur.

When she wrote this letter, Elizabeth had been for four years in an extraordinarily unusual and privileged position for a woman: not despised old maid, not obedient wife and not pitiable widow, but an independent woman, running her life to suit herself. Now her husband—overbearing and manipulative, owner and master of the Macarthur empire—had just returned. So when I came to the sentence 'you may imagine how great was my joy on the arrival of McArthur...' I could only read it ironically.

But who knows what she really felt?

Dear Sir, accept of a few hasty lines from me just to acknowledge the receipt of your last—for altho' I have <u>much to tell</u> and <u>many things</u> I could wish to relate, yet I cannot make up my mind to write a long letter.

I now have pleasure in communicating to you all that relates to us and of all the important changes that have taken place. You may imagine how great was my joy on the arrival of McArthur and Elizabeth. I had only about half an hour's notice of their approach & knew not that the colours were up, until the ship's arrival was announced to me.

Mr M arrived in but indifferent health—Elizabeth is much improved in her manners & appearance, & is as good humoured & lively as ever—I enclose a letter from her—Edward we expect to come out in a few months—I hear the most favourable accounts of both him & John. So sudden an increase to my family has made me sob about a little.

A lady of the name Miss Lucas came out with

Elizabeth—a very respectable person, though a little ancient <u>for a Miss</u>. We have also two young gentlemen in the family—a nephew of Mr McArthur's, a fine youth of 29, & a Mr Davidson, a nephew of Sir Walter Farquar's—also a Mr Wood, a professional gentleman in the wool business, who at present resides with the family—you may suppose that I am much exercised how to dispose of them all. We often wish you were among us. We are quite a little circle in our own society. I have little occasion to seek for amusement out of it.

Kitty is quite well. Mrs Marsden will tell you that Jock is at the Creek and indeed all our horses excepting the stable horses are at the Creek also. Young Smiler has produced a second foal, a very promising one. Your Kitty has taken an unaccountable liking to feed on that part of our estate called Tipperary, just opposite Arndell's Farm.

Accept of my kindest and best wishes for your health and prosperity & believe me to be your sincere & affectionate friend,

E. McArthur.

29 January 1807, to Bridget Kingdon

Not long before this letter was written, Edward Macarthur arrived back in Sydney after more than a decade in England. He was seventeen.

In 1806 a new governor, Captain William Bligh, had arrived in the colony. Bligh and John Macarthur were immediately at odds with each other: like earlier governors, Bligh was determined to limit the power of the New South Wales Corps, especially in its trade in rum. Macarthur was no longer a member of the Corps, but he still benefited from its power through his links with its officers. He and Bligh were on a collision course from the first day, not helped by the inflammatory personalities of both men.

It seems clear from this letter that—as was quite usual at the time—Elizabeth needed permission, and her husband's promises, to make important decisions. After her four years of autonomy, it's hard to imagine that didn't grate.

Parramatta, 29th January 1807

You will be pleased to learn that our dear Edward arrived here in health and safety but apparently not so strong in constitution as I could have wished.

Governor King and his family go to England by this ship the *Buffalo* and we part very good friends, we have since Mr McArthur's return to the colony lived on terms of great civility, and we part with regret.

Our harvest is now getting in—wheat is sold from 25/- to

85

30/- the bushel. No sort of animal food is to be procured under 2/- the lb, 5/- for a fowl, 10/- to 15/- for a goose.

Our system of government is very wretched—much as Mr McArthur strove when in England to direct the attention of the administration towards this colony, they seem to think little about us, having no doubt affairs of more consequence on their hands. The expenses however that are incurred may rouse them again into a little exertion for our good.

I have great hopes of being again permitted to see 'Old England'. Mr McArthur has promised I shall go in a year or two, whether he can or cannot accompany me. If the latter it will be a great diminution of the pleasure, but so it is—some drawbacks always attend our most promised enjoyments.

This country has undergone so many changes for the worse that with difficulty I recognise it to be the place it was some six or seven years since.

Our new Governor Bligh is a Cornishman by birth, and his daughter Mrs Putland, who accompanied him is a very accomplished person. The Governor has already shown the inhabitants of Sydney that he is violent, rash, tyrannical. No very pleasant prospect at the beginning of his reign.

Food, clothing and every necessary of life bear a price truly astonishing. All these melancholy changes may be considered the effect of tyranny and an improper administration of the law. Liberty has retired from amongst us into the pathless wilds, amongst the poor native inhabitants, who certainly maintain their independence, and have hitherto resisted any infringement on their rights. Nor will they become servants for any continuance, whatever temptation may be offered them.

5 February 1808, to Captain John Piper

Ten days before Elizabeth wrote this letter, conflict between the New South Wales Corps and Macarthur, on the one hand, and Governor Bligh, on the other, reached a climax when Bligh had Macarthur arrested. The officers of the Corps—under the leadership of Major George Johnston but incited by John Macarthur—then arrested and imprisoned Governor Bligh. Macarthur was quickly released.

In all her letters, whenever she refers to her husband's many conflicts with others, Elizabeth loyally takes her husband's side. How much she knew of the full picture, and what she really thought about it, we can only guess.

Dear Sir,

I came down from Parramatta a week since with our poor Elizabeth who has been exceedingly ill, ever since the month of May last, in order to try what change of air might do for her, little dreaming of a revolution, although the excessive despotism of the ruling power called aloud for reform, but it never entered my head to imagine that the inhabitants would so effectually rouse themselves from the despairing lethargy they had fallen into, as to adopt so spirited a measure.

Mr McArthur I fear will not be able to write to you. The criminal court is now sitting and he before it as a prisoner, but I trust it will be for <u>no serious offences</u>. Although he has been most rigorously treated, you are to understand this work began before the change of affairs—and for aught I know was one means of accelerating it—so the very semblance of <u>Law</u> <u>& Justice</u> were from the beginning set aside.

The Governor is to be sent to England as soon as possible, under charge of an officer. I know of no one so fit for so gallant an action as yourself—what a pity that you are not on the spot!!

Believe me to be, my dear sir, very sincerely your friend,
E. McArthur

30 May 1809, to Garnham Blaxcell

For a time after the coup John Macarthur was virtual emperor of New South Wales, but a year later he was obliged to go to England again to take part in an inquiry into his part in Bligh's arrest. He took with him their two youngest sons, James (eleven years old) and William (nine). The only children at home were Elizabeth (sixteen), Mary (fourteen) and the baby Emmeline; Edward had returned to England.

Once again Elizabeth was running the family enterprise— thanks to Lord Camden's colossal grant of land, this was the biggest and wealthiest in New South Wales—on her own.

Her reference to the Hawkesbury is about the floods that had just taken place there, destroying a large part of New South Wales's grain crop.

Garnham Blaxcell was a successful merchant and trader in Sydney, a favoured partner in various enterprises of John Macarthur. I've included this note because it shows how skilfully Elizabeth struck exactly the right tone for the job: businesslike, but with enough acknowledgment of her husband to be politic, enough acknowledging of Blaxcell's importance to flatter him, and just enough feminine helplessness to maintain the fiction of herself as the conventional wife.

Dear Sir, I enclose the memorandums relative to the two grants, which I would have sent yesterday, but was prevented, for not very readily knowing where to put my hand on the papers.

I will not say that I have not thought of the little business we have to transact, because I am most anxious that every thing pointed out to me by Mr McArthur should be executed as soon as possible and every day I feel such an accumulated weight of responsibility and care, that whatever tends to lighten any part of it, is desirable.

My knowledge of the various claims upon your time, and the difficulty & delay which usually occur in fitting out ships for sea had made me unwilling to arrest your attention for a subject which I felt assured you would consider, as soon as you were more at leisure.

I am concerned to hear the reports from the Hawkesbury. I have no grain in hand & am very fearful of much difficulty in procuring the quantity I want.

Believe me, etc., EM

13 November 1811, to John Piper

When Elizabeth wrote this letter John Piper was on his way to England on leave, although he came back to New South Wales a few years later. The 'dear John' she refers to here is her son, not her husband. Their daughter Elizabeth seems to have had some recurring or chronic disorder which was the source of great concern to both her parents.

In London the inquiry into the coup against Governor Bligh dragged on. News about it—including the outcome of the trial against George Johnston, the officer who had done Macarthur's bidding—was slow to reach New South Wales, and the implications for Macarthur remained unclear. By this time Elizabeth's husband had been away for around two years. If, as I suspect, his absence was by way of reprieve, the uncertainty would indeed have been cruelly 'tantalising and disrupting'.

A new governor, Lachlan Macquarie, had replaced Commodore Bligh.

Elizabeth might have said now and then that she wanted to return to 'Old England', but throughout her letters from now on there are spontaneous and heartfelt expressions of love for the land she'd come to know.

Sydney, Nov 13th 1811

My dear Sir,

By the *Concord*, which is to sail in the morning, I avail myself of the opportunity of writing a few lines to you, thinking it probable that it may meet you at St Helena, where a letter with intelligence from the friends you have left here will be, I flatter myself, the more pleasing as it will be unexpected.

You will hardly believe that I continue at Sydney, where Elizabeth has remained ever since your departure, and myself also, with the exception of a few days, I have passed in two visits to Parramatta. My abode here is for medical attendance to Elizabeth in order that she may be relieved from that affliction which has weakened her very much. I think she is getting better. Mary and Miss Lucas are at Parramatta & quite well. I returned from thence yesterday. You cannot fancy how reluctantly I came away, or how beautiful and verdant the scenery is just now about our farm—we have had some refreshing rain since you left us, which has given a new face to the country.

You may believe me when I say, that we experience a great blank in the loss of your society. For the first week there was nothing but lamentation—Captain Piper—such a loss! Then it was God bless him. Poor Captain Glenholme really looked like the most disconsolate being you can well imagine—I am told that Lt McCreery has taken up his abode with him, & I believe he is a little comforted.

I know that the friendly sentiments you feel for me & my family will lead you to rejoice when I tell you that the good people at Sydney have been uncommonly attentive & kind.

We have received a few letters and some papers containing an account of Colonel Johnston's trial, the sentence not known—how very tantalising & disrupting to me who am so much interested in the event. The commodore is surely exposed however the affairs terminate.

You will probably know before this reaches your hand, I received a letter from my dear John—he was in London—and only two lines from his dear father, who was so much engaged in attending the court martial that his time was exclusively devoted to that object. I will not dwell on this subject, which so much bewilders and disturbs me.

God send you all health & a pleasant voyage. Elizabeth writes with me in every friendly wish towards you, & the boys their remembrance to you. You cannot think how pleased we were & how much it gratified us to hear the Three Cheers you gave us outside the heads of Port Jackson.

I know of nothing more to say, but to repeat my wish that every good may attend you—and that you believe me to be, my dear sir,

Your sincere and obliged E M.

I know not what to think whether Mr McArthur will, or will not, have left England. How cruel is this perpetual state of uncertainty. Excuse this scrawl—Mr Campbell will fill up the directions to you, & put the letter on board the *Concord*.

March 1816, to Eliza Kingdon

In their young days in Bridgerule, Elizabeth and John Macarthur had stood as godparents to Bridget Kingdon's youngest sister, Elizabeth (usually called Eliza). Bridget had died in 1802, but Eliza was now twenty-eight, and she and her godmother began to correspond.

After staying in Australia for a few years, Edward was back in England, along with his father and all his brothers.

Governor Macquarie and his wife had become friendly with Elizabeth. Macquarie made a point of including ex-convicts as part of respectable society, even inviting them to Government House. Not all settlers approved of this—John Macarthur was outraged.

The tone of the reference to 'the natives' in this letter is much harsher than the earlier one in which she describes a visit from Daringa. Whereas then Elizabeth thought of herself as a temporary visitor to a place offering new and exotic experiences, by 1816 she was well and truly settled in the country, and better off financially from it than she could ever have predicted. The only problem was that the land from which her family was so mightily profiting had belonged for many thousands of years to the Indigenous people. They continued to battle their dispossession by the colonists in any way they could.

If you think of yourself as a visitor, planning only to stay a few years, you can take a generous tone towards the people whose homeland it is. But once you're competing with them for control of that land, and they're fighting back, your attitude is likely to harden.

From the records that exist, it's hard to gauge exactly how Elizabeth Macarthur felt about the Indigenous people she displaced. My guess is that her feelings changed over time, as she became a settler rather than a visitor, and that her initial impulse towards sympathy was later complicated and obscured by self-interest.

In writing about the Indigenous people in the novel, I was prepared to go beyond what can be definitely established about her views. I gave Elizabeth, in her old age, an insight she never expresses in her letters: that she's living on stolen land. I did this because, although A Room Made of Leaves *is set in the past, its real subject is the present—the situation that the past created.*

Present-day non-Indigenous Australians are in the situation Elizabeth articulates at the end of the novel: 'I can see no way to put right all the wrongs done, no more than I could all those years ago when I picked up the stick belonging to a Burramatagal woman and heard what it was saying. The difference is that now I do not turn away. I am prepared to look in the eye what we have done. That repairs no part of the sorrow of it, I know. But it is the first thing, the first hard truth, without which no repair can ever be hoped for.'

Parramatta, March, 1816

My dear Eliza,

I know not what I can say of our mode of life, that will give you a correct idea of it. It is a mixture of town and country life, and yet in many respects unlike anything you can have experienced. Our climate is delightful, and we have in high perfection and in great abundance the fruits of warm and cold climates, even to profusion, so much that our pigs are fed on peaches, apricots and melons in the season. We grow wheat, barley, oats, we make hay, at least I do, but the practice is not general. We feed hogs, we have cattle, keep a dairy, fatten beef and mutton and export fine wool. A variety of avocations arising from these pursuits keeps the mind pretty busily employed.

Our society as the country has increased in population has become more extended. On particular days, such as the King's or Queen's birthday there are parties at Government House, numbering occasionally 150 persons. I will not say that these assemblies have been very select. However there is a sufficiency of pleasant, agreeable persons to visit and be visited by, to satisfy one who is not ambitious to have a very numerous visiting acquaintance.

Governor Macquarie is one of the most pleasing men, but then he is the Governor, and it is not possible to forget that he is so. Mrs Macquarie is very amiable, very benevolent, in short a very good woman. They have a lovely boy, now ten years old.

Attempts have been made to civilise the natives of this country, but they are complete savages, and are as lawless and troublesome as when the Colony was first established. Our out-settlements are constantly subjected to their depredations.

Edward always recollects you with kindness. I think whenever he has leave of absence and can command a little spare cash he will pay a visit to the neighbourhood of Bridgerule. You may fancy how much I wish to see those dear children, from whom I have been so long separated. Edward last quitted me about seven years since. John left this country at the early age of seven years and a half, and has not since returned. He is now 22. James and William went home with their father, and when I last heard of them were with him in Switzerland. John is my faithful and most affectionate correspondent. My daughters Elizabeth, Mary and Emmeline are still with me, and a single lady about my own age, who shares all my cares.

It is not wealth, nor large possessions that entail happiness but health, industry, and the blessing of God.

I am much oppressed with care on account of our stock establishments at our distant farms, at the Cowpastures, having been disturbed by the incursions of the natives. The savages have burnt and destroyed the shepherds' habitations, and I daily hear of some fresh calamity. Yesterday the Governor was pleased to order a non-commissioned officer and six soldiers out to protect our establishments from further injuries. Two years ago a faithful old servant who had lived with us since we first came to the colony was barbarously murdered by them and a poor defenceless woman also. Three of my people are now reported to be missing, but I trust they will be found unhurt.

My cares are many and anxious and I have so long been deprived of assistance from any male branch of the family that I cannot say I am comfortable or happy.

God bless you my dearest Eliza
Your affectionate friend
Elizabeth McArthur.

11 December 1817, to Eliza Kingdon

*In 1817 John Macarthur returned from his second long absence,
bringing with him his two youngest sons, James (now nineteen)
and William (seventeen). His sons John and Edward remained in
England. The youngest child, Emmeline, was a newborn when
her father had left. She was now nine.*

*A sceptical reader of Elizabeth Macarthur's letters (such as
the author of* A Room Made of Leaves*) might read with interest
that when her husband returned from a nine-year absence, she
couldn't feel the happiness she knew she ought to.*

Parramatta,
11th December 1817

My dear Eliza,
I was favoured with your letter by the *Lord Eldon* transport,
the very same vessel which restored to me your godfather and
my Husband, together with our two youngest sons, after a
cruel separation of nine years. I am yet scarcely sensible of
the extent of my happiness, and indeed I can hardly persuade
myself that so many of the dear members of our family are
united again under the same roof. Mr McArthur is occasionally afflicted with gout, otherwise I perceive little change in
him during this length of time.

James and William from little boys when they left me,
returned fine young men, James six feet high and stout
withall, William more slender but evidently giving promise

of being stout also. They are delighted to return to their native land, and breathe not a regret for the gay scenes of the English metropolis. Nothing they saw in France or Switzerland effaced the strong desire they had to return to their native wild woods in New South Wales. So much for the Love of Country.

I cannot even now repress the ardent desire which I have once more to see the place of my birth. So many and so great have been the obstacles that I have never dared to cherish the hope.

In our *Colonial Gazette* of the 11th and 18th of August there is an account of a tour or expedition by our Surveyor General to the westward of the Blue Mountains—the party was absent nineteen weeks from the settlement at Bathurst, and passed through a great variety of country.

Emmeline is not yet sufficiently composed to write by this opportunity—she is so much engaged in running about, and showing her brothers everything that she can think will amuse them. Pray pardon this confused letter—I have some difficulty in collecting my own scattered thoughts at a moment like the present.

Adieu.

17 May 1818, to Eliza Kingdon

Elizabeth Macarthur's daughter Elizabeth seems to have had a more positive (although patronising) attitude to the Indigenous people than her mother. Both women corresponded with Eliza Kingdon. The younger Elizabeth wrote (in March 1817), offering Eliza her views:

> *They are a singular race utterly ignorant of the arts, living constantly in the open air, and without any other covering than occasionally cloaks of the skin of wild animals, but even these are not universally worn, it is not uncommon to see them without any covering at all. They are nevertheless very intelligent and not obtrusive. They have great vivacity and a peculiar turn for mimicry, acquiring our language, tones and expressions with singular facility. Their carriage is very graceful, and perhaps they possess more native politeness than is found amongst any people. They deem it a great want of good breeding to contradict. In all the European modes of salutation they make themselves perfect. The benevolent exertions of Governor Macquarie have induced some of these people to send their children to a school which has formed for their reception and instruction. The little creatures have been taught to read and write, with a readiness truly astonishing, and in the hands of Providence let us hope they may be instrumental in civilizing their countrymen. Pray pardon the partiality of a native for native subjects.*

Eliza Kingdon seems to have been curious about the life her godparents lived, and the older Elizabeth obliged.

Parramatta, 17th May, 1818

You wish to know how we pass our time? Not very much unlike what you do in the country. James and William assist their father in the management of his farm and stock. By way of amusement, they ride, shoot wild fowl, fish and occasionally associate with the officers of the 48th Regiment which is now here. We have an excellent collection of books—we receive most of the new publications from England. James and William amuse us with an account of their travels in France, and of the manners of the Swiss, amongst whom they resided many months. As we have frequently ships from various parts of India and China, we see many passengers who come here to re-establish their health. This makes a little change in our society.

We have also frequent communication with the South Sea islanders, and inhabitants of New Zealand. The latter are a stout hardy race very different from the natives of New Holland. They avail themselves of the opportunity of visiting this colony, in a vessel belonging to the Missionary Society, which goes to and fro. These savages, for such in truth they are, generally pay us a visit, and amuse us much.

We frequently visit Sydney, a very agreeable distance to ride or drive.

February 1821, to Eliza Kingdon

Elizabeth's stepfather, Edmund Leach, the father of her half-sister, Isabella, had died in 1791 and Elizabeth's mother had married for a third time, to John Bond. Elizabeth must have known Bond before she left Bridgerule—he was one of the witnesses to her mother's marriage to Leach. She didn't seem to think much of him—see the letter of 21 September 1822, below.

Given that the Macarthurs had done so well in New South Wales, it's surprising that Elizabeth is so discouraging in this letter and the following two about 'young men of good family and of small capital' trying their luck there. Perhaps she (or her husband, whose tone—judgmental, dogmatic and rather flowery—can be heard in this part of the letter) was concerned that they might be asked to provide assistance to such a young man. Certainly these letters to Eliza had a tone of being written by a 'we' rather than an 'I'.

Parramatta,
February, 1821

My dear Eliza,
In your last letter from 'Ham Common' you request our opinion of this being an eligible place for young men of good family and of small capital. To this I answer that at present their emigrating to this country would be a most hazardous experiment. Things are too unsettled. The lands in the vicinity of the townships are granted, so that a new settler would have to go back a long distance into the woods—cut

off from society, and compelled to dwell in a bark hut, with convict servants, and surrounded by gum trees, the emu, the kangaroo of the forest. The little capital a new settler might bring with him would melt away in the town like snow before the sun, for Sydney is a most expensive place, and most of the inhabitants are vicious. We are hoping for a reform: when that shall have taken place, and some exports have been established, a fairer prospect will be opened.

Wool is at present our sole export, and that may be said to be in a languishing state—few pursue this branch of industry with vigour, and they being obliged to depasture the waste lands with flocks, under the care of men as shepherds, who are for the most part worthless and careless, is a great drawback upon enterprise. Be assured I have been careful not to let a word escape me, which might tend to mislead you in England. Be assured that when things mend you shall hear from me.

You are so good to say that my letters are acceptable to you, and I am sure I cannot do less than write to thank you a thousand times for your kindness to my dear Mother. A visit from you must cheer her so much. It makes my heart dilate when I think of it. How sad a reflection to me that she should prefer to surround herself with the persons whom you describe, and who must render any assistance to her so much less availing. I will write to her soon, and pray that you will communicate to her such parts of my letter, as you think will be of interest to her.

Believe me etc.
EM.

4 September 1822, to Eliza Kingdon

It's a mark of how significant the Macarthurs were (or certainly felt themselves to be) in the colony that Elizabeth's tone in this letter towards the governor is so patronising.

The issue of ex-convicts being made magistrates—an initiative of Governor Macquarie—was a particular source of outrage to John Macarthur. He felt that the new antipodean society should copy the one back in England, with an aristocracy (of which he would of course be one of the leaders) set above the riffraff. Elizabeth may have agreed with him, but whether she did or not, she wouldn't have gone against him in a letter that he might ask to read.

John Macarthur's nephew Hannibal had settled in New South Wales. He'd married Anna Maria King (a daughter of the former Governor King) in 1812. He now had good properties near the Macarthurs and a growing family.

My dear Eliza,
We have received the sad intelligence of the loss of the ship *Grace*, laden with colonial produce and having besides letters from our friends.

Would we but meet, how interesting to me to listen to all the details of your domestic affairs—whilst I in turn should relate our Australian Wonders—depict our mode of life, our occupations, our wanderings amidst the woods, attentive to the notes of the Bell Bird, and tracing the steps of the kangaroo and emu.

Our two youngest sons make 'Camden' their principal residence. They are excellent young men, with minds highly cultivated. They devote themselves to the management of a very large agricultural establishment with unceasing assiduity. Mr McArthur talks of making Camden the residence of all the family: as yet there is not a suitable house, nor do I know when we shall be enabled to build one. It is what we much want, for our poor Parramatta house is tumbling down—it is quite a ruin.

The Clan McArthur is not likely to be much enlarged by our family—they all seem prudently to think these are not marrying times. Hannibal McArthur, whom you know, has six children—they live near us. We continue to like our present Governor Sir Thomas Brisbane. Lady Brisbane and her sister Miss Macdougall are gentle and amiable—perfectly unaffected in their manners and habits, yet possessing all the acquirements of wellborn and well educated persons.

The public measures of Governor Macquarie have been severely reprobated—particularly for making convict magistrates, and for otherwise bringing forward that description of persons. Even his bounties have been forgotten by many on whom he bestowed them with profusion.

Mr McArthur I am happy to say has had better health than heretofore. He desires to be most kindly remembered to you. How did I wish 'that I had wings like a bird' that I might sit myself down beside you, at the bridge so often passed and repassed in my younger days, and there fondly embrace you.

I have more than once written on the subject of young gentlemen migrating here with small capital. It requires, perhaps, more than ordinary fortitude to go back to settle in the interior of the colony. Several officers of the 48th Regiment reduced in the Peace Establishment are about to become settlers, but the greater part return to England by the ship by which I now write.

I have already said that we are much pleased with Sir Thomas Brisbane and his family—the ladies are fond of and live in great retirement. They mix little in society and give none of those large entertainments which Mrs Macquarie used to do—Lady Brisbane has a good piano on which she occasionally plays and accompanies the instrument with her voice. Miss Macdougall plays the harp, and Mr Rumker—a German gentleman who came to this country with Sir Thomas—the Piano in turn. The Germans are passionately fond of music.

21 September 1822, to Eliza Kingdon

Once again there's a sense of John Macarthur leaning over Elizabeth as she wrote and offering her his opinions, and even turns of phrase that are more extreme and colourful than the kind she generally used.

It's also possible that she'd simply taken on his opinions and tone as her own, at least in public. In a marriage between a woman with no power and a strongly assertive man such things aren't completely unknown, even today.

Commissioner John Thomas Bigge had been sent to New South Wales a few years earlier to report back to the London authorities on the state of the colony. John Macarthur had spared no effort or expense to get him on side, so that Bigge's report would echo the opinions of Macarthur and bring about the changes he wanted to see.

Mr Boughton is John Herring Boughton, an acquaintance of the Kingdons who arrived in September 1822 as a free settler.

It's now apparent who the 'young gentlemen' were: Eliza Kingdon's nephews.

If Elizabeth wrote directly to her mother after the handful of letters of the early years, or if her mother ever wrote back, none of those letters have come to light.

Elizabeth's half-sister, Isabella, had married a man called Thomas Hacker. Both Elizabeth's mother (now getting on in years) and her sister seem to have married badly—certainly Elizabeth thought so—and they laboured under financial and perhaps other difficulties. Eliza became the source of information about them for Elizabeth, and cleared the way for assistance to be given to both women.

Saturday Sept 21st, 1822

Since my last letter, written about a fortnight since, we have had the pleasure to see Mr Boughton who brought us a most welcome letter from you.

Mr McArthur and myself were glad to see your brother Roger's handwriting once again. He will consider the subject of his sons' coming to this colony, but at present they are too young. My husband is decidedly of the opinion that no young man should become a settler in this colony under the age of one or two and twenty. In truth we see no pleasing prospect held out to respectable persons. There are a world of difficulties to be encountered when they arrive at this far distant place. Still we hope for favourable changes.

The report of Mr Commissioner Bigge has not yet been acted on. We flatter ourselves that the report will notice many existing evils which it depends on Government to correct, and to turn their attention to many beneficial changes. The want of exports keeps us like beggars and depending on the expenditure of Great Britain. When Mr Boughton travels into the interior, he will be delighted with its appearance. It is with the country, not with the towns, that strangers are pleased. I hope he may form a correct judgement and neither deceive himself or others.

The accounts from England are so gloomy that I wonder not at the desire to emigrate. If we could persuade ourselves to live altogether as shepherds, and be contented with bread, milk, meat, vegetables and the variety of fruits that are raised in perfection in his climate, it would be all very well. But we must have a number of imported luxuries. Even our servants will have tea, sugar and other things, which many of them have never in their former lives been accustomed to indulge in.

It seems that my mother is well and cheerful for which I am most thankful to the Almighty. I would not she should feel her misalliance (without reproach altho' it be) with the same bitterness of spirit that I do.

Through the generosity of Mr McArthur, my mother has now been given an allowance, which, added to her small dower, should render her circumstances easy. But I have long been aware how she has been surrounded, and my heart has grieved more than I can find words to tell or express. Mr Bond was always an idler. But whom my sister married I could never make out: whether an industrious person or otherwise. I never knew the name of Hacker, excepting one person, who was a brother of Mr Bond's first wife. He as far as I can recollect was a drone also.

Adieu
EM

12 February 1823, to her son John

When Elizabeth wrote this letter and the following one, her husband and sons James and William were in dispute with the governor about land.

In 1803, when ten thousand acres at Cowpastures had been granted to John Macarthur by Lord Camden, many voices (including that of Sir Joseph Banks) had been raised against such an unprecedentedly huge acreage going to one man. The upshot was that Macarthur had been told he could have five thousand acres then and the other five thousand at some point in the future.

When John Macarthur was away in England for the second time, Elizabeth had conversations with then-governor Macquarie and took away from those conversations a belief that the full Cowpastures grant would go ahead.

Now a complicated situation has blown up with the new governor, Sir Thomas Brisbane, about land, and Elizabeth is putting on the record those conversations she'd had with Macquarie. She wants her son John (now a lawyer in London with good contacts in government) to know her side of the story, so he can push back against letters from the governor that will soon arrive in London.

Major Frederick Goulburn was secretary to the governor, and in charge of administering land grants.

John Macarthur's longstanding health problems were now becoming more pronounced. Since the time of the Macarthurs' voyage to New South Wales in 1790 and his illness at the Cape, he'd suffered various bodily ailments—gout, the general joint pains of 'flying gout', and digestive upsets—but now it was becoming more apparent that there were disorders of the mind too. His behaviour alternated between manic energy and deep depression. These days he might be diagnosed with bipolar disorder.

The uncertainty over the land grant has exacerbated Macarthur's always-unstable moods to such an extent that Elizabeth has to go behind his back in this letter to try to find a way to minimise the damage. It's a fine balancing act she's performing, probably not for the first time.

At the same time, the situation with her mother seems to have arrived at some kind of crisis.

Parramatta, Wednesday morning, Feb 12th 1823

Yesterday, my beloved son, we wrote you a hasty letter, & sent it off to go by the *Minerva* this morning. Since it was dispatched a letter has been received from Major Goulburn to which your father wrote a reply this morning. Copies of both letters are here. We are in hopes it will yet be in time for the ship, also your father's remarks to you, thereupon.

What can I add upon this unpleasant subject? One upon which I can only say I had not the least apprehension that any difficulty would have arisen.

Your dear father is now asleep. He did not rest during the night, but I <u>think</u> he will be more composed and tranquil now that an answer is given—unworthy as it is. Why Major Goulburn is inimical to your father, I cannot tell—still less can I account for that extreme vacillation on the part of Sir Thomas Brisbane.

Your father's estate was an object of jealousy to the late government, but I never expected it would have been to the present. The last time I ever saw Governor Macquarie he said to me—'Mrs McArthur, I believed your two sons had <u>taken</u> or <u>chosen</u> their land in Mr Throsby's country. As it is, I am sorry they have it not where D'Arrieta and Douglass are fixed—still, I think hereafter these lands may be purchased on advantageous terms.' He said this to me in a kind and conciliatory manner and I thought he meant to impress upon my mind that Mr Oxley had given him to understand James & William had chosen their land in Westmoreland, before it had been decided to grant away the Cowpastures.

Mr Oxley, when I told him, laboured to make me believe it was the 'rancorous feeling' of Governor and Mrs Macquarie towards us that made them take this measure to injure and annoy us, and that he himself was altogether 'ignorant, he declared to God' of any intention there was to grant away the Cowpastures…How much of either of those stories is true I cannot tell. But you may infer that Governor Macquarie and also Mr Oxley the Surveyor General thought your brothers had just cause to complain of ill-treatment and injustice.

It is certain Gov Macquarie left a remark among many others, for the guidance of his successor, Sir Thomas Brisbane & that your father was entitled to land—but 'he had not promised that it should be given at the Cowpastures'. After some little deliberation, however, Sir Thomas thought fit to allow you to have the tract marked 'Brisbane' on the chart—this is all upland, of little use in dry seasons.

Which reason can be given for not allowing the 5000 acres

to be measured adjoining the Camden Estate, I cannot think. The reserving it for government purpose is a pretence. Mr Oxley is looking to have it himself I cannot but think.

I am quite certain your father has never by word or act given Sir T. Brisbane cause of complaint—I hope that things will be smooth between them—but after such a breach of promise I can hardly tell how the governor can meet your father. However, that is his affair, between ourselves. I was afraid when the letter of 'remonstrance', as it was called, was written, that it would not read very agreeably.

I lament dearest John that this which has already caused you so much trouble and anxious solicitude, should still be productive of more.

Ever your affectionate mother
E McA

p.s. I hasten to remark that we lost fifty or sixty fine ewes some months since by a shepherd forcing them down one of the steep ravines of 'Brisbane'. I remark this to show how liable we are to receive injuries by grazing sheep on such lands, entrusted to such shepherds as we have here.

Assure yourself my beloved son of the united love of all here—they are all now asleep—knowing not that I am writing—they would persuade me from it, under the belief there is no chance of this being received before what may be written by the *Courier.*

I was very glad to receive Miss Kingdon's letter but mortified & hurt that she should have had so much trouble. I will write to her by the *Courier.* It is a melancholy picture she draws of my poor relatives. I trust my mother will at last be comfortable. The thought that she has not been has embittered many an hour.

Once more adieu, my dear John. I cannot read over what I have written, my eyes will not allow of it by candlelight.

26 March 1824, to her son John

The matter of the land continued to be an issue, but Elizabeth reassures John that it's likely to end well. She allows herself some pretty pithy judgements on the men setting themselves against the Macarthurs, including Major Goulburn and his colleague Henry Douglass.

Parramatta, March 26th, 1824

My dearest John,

I am just apprized of the ship *William Shand* being about to sail for Batavia and am induced at this very short notice, even, to risk a letter—and particularly as the *Courier* will not go before the second week in April and perhaps not then.

My first communication shall be to tell you my beloved son, that we are all well. Your father, James & William are at Camden.

I am in hopes the land is at length in a fair way to be settled—Major Goulburn however has resisted in every way he could and now withholds the buildings & paddock & requires your father to enter into some securities with the Crown Solicitor—his letters are a tirade of nonsense.

The *Competitor*, on board of which our wool was sent, sailed the 4th of February—you will have to wade through a vast heap of letters and papers by that vessel. These letters will vex & perplex you about the land, but I hope it will all end well. As the redoubtable Major is set in motion, in truth

I wish your father & him could adjust matters amicably.

James sent in his card to the office on Tuesday and wished to speak to him, but the man is so stubborn and mulish in his habits that there is no doing any thing with him, unless it be in the way of a joke—he dearly loves a pun, too. Seriously, on account of many things, I wish he had not set himself so much against your father. Indeed, I think Douglass has been a principal cause of the great disunion in the respectable part of the community here—I think it probable he will call on you in London with some fine tale—he is highly theatrical and very sentimental.

I must hasten to finish off this scrawl—I write by candle-light, the family all in bed—this has been my excuse for a blundering letter. Your father has had better health & for a longer time together than I have known him to enjoy for a very long time.

You will have learnt that we had a scorching dry summer—a few showers which have lately fallen, have given us a little verdure but we want rain still, very much. The lambing season is about commencing, so that being put in possession of the Camden estate will be of great importance. I trust it will take place without further delay. You ask me if the high lands would be desirable at Camden? Doubtless they would be—but bad neighbours would be a nuisance and none but bad ones would take a grant in such situation. Your father will write on this subject, when the one on hand is settled.

God bless & preserve you, my beloved son, prays
Your ever affectionate mother
E. MacArthur.

7 June 1824, to Eliza Kingdon

Edward Macarthur had become a high-ranking officer in the British army, but in 1824 returned to Australia for a visit. Unlike her response to the return of her husband a few years before, there's no ambiguity in Elizabeth's joy at seeing Edward again. When she wanted to, she was more than capable of saying exactly what she meant, leaving no room for ironic double meanings.

The 'spell of celibacy' that Elizabeth refers to was created at least in part by her husband, who'd refused several suitors for their daughters.

Over the years in New South Wales, Elizabeth's attitude towards Indigenous people seems progressively to have hardened. At this time many colonists were hostile to 'the natives', but there'd always been some who recognised that Indigenous people were fighting for their homeland. Even Governor Philip Gidley King had said two decades earlier that he 'had ever considered [them] the real Proprietors of the Soil'. Elizabeth shows no such understanding here.

Parramatta
June 7th 1824

My dear Eliza,
The return of our beloved son Edward after an absence of sixteen years, was an event so joyful to us that I hardly yet can think of it calmly. He arrived on the sixth of April, yet it seems to me but as yesterday.

Since my last letter to you, our second daughter Mary has broken through the spell of celibacy which seemed to encompass the house. She was united in marriage to the principal surgeon of this establishment, Mr Bowman, in November last and I trust with a fair prospect of happiness. I cannot however quite reconcile myself to the blank it has made in our home circle.

Mr MacArthur and our two youngest sons are at present at our estate at Camden, the former I am happy to say enjoying much better health than he has done for years.

Last week we received some very alarming accounts from the settlement at Bathurst. The natives had barbarously put to death a number of stockmen in the service of individuals settled in that neighbourhood—plundered the huts—set fire to them—killed numbers of sheep and cattle—spreading terror and devastation around. A young gentleman, a proprietor at Bathurst, called here on Saturday last. He had come from thence with several others to solicit the Governor for aid and assistance. He said he had seen the bodies of seven white men brought into the settlement the morning he set off.

I know not what measures will be resorted to, in order to check these barbarities, which upon the whole are of a far more aggressive nature than any that have before taken place. Heretofore when guilty of these outrages the natives have not been checked by lenient measures, on the contrary emboldened by success they have proceeded to commit further atrocities, until at length it has been found necessary to send a military force to terrify them into submission, and to prevent further acts of barbarity.

It is now many years since so alarming a circumstance has taken place. Twice we have had our own stations molested, each time two lives were taken, the huts plundered and set fire to. This happened when Mr MacArthur was in England. The military were obliged to interfere, to prevent the further effusion of innocent blood.

As for my sister, I think of her, poor soul, her poverty, her distress, without in the least discovering how her situation can be substantially benefited. Were it my sister only I could see my way. But for so numerous a family what can be done? They must learn to earn their own bread, for our means are not unlimited.

Adieu
EM

7 June 1824, to her son John

As John Macarthur's mental illness gradually grew worse, he became more difficult to deal with—he was highly excitable and fell out with many people, including his nephews Hannibal and Charles. Elizabeth did her best to smooth things over, but her task was becoming increasingly difficult. Still, she doesn't dwell on it in her letters. Her son John is in London, too far away to help, and she must have been conscious of filling her letter with news and amusing gossip, rather than the anxieties of her situation.

This letter shows that Elizabeth could understand, and feel sympathy for, a woman who'd taken the 'false steps' that resulted in her becoming a convict. Her husband didn't ever show any such understanding—for him, a convict was permanently tainted.

Elizabeth's attraction to a title or nobility, and to the importance of 'respectability', is evident in this and other letters. This was an aspect of her character that was typical of the time and not unknown today, but it didn't find its way into A Room Made of Leaves.

Parramatta, 7th June 1824

My beloved son, I enclose you a letter, addressed to me by a Mrs Marr, who goes to England with one of her sons— purporting both to return again to this country. The letter, you will say, is a curious production—truly an original, as is the writer. She is very desirous to see you and will probably wait upon you at your chambers. I shall therefore tell you briefly who she is, and sketch her character.

She is the <u>foster sister</u> of the present Earl of Winchelsea by whom she is still patronised. Her mother and father were very many years servants in the family of the late Lady Charlotte Finch, his lordship's mother. The subject of my letter was born in the family, brought up in it, and remained, while some unhappy occurrence led her astray and she was tempted from one false step to another, which finally led to her being sent hither, <u>a convict</u>. She came at the first settlement with Governor Phillip. I remember her well, on my first arrival—I used to occasionally employ her in needlework. She was rather pretty, very volatile & good tempered—married a very decent tradesman named Henry Marr, a clever person, and one of the steadiest general dealers in Sydney. This is the first trip the old lady has made, having been many years a free person.

She is very clever as a needlewoman & has a clear head. She has lately buried her two daughters, both of whom were respectably married. Grief on this account, and a letter she has lately received from 'The Earl' induces her once more to visit old England.

I shall take the opportunity of noticing our entire satisfaction in the various articles purchased by Mrs Harris which we have received by Edward—every thing has been carefully put up & specifically marked for the purposes designed, good in quality and not we think overcharged. It is of consequence that what we have for our personal use be appropriate and of superior quality. We <u>wear</u> our things <u>out</u>, and therefore wear them long—we have no opportunity of changing often. When Edward returns, he will be able to explain all this. At this distance from the mother country mere articles of show are ridiculous—our household linen & clothes should be of good quality—both because they are better taken care of & are in the end more useful, certainly more respectable and in the object of packages & freight, cost no more than trash.

I should have written decidedly for regular half-yearly supplies before now, but that I have been held back from prudential considerations. Your dear father likes to order and sometimes he exceeds in quantity at one time. For personal and household supplies some female friend is necessary to select—the last cambric muslins we were greatly deceived in. Your sister made them up into dresses, but they washed to pieces immediately—injured I suppose in bleaching.

Your father read over the accompanying list, which was to have been given to Mr Macleay for the purpose of him obtaining them from Scotland. Edward however thinks they can be procured from London equally cheap, stout & good. If that be the case, it is folly to incur obligation, and go out of one's way for nothing.

June 29th

The foregoing you will perceive, my dearest John, was written three weeks ago. The *Midas* was then supposed to be going immediately to sea—but from some appearances there was cause to apprehend that the oil casks were leaking. The ship was unloaded & the whole cargo re-examined which then caused her detention until now.

Your father was at Camden when I began this letter. He is now at home. Edward has been at Camden since Saturday week. James came here on Saturday, stayed just to make up his & Edward's packet of letters for you, & set off back again this morning—Emmeline is in Sydney with Mary.

I know not what to say of the state of politics now. Mr Forbes has been solicitous that the Governor should reside more at Sydney. He has generally been here two days in the week. I do not think the family will remove. Lady Brisbane likes the quiet of Parramatta best. Your father keeps quite aloof and meddles not, which is very satisfactory to me.

I am sorry to say your father has felt deeply offended with Hannibal & Charles, on account of the <u>foolishness</u> of the latter—in expressing his embittered feelings towards Mr Barnard—and by the increased intimacy of Hannibal with Mr Field after the breach between your father and him. I have done all I could to prevent these misunderstandings. Mr Oxley has met your father again—they speak, and so forth.

God bless & preserve you, my beloved John
So prays your ever affectionate mother
E. MacArthur

6 February 1825, to Eliza Kingdon

In February 1825 Edward Macarthur returned to England. By then his father's mental health had deteriorated markedly. Here for the first time Elizabeth acknowledges the effect on her own wellbeing of the 'accumulated gloom'. That sounds like the true voice of a woman who not only has the steadiness to deal with an increasingly impossible situation, but also the insight to recognise what it's doing to her, and the honesty to admit to it. The more I read these letters, the more I admired Elizabeth Macarthur.

Although A Room Made of Leaves *ends twenty-five years before these challenging times for Elizabeth, they were in my mind as I thought about the sort of person she might have been. Her letters show her to be courageous and calm, even though her life was beset by difficulties that might have made a less-resolute woman despair. That was the person I put at the centre of the novel.*

In this letter Elizabeth speaks of being tempted to visit England. She hadn't been there since she left in December 1789, thirty-six years before. She might have been tempted, but she never did return, not even for a visit.

Parramatta,
February 6th, 1825

My dear Eliza,
I write you a hurried letter by my dear Edward who is preparing to leave us the day after tomorrow. He has been

with us ten months. When I look back I can scarcely credit it. His father was very ill when he arrived, and I grieve to add is now confined to his bed, so that it has thrown an accumulated gloom around me.

There is now such a perpetual influx of strangers of various classes in society, they are obliged to go back a great distance, and are subject to a thousand difficulties. But what situation has not its difficulties? This country seems of late to have attracted considerable attention, and such seems the increased desire, or necessity, for emigration, that every ship brings a host of passengers.

Van Diemen's Land has hitherto been the favourite settlement for emigrants with capital. The climate being colder was an additional recommendation to Scotch settlers, in particular.

Your account of the Bude Canal amuses me much! The powers of steam have now become such in their application to navigation that I know not whether I may not be tempted to revisit England—especially now that we are told the voyage will be rendered practicable by way of the Isthmus of Darien or by Panama.

This letter which was commended to be conveyed to you by our beloved son Edward, I was unable sufficiently to command my feelings to finish. I was pained so much before our parting that I could write to no one. It is now five weeks since we bade him farewell. We hope he is well on his voyage.

Adieu
EM

4 February 1826, to Eliza Kingdon

Elizabeth's strong feelings against the Indigenous people when they were presenting a threat to settlers gave way to a somewhat condescending interest when the threat abated, and the corroborees she witnessed became just an interesting morsel of exotica to entertain Eliza. Her assertion that a corroboree was 'always to do honour to and entertain strangers' may not have been the whole story. 'Myall' was a word often used by colonists to describe Indigenous people living beyond the settlements—those who were usually the ones accused of violence against the colonists.

In letter after letter from this time, Elizabeth asserts that her husband is healthier than he's been for years. This may be a head-in-the-sand attitude on her part, but it may also be because of the stigma at that time against mental illness.

Parramatta
February 4th, 1826

My dear Eliza,
Nothing like the splendour and gaiety you describe as contemplated at the ball at Bude can be exhibited for many years in Australia. But let me give you some account of one of our native dances—a 'Corroboree' as they call it, when it is not unusual for two or three hundred to collect, to paint and deck themselves with green boughs, and in sets perform various grotesque figure dances, in most excellent time, which is given by others who sit apart and chant a sort of wild cadence.

These corroborees are always on bright moonlight nights, and some agreeable spot is always chosen for the exhibition amongst the woods. The number of small fires which are kindled causes just enough brilliancy to give effect to our beautiful woodland scenery, and throw sufficient light on the sable performers. This festivity is generally prolonged until past midnight, and always given to do honour to and entertain strangers, whom they call 'Myall'.

Some time ago the natives in the vicinity of Hunter's River as well as those beyond Bathurst were in open hostilities with the settlers. They have since been reconciled, but the country is now infested by another and more formidable Banditti, consisting of runaway convicts from the penal settlements who have been joined by others from road parties, clearing gangs, and government establishments. These desperadoes have contrived to arm themselves, some are mounted, and embodied in parties of from eight to fourteen. About dusk they take forcible possession of some farm, constrain the servants, place guard over them, and compel the proprietors to bring forth all their stores, which they appropriate at their pleasure. After rioting and destroying and carrying off all they can, they leave the distressed family to lament, and seek redress at their peril, for these ruffians denounce all manner of vengeance in the way of reprisal. Only last week the farm of Captain King was so plundered. It ends with capture, and the ultimate death or banishment of these plunderers. Such are the perils to which settlers are occasionally exposed.

I hope you will continue to write to me as usual. Your letters always give me great pleasure by reminding me of scenes long past. The reflections which they bring with them are always useful, and I find they have a salutary effect upon my mind.

My husband, I rejoice to say, enjoys better health at present than he has done for years. He unites with me in every affectionate remembrance.

Adieu

16 December 1826, to her son John

Not surprisingly, Elizabeth can be very much franker about her husband's disorder with her son than she was with Eliza.

The 'Government Hospital' was where her surgeon son-in-law James Bowman had his practice. When in Sydney, Elizabeth and her husband stayed with the Bowmans and their house in the present-day suburb of Woolloomooloo.

Government Hospital
Sydney
December 16th 1826.

My dearest John,
I am not a little mortified that a vessel sailed direct for England on the 5th of this month, without taking a single line from <u>any</u> of us. I was about to write the day before her departure, when the Archdeacon told me he had learnt she would not sail for two or three days—I was therefore prevented from writing by the extraordinary punctuality of the Commander, who sailed on the day he advertised to do.

It is now nine o'clock. Your dear father is gone to bed not in good spirits—I asked him whether he should write to you—his reply was, I am not in spirits to write and I know not what to say. He is suffering again from one of those fits of despondency which are sure to succeed extraordinary exertion and over-excitement. We have looked for it, and the sudden depression in the value of our produce, the gloomy accounts of the state of the things in England and the perplexed state of affairs here have united to depress his spirits. I am unhappy to see that he is in such a state of suffering. I trust a change will soon take place again for the better. He is relieved certainly since he came here, and was well enough to dine at Government House on Wednesday last, when the Governor and everyone was very attentive, as he told me.

Your sister Mary I am glad to say is quite well and your nephew Edward is a fine infant. The Doctor is also very well. They desire their kindest remembrances—and now my beloved son I shall conclude this incoherent scrawl for it ill agrees with my eyes to write by candlelight, and the confused way I am expressing myself I fear can give you little pleasure or information—I only was anxious to assure you we are all well, and that all our affairs are so likewise. God grant that this may find you in health and also your dear brother. We think of you continually believe, ever to remain

My dearest John
Your dearest mother
E. MacArthur

17 December 1826, to her son Edward

Earlier in 1826 John Macarthur decided to remodel Elizabeth Farm, and Elizabeth was obliged to go to Sydney to stay with her daughter Mary and son-in-law James Bowman. John Macarthur wouldn't let her come home until his frenzied but ineffective repairs to their home were finished.

His 'old tormenting complaint' could be the gout and other joint pains that had recurred since his illness at the Cape on the first voyage to New South Wales. It could also be the recurring deep depression that he himself described in his letters as worse than any physical ailment.

'This is disease unquestionably'—you can hear Elizabeth's sad acceptance of something she'd tried so hard to deny.

Government Hospital Sydney
Sunday 17th Dec 1826

My dearest Edward,

I wrote a most hurried letter to John yesterday and sealed it up last night, without being able to read it over, under the impression that the *Regalia* would sail very early this morning—but we received a message that the vessel would not sail before tomorrow morning. I have therefore determined to scribble a letter to you.

You will perceive that I am still at Sydney—I have been sojourning here two months & yet I am not permitted to return. The repairs at home were commenced with too much vigour—too many workmen employed and too much ardent activity bestowed on that which could best advance slowly step by step, while the family continued to occupy a part of the house—at length your father saw his error—discharged the greater part of the workmen—thereby reducing the monthly expenditure & the repairs are still going on well, although slowly. I am told that if I return, your dear father will not proceed. I have lived so long in a ruin of a cottage that I think it best to stay where I am until I have a bedroom finished.

You will observe by my letter to John that your dear father has had a severe attack of his old tormenting complaint, with all the accustoming attendants of despondency and low spiritness.

Do not be vexed that your father, nor any other part of the family write—there is another ship will sail very soon. I have let your father know I am writing. He only says, 'Poor fellows! What have I of a pleasing nature to write to them about?' This is disease unquestionably.

Captain Langdon has sold the merino sheep he imported on the *Hugh Crawford* to Mr Jones for eighteen pounds a head. Mr Dawson says the wool is far inferior to any of ours.

Your father took a little walk yesterday round the Govt Domain and looked at the shipping in the cove—he seemed better afterwards—he has slept better tonight—is not yet risen.

I sign myself
Your affectionate mother
E MacArthur

8 January 1827, to her daughter Elizabeth

In this letter to her daughter Elizabeth, who was probably with her married sister in Sydney, Elizabeth is frank about the difficulties in dealing with her husband. It was now generally known around Sydney that John Macarthur was too erratic to deal with. 'Chequered times' is a masterly understatement. Still, Elizabeth had to ask his permission to forward letters by the coach—he might have been in the grip of mental illness, but he was still in charge.

It's also clear from the note on the cover (and in many other places in her letters) that her involvement with the family's wool production was something she threw herself into knowledgeably and enthusiastically.

How knowledgeable, though, really? The answer to that might lie in the letters she wrote to her husband during the years that he was in England, when she was in charge of the flocks. How frustrating that not a single one has come down to us!

Her background as a farmer's daughter and granddaughter would have given her some familiarity with sheep farming, but not real expertise. Her letters never get more specific or detailed about sheep than the kind of remarks she makes here. (John Macarthur might also have had some knowledge—he lived for a few years in his late teens near Bridgerule, in farming country—but he wouldn't have had a great deal of hands-on experience.)

The most likely scenario, in my mind, is that the nitty-gritty of breeding fine wool, the detail of day-to-day culling and keeping, was done by someone on the Macarthur lands who really knew about wool. John Macarthur would have had a general policy—for example, 'keeping the merinos pure'—and Elizabeth

clearly enjoyed being out in the paddocks and in the wool shed.
But it's probable that neither of them can claim the credit. There
was someone else—probably several someones, and probably
convicts or ex-convicts—who should have been credited on the
old two-dollar note as 'the father of the wool industry'.

My dear Elizabeth,

The Archdeacon has sent to acquaint me he goes to Parramatta at six tomorrow, and will take any parcels or letters. You have the letters already forwarded to you, but not those from John. I will ask your father, if I may send those by the Archdeacon. He is in bed and has been suffering very much today and perhaps I may not be able to ask him in time. The general tenor is agreeable & lively but there are chequered times.

I wrote to dear Mary today—I have nothing particular to tell for her information and I hope someone will write to her this evening—I am truly vexed about the lost letter to Emmeline. I will in future, be more particular about letters. Let Emmeline see this. I cannot very well write to her this evening. Mr Dawson is talking and it is getting late.

God keep you well—
Ever your affectionate mother
E MacArthur

p.s. Please take no notice of any discussion you may hear on board the *Australia*—all is smoothed over. The sheep are in beautiful condition, their wool is beautiful—the wool of the male sheep superb!!!

4 March 1827, to her son Edward

Elizabeth continues to walk a fine line between not worrying her faraway son and telling him the truth of the situation. For a paragraph or two she can distract herself with local gossip, but she can never forget for long the situation with her husband. By this time, John Macarthur's psychological instability was clearly abnormal, although Elizabeth continues to put the best face on things and seems reluctant to admit—at least to her son—that her husband's wild energy was a sign of trouble, not health.

Bannister was one of several suitors for a Macarthur daughter who wasn't considered suitable. Emmeline did finally marry: Henry Watson Parker. The family didn't think he was suitable either, but it seems to have been a happy partnership.

John Macarthur's nephew Charles was involved in pastoral enterprises with Hannibal Macarthur.

Sydney March 4th 1827

My dearest Edward,
It was with great joy I received your most welcome packet by Charles MacArthur—Mr Bowman's horse was at the door, on which he was about to take a ride to Parramatta when Charles arrived with his nephew James. After the Doctor's departure, your dear sister Mary & myself quietly then perused your letters.

Most thankful we were, that your communications were of so pleasing a nature, for never did your poor father so much need distraction—he has for some months past given way to the most gloomy apprehensions—one of those peculiar & sudden alterations which we have before witnessed.

This time twelve months ago he was in excellent health and in exceeding good spirits, but for the last four or five months quite the reverse has been the case.

That he suffers excessively and even more than we can well judge is certain, but it is the mind preying upon the body and disturbing its proper functions.

The depressed state of the markets in England and a very dry adverse season here have conspired to feed this melancholy. He is however better, and I hope & pray he will continue to mend—he spent a month or more here lately to try the benefit of change.

I trust John and yourself will receive all the letters safe—I did not myself write, as James had said all that was to be said and we had constantly persons calling on one account or another, so that I kept myself disengaged to talk—which occasionally you know, Edward, I am very fond of.

Mr Henderson is busied in searching for coals in the vicinity of Port Jackson. Mr Henderson showed me yesterday a fine specimen he found on Mr John Blaxland's estate near Parramatta. He found some also on Mr Marsden's. He said the vein must pass through our land—I wish it may be discovered to do so, as it may render that coarse part of our estate near the Duck River more valuable.

It is Sunday, we have just had a visit from Mrs Abel— she generally comes in once a week and chats with us. I fear Mr Balcomb has entangled himself in debt—this is merely conjecture. She has been amusing Mary & I with an account of two or three parties she has been at this week, one at Mrs Jones's—a strange mixture of finery, ostentation and vulgarity according to her account.

Dear Edward, I picture to myself your great consternation, when you received the intelligence of the intention of your father to return to England—I trust it may not distract you—these sudden changes and resolves. We none of us liked the thought and were exceedingly pleased when he abandoned the idea. It made a great talk & chatter here for a time.

You will perceive I still write from Sydney—it is not yet convenient for me to return home—the repairs which were commenced with too much vigour, could not proceed with a velocity corresponding to your father's wishes—he then began to tire & would stop the same & come here, stay a few weeks, & return to expedite the work. It is proceeding, and I have a prospect of being enabled to return with some degree of comfort soon.

I have had a few lines from Miss Bannister—poor Bannister, I profess I understand him not—nor how he has involved himself in embarrassments, I feel of a very serious nature, I mean in a pecuniary sense. I wish for his sake and his sisters' that it may not be so. He made proposals for your sister Emmeline to your father by letter, who very warmly in a reply stated to Mr B his reasons for declining them—in which reasons Mr B in another letter fully acquiesced. Your father was very much vexed. He consulted me—in fact we were all of one opinion. Mr B and Emmeline had never been thrown into each other's company, nor could we discover the least partiality, more than of a very general nature. We none of us dropped the least hint to her, not thinking it necessary as Mr Bannister was so soon to quit the country—circumstances occurred which averted more vexatious feeling between the Governor and Mr B and he suddenly determined to go by the first ship, leaving his sisters behind. Miss B made an appeal to your father for protection, which distressed him very much— she said she wished to hire a cottage at Parramatta & that her sister Harriet would go to the Pedders in Hobart Town. I gave no encouragement to a scheme which appeared to me so odd and even impracticable, and I really was very glad when the sisters accepted of a proposal to remove to Hobart Town. I cannot understand these very eccentric people. I should rejoice to hear that Bannister has extricated himself from his difficulties, for his own sake as well as his sisters'.

This, my dear son, you will say is a proper old woman's gossiping letter. When I take up my pen, I know not when to have done when addressing those that are dear to me—the misfortune is that I feel I neglect to notice the things which it would be most acceptable to you to hear, and tease you with a repetition of uninteresting matter.

I hear that the vessel is off, therefore I hastily subscribe myself, my dearest son
your Affectionate mother

November 1830, to her daughter Elizabeth

When Elizabeth writes about the practicalities of life on the Macarthur estates and the day-to-day discussions with people working for her, you can hear the pleasure she has in that aspect of her life, and her writing takes on an energy and a spontaneous directness.

Her long-ago lessons in botany with Mr Dawes can often be sensed behind her many descriptions (not all reproduced in this selection) of botanical subjects.

Camden
Friday morning, November

My dearest Elizabeth,
All your various communications up to the time Mr Koltz left Parramatta, I have to thank you for—they arrived in rapid succession, and we had hardly finished the discussion which one provoked and William set forth to overlook his out-of-door concerns—when on his return something more would have arrived.

I believe I have now spelled over quickly all the letters and begin to understand their contents. Dear dear James told much, and how well he has written—& how gratifying and how much to the purpose is the letter of our beloved John, and dear sensitive, single-hearted Edward how like himself—I must not indulge a vein of thinking <u>no wise healthy</u> to the mind.

Yesterday it was fair, & the people said it promised to continue thus. I feared otherwise from certain atmospheric influences upon my system. However after dinner William & I determined on a walk over the range and through some fairly dry roads winding round the hills, and after staying and admiring the bunches of grapes & the size of the vine leaves, we descended the hill towards home.

I have little to tell you in the way of adventure, for with the exception of yesterday & the day before, I have not been out since I visited the Merino flocks. The evening before last, I took a drive, the road was rather wet & splashy—the long grass either side the road waving in the breeze like a field of tall grain. Here we came upon two beautiful cock pheasants dancing through the grass. Apropos of pheasants, Lowick is quite doleful in consequence of the little increase he is likely to have from the hens this season—'The thunder has spoiled the eggs'—and the few that have produced birds have been so tender and delicate—that, to use his own words, he fears 'they will come to nothing'. This is attributable to the rain, not to any want of care or attention. The ducks are the one thing that seem to thrive in this weather—'fine weather for ducks'.

The pride of the garden just now is the Magnolia—it has been in flower a week or two…the bud is about the size of an ostrich egg, pure white when it expands. I know not what to compare it to, the petals are thick and resemble white kid leather. The scent is a combination of sweetness and fragrance, something like essence of orange flower and bergamot. The flower closes at night & opens again in the morning. William gathered a branch with a flower bud—last week it kept alive several days & perfumed the cottage.

So much rain really makes one nervous & apprehensive but God's will be done—it is not wise that we should repine.

27 December 1830, to her son Edward

Elizabeth was much too discreet a correspondent to spell out what seems pretty clear: she was away from her husband as much as possible, either in Sydney or at Camden. The strain of living with him, and needing to keep his increasingly erratic behaviour from the eyes of the world, was taking its toll on her own health.

In any case, she clearly enjoyed the free and somewhat socially isolated life at Camden with only family for company, and plenty of activities to do with the sheep and the crops. She didn't want a fine house or luxuries: the farmer's daughter she was at heart took most pleasure from watching the farm thrive.

Charles Frederick Koelz (Elizabeth misspelled his name) was a recently arrived German wool classer engaged by the Macarthurs.

Camden
Dec 27th 1830

My beloved Edward,
I know it will give you pleasure, additional I should have said, to receive a letter from me written from hence. I have been staying with William and Frederick Thompson nearly two months, and I expect it will be two or three weeks more before I shall make up my mind to return to Parramatta, so well am I pleased with my sojourn here and so much has my health been benefited by the change.

I cannot tell you how delighted I have been with the wonderful improvements I daily discover—not in a fine house,

mind, for the same little cottage is still all the residence—
neatly kept—but it is solid improvements I see in every part
of the estate I have as yet visited, such as will be infinitely
more striking and imposing to the eyes of a stranger, some
years hence than now—but to me they are so apparent where
so e'er I bend my steps, that I cannot but feel astonished at
the persevering industry of your brother William who has
so beneficially devoted his time and been so successful in
planting and propagating to a very great extent.

I write this to go by Dr Cook who is known to you, he
paid us a visit here last week. The weather was warm and
William very busy with sheep shearing and harvesting—the
former operation has been protracted to an unusually late
period on account of a succession of rainy weather, by which
the river has kept at a height which prevented the sheep from
being washed. The last fortnight has been propitious and I
believe this day finishes the shearing of the grown sheep—
tomorrow the shearers commence with the lambs.

You would not be a little surprised to see the wool house
just now—every bin full up to the brim with fleeces, even to
crowding, all evenly and neatly piled and covered with cloths to
prevent dust from soiling its present purity of appearance. There
is a very manifest improvement in the wool, which you would
not fail to discern. This is a source of solid satisfaction to us all,
for which and for many other blessings, my heart dilates with
thankfulness to Almighty God, the Giver of all Good.

I am not aware whether any part of the family will write
by Dr Cook but myself—and your father writes to John by
the same ship about the insurance for the wool. I heard from

Parramatta on Friday last—all the dear circle there was well excepting that your father is <u>low</u> and complaining.

Maria stayed a week here on her way, being partly detained by rain. The party consisted of Hannibal, Maria, James (who is becoming a fine young man), Charles, George and the infant Arthur and nurse—we made it out very well, were very merry, the cottage pretty full as you may guess.

Mr MacAlister has not descended from the highland since I have been at Camden—poor fellow he has had a narrow escape in a skirmish with a desperate set of Bushrangers, in which he was wounded but not severely. One of the mounted police under his command was also wounded and a constable severely so. The desperadoes were all finally captured—tried at Bathurst and executed. There are a few men out there committing depredations on the most frequented roads in broad and open daylight—our government is so feeble and inefficient—you would hardly credit that such things could be done with impunity for any length of time.

Another revolution in France! I can scarce say I am surprised at it—Spain and Portugal next I think will follow their example. What an eventful life has that of the Duke of Orleans been. I have read so many of the works of the late Madame de Genlis that the history of the Orleans family is familiar to me.

And now my dear, dear Edward, let me thank you for the kind communications entrusted to Mr Koltz—for the valuable book—and the pens, with one of which I am now writing—whilst the paper that enrolled them lies before me with your caution, that they be 'carefully wiped'—so like yourself. All your gifts prove useful, and indeed this is particularly so—I cannot see to round a pen, and this has frequently prevented me from writing.

Frederick's account of your father, is that he is still very low, wondering 'what takes John to Paris at this agitated time' and more at a loss why James should accompany him. He goes not out—but yet I am convinced it is not a bodily ailment—altogether hypochondria.

We congratulate you on your appointment, your friend the Marquis certainly has shown you very marked attentions. I should think him a kind and good man.

Dear John's letter to his sister was a treasure—your father was gratified—he wrote to tell me so. Your warm-hearted friend McAlister will scream with joy at your remembrance of him when he gets the pocket book. A number of old servants enquire for you, amongst the number T. Herbert who has been in our service 28 years.

And now beloved Edward, I shall conclude with earnest prayers for the health and prosperity of yourself and our beloved John, to whom I do not write because this letter will answer the same purpose of assurance that you are as dear as ever to me though so long separated.

It is nearly dark and I cannot write by candlelight therefore I conclude myself, my dearest Edward,

Your affectionate mother,
E. MacArthur.

I cannot even read over to correct what I have written—make allowances for all errors.

Sometime in 1830, to John Macarthur

Of all the many letters that Elizabeth Macarthur must have written to her husband over the years, this is the only one that's come to light. She was in Camden; he was in Parramatta.

Re-reading this now, I have a pang of misgiving: did I get it wrong, the relationship between Elizabeth and John? Did she in fact love him deeply?

I've read this note many times, trying to hear its tone. The sentence about their sons, giving credit to her husband for their good qualities—is that heartfelt praise, coming from a loving and admiring wife? Or is it (as the suddenly rather elaborate syntax and flowery language suggests) exaggeratedly cheering and flattering, the way you might try to buck up someone in the grip of 'oppression'?

Well, both things can be true—you can be trying to buck someone up because you care deeply for them. As with so many sentences in Elizabeth's letters, that one can be read in several ways.

I began my thinking about Elizabeth, back in 2001, by coming to the conclusion that she was hiding her true self from the readers of her letters. Now I think how right I was—even the author who thought she was glimpsing Elizabeth's true self might very well be mistaken.

But if I was, it was in the service of a story that I felt (and feel) was worth telling: one about the way stories and documents from the past can be a mask or a decoy, rather than a window.

This is one of the few letters in this selection that I've reproduced in its entirety.

Camden, Friday, 1830

My dearest MacArthur,

We had the pleasure to receive Mr Koltz on our return from a little ramble, which we had been induced to take after dinner over the Stony Range—and to return and take a look at the vineyard, to observe how the vines looked after so much rain. We did not think Mr Koltz would have made his way out so soon—however, William was well pleased to see him—and they soon entered into interesting conversation concerning the wool. This morning, as nothing else was to be done, they have been examining what wool remains in the wool house unpacked. Mr Koltz seems to approve of its condition and general character—the rain having again recommenced, there is little or nothing to be done. Mr Koltz appears all that you say—and I hope he will prove a valuable acquisition to this establishment, and relieve our dear William from some portion of his cares.

I have read all the English letters which cost me a great application of eyesight—I could not get through them at all last night. Our dear and beloved sons—their images seemed to hover round me when I retired to rest. God bless them, and strengthen them in those virtuous dispositions and honourable qualities, which you have at an early age impressed upon their minds and imparted to them by example.

I hope dear James is on his way out by this time—John's letter to his sister tho' short is full of information—he seems to think the affairs of England in a very unsettled state, I perceive.

I hope you have recovered from the oppression you were suffering from yesterday—I had something of it myself and I expected from my feelings, that a change again in the weather was about to take place. We had a great deal of lightning last night.

Many thanks for your offer of sending Macdonald up with the new carriage for my accommodation. If it would please God to let us have fair and somewhat settled weather again I should indeed be very glad to have it here and I see no reason why Mary & Edward might not in that case, come in it—we expect Frederick will return from Argyle as soon as the weather holds up, he will cheerfully go down to escort her—and Hyles can be in attendance also—I should like her to come, whilst I am here. When our dear James returns the little cottage will be pretty well occupied.

William will I dare say write and tell you all that all here is well as can be expected—I have written a gossiping letter to Elizabeth and must write a line or two to Em.

Believe me to be, my dearest MacArthur,
Your ever affectionate wife,
E. MacArthur

23 April 1831, to her son Edward

As always, Elizabeth is full of the news of the town—who's given birth, who's married, who's died—much more than I've included. Occasionally she allows herself a moment's cattiness, here and elsewhere.

'These are not marrying times,' she says—and in fact, of her seven children, only three married.

Parramatta
Saturday 23rd April 1831

My dearest Edward,
Again I take up my pen to address a few lines to you, well knowing my scribble will be welcome. I know not who has written to you, and who intends to write. They are all talking about it, and wandering about discussing on the subject— and on the weather, we have had a week of almost incessant rain—it commenced on Saturday last and now it is Saturday again—the eighth day.

We have had a flood at Camden—and then here— neither of them particularly distinctive that I have heard—and upon the whole it is to be hoped the combined rain will be beneficial. We must, however, expect heavy losses amongst our flocks and particularly in the breeding ewes, as it is the season of lambing.

James came from Camden on Thursday, leaving William & Frederick Thompson there, quite well. The latter was to have accompanied James, having accepted the invitation to a ball & supper given at Government House last evening to celebrate His Majesty's birthday, but the weather caused us all to decline. Your father at all events would not have gone. He has not been from home for many months.

We are very thankful that you dear Edward have an occupation—although not very profitable, yet is it an honourable and I should think an agreeable one, to have been favoured with the friendship of the Marquis of Cholmondeley for so long a time. This position enables you to do some kind offices, I perceive, for your friends—perhaps more valued & feeling themselves more flattered by the distinction than they would be to receive a costly present. Thank you for the ticket for the prorogation of Parliament by his present Majesty. I suppose there will be a coronation of their present majesties—James and your sisters laugh at me and say I am looking out for velvet and trappings!

James tells us, you had doubts whether I had ever written to Lady Brisbane since receiving the shawl and those other marks of her kind recollection. I assure you I wrote almost immediately afterwards. Emmeline at the time was at Camden, Elizabeth also wrote, but whether by the same ship I cannot say—neither am I certain whether we sent the letters by one of the Scotch Company's ships or by a Liverpool ship. Emmeline now fears that there may have been a miscarriage of some of our former letters.

It gave me great pleasure to hear of the safe arrival of Captain King and his son Phillip. I sincerely congratulate Mrs King on that joyful event and also on the recovery of her daughter from a very dangerous illness. James and Emmeline paid Mrs P. King & her a visit a short time since. You may be assured I was very glad that James returned to us a bachelor—indeed, dear Edward, these are not marrying times for persons possessing much sensibility or reflection. For those of hard materials, that can browbeat and elbow their way, or that can labour to get their own living, the affair is somewhat different.

Rumour acquaints us that we are to have a new governor soon. All the Dumaresqs are married. The captain has married one of the Miss MacLeays and they are going forthwith to Hunter's River to abide—the lady is much pitied by those who know her well. Captn D is universally disliked. The governor & Mrs Darling called about three weeks since. They were very kind and seemingly friendly.

I have not for a long time been at Sydney. Mr Bowman & Mary pay us visits of a day at intervals of a week or two. They have a quick little phaeton of their own—Joseph Bigge who was coachman to Governor and Mrs Macquarie keeps a livery stable & is become a sober man—himself and a pair of his horses are always ready to bring Mary or any of the family, and the doctor finds it much cheaper than keeping a coachman & horses. Elizabeth is well and so is Emmeline and our great friend Mrs Lucas.

I fear my long details must fatigue you—I will hasten to conclude. The trouble is I know not when to have done when I enter up gossiping details—pray do not think your own letters are ever thought to be long. We are sorry they are not more diffuse and lengthy.

God bless you my dearest & dear Edward—that this may find you well.

Cheerful is the prayer of your ever affectionate mother
E MacArthur.

23 April 1831, to her son John

Elizabeth had last seen her son John in 1801, when aged seven he went with his father to England to be placed in a boarding school. Unlike Edward, he'd never returned to Australia. He was now thirty-eight. In her comments about the portrait, Elizabeth's sadness—almost bewilderment—at this endless separation can be felt.

THS is Archdeacon Thomas Hobbes Scott, a longtime friend of the Macarthur family.

Parramatta 23rd April 1831

My dearest John,

I need not tell you how happy the return of dear James, after a three years' absence, made us. Your own heart will enable you to judge of this feeling—he is now quietly settled and taking his usual active part in the affairs of the family, so that it seems as if he had not been away.

A letter from Edward, by a late arrival, has apprized us of your return from the continent with amended health and improved appearance. We hope that you will not again be a sufferer from indispositions.

I have to thank you my dear son for the bracelets and other ornaments sent by James. I shall think of you when I wear them, not that I needed these emblems to keep you alive in my remembrance.

I cannot recognise the boy I parted with in 1801 in the

likeness of yourself brought by James. Elizabeth is not satisfied that it can be a likeness—neither does your father think
the expression of the countenance a correct one. However the
Governor says it is a good likeness and Mrs Mathieson says it
is & some others who have seen you so that I must suppose it
to be so and I am very glad to have it.

When you see Mr Davidson pray remember me kindly
to him—Mrs Davidson's mother has been with us very lately
and will I believe be going to Camden soon, to spend some
time with James & William.

I hope our friend THS has at length safely reached
England, after his many disasters & prolonged voyage. We
miss his society very much, more even than I had anticipated
we should have done—it is, I believe, at my season of life too
late to form new friendships.

Your father & sisters join in kindest love & best wishes to you
with
My dearest John
your ever affectionate mother
E. MacArthur.

26 September 1831, to her son Edward

Elizabeth wrote to her son John in April 1831, but he never received the letter—in that same month he died suddenly in London. The portrait, whatever its shortcomings, was now all she'd ever know of him as an adult.

George Watson Taylor was private secretary to Lord Camden, whose gigantic grant of land made the Macarthurs pre-eminent in the colony.

Parramatta, Sept 26th 1831

I think I have regained sufficient composure to address you, my beloved Edward, and therefore I seize the moment to share the detail, of the irreparable loss we have sustained. The Almighty I trust will in his own good time give us the consolation we pray for and enable us to look on this sad event meekly, & with entire resignation.

Your poor father sustained the first communication, which was made to him by dear James, with manly firmness, & for a day or two he talked over the many amiable qualities of our dear departed John, read every kind note & every letter addressed to him, yourself, or James on the affecting subject, occasionally giving way to a burst of tears—which he declared gave him great relief—and that he derived an unspeakable solace in reading all the testimonies of esteem and affection, which those communications contained—but for a day or two past he has given way to a despondency from which we cannot awaken him. He blesses you and said he would write to you, to say how much he praised you for all your exertions. He also said he would write to our kind friend George Watson Taylor. I feel persuaded he will not be able to do so and before this fit of malady presently gives way to a more rational feeling the ship will have sailed.

Dear James will have enough to do—this will inform you that myself, he & Emmeline received the afflicting intelligence at Woolloomoolah. We had gone down to visit Mary after her confinement, which took place the previous day. A despatch was immediately forwarded to Camden & when we returned the next morning, we found dear William already there. I need not tell you of our meeting—your own affectionate heart will best depict the scene.

I trust I feel as I ought to do, the kindness of the friends that supported me in the last sad duties. God bless them for it. I cannot repay their manifold kindnesses.

Emmeline has said how deeply she felt the loss of her brother, although she had never known him. Neither had Mary any recollection of the beloved object of our regrets— her little one must soon divert the current of her thoughts into other channels, and it is well that it should be so. James, on whom the images of his poor brother are vivid and fresh, naturally suffers the most—and he is under the necessity of keeping his sorrows in check, to give consolation to others, & transact business necessary to be done. Elizabeth, you may be sure, grieves sorely, and tells over the many interesting situations in which she and her poor brother were together placed—the friends they mutually held.

William and James have formed a basis of brotherly affection to which every succeeding year seems to have added strength. His chief solace will be in the care of the garden and in the companionship of his little nephew Edward, who is much attracted to him. Dear Mrs Lucas feels for us all with the sympathy of true friendship, showing itself more by constant acts of kindness than mere words of sorrow and condolence.

Dearest Edward!—accuse me not of dwelling so long on a subject, which to write renews your grief—& opens anew the wound which the lapse of time might have healed. I would endeavour to write of something else—but my poor John's image is at present too vividly depicted to my imagination.

Saturday 1st Oct

You will perceive the foregoing was written on Wednesday last—your poor father—after a severe paroxysm of suffering is now, I trust, in a way to be relieved—his mind begins to right itself. He has just called me to his bedside, & desired me to mention to you, that he wished you to express his grateful thanks to Lord Wynford for his remembrance & kindness—also to General Macdonald and Archdeacon and Mrs Hamilton—Sir T and Lady Farquhar—& to every other—where his thanks should be given. I assure you, my dear Edward, that I feel I can scarcely say how grateful I am to Mr Bigge—his letter to James was written with so much true family feeling—and conveyed so ample a testimony to the work and merit of the dear departed—that to us, it is a treasure.

Should your father continue to improve, I propose going to visit Mary on Monday. Emmeline returned from Wooloomooluh last evening—her and the infant pretty well. I shall not add more at this time. Accept our affectionate love and believe me My dearest Edward

Your affectionate mother

4 May 1832, to her son Edward

John Macarthur had remodelled Elizabeth Farm several times and now embarked on a grandiose plan for an impressive mansion at Camden. 'We all bear the tempest, I may say, wonderfully well,' Elizabeth says to her son in this frank report, although it's clear how difficult things must have been for her.

Elizabeth has taken up the cause of a Mrs Bennet, helping her in her legal battle to obtain a legacy. In among the chronic anxiety about her husband and grief about losing her son, helping someone else might have been a welcome distraction.

'Woolloomalah' was the name of the house in Sydney where Elizabeth's daughter Mary lived with her husband and their children. Elizabeth experimented with a couple of different ways of spelling the Gadigal word.

Woolloomalah
Friday May 4th 1832

My beloved Edward,
I gladly avail myself of an especial inducement I have to write to you now by a medical gentleman, whom I have <u>just</u> seen, & who is to embark in the *Erin* tomorrow—to sail early on Tuesday morning. He politely offered to take charge of my letters—and said he would undertake to see you.

In the first place I hasten to assure you of my health, together with the general good health of all the family & that I left Parramatta Thursday morning proposing to pass a few weeks with Mary & Bowman, which they have long solicited me to do—your sister Emmeline & William & young Edward accompanied me in the German carriage.

The letters you will have recently received will perhaps have apprized you of your dear father's return to health and even to an excited state of activity—which is much more appalling to his devoted family than when suffering a little from rheumatism, or other casual complaints which compel quietude and consistency. But do not be alarmed, my dear Edward, nor grieve yourself—we all bear the tempest, I may say, wonderfully well. It is the old story—setting a variety of wheels in motion, with a <u>Steam Engine</u> power—planning & building—making believe to do at least—altering, directing, driving about at all hours, changing his mind continually—and in short keeping his family in a perpetual worry: for rest I am sorry to say he does not, neither does he indulge in wine or other stimulants save smoking cigars.

We cannot attribute this excitement to any one particular cause. He bore our beloved son John's death with becoming fortitude, and certainly he grieved at heart <u>deeply</u>, but soon, we thought, endeavoured to <u>conquer</u> his feelings by throwing off sorrow and indulging himself at the expense of ours in talking of the dear departed, <u>continually</u>—reading all the letters and saying those and his bright name were his solace. He became more and more restless, anxious to get abroad and talk anywhere, and with every person, who came in his way.

I cannot but consider that he labours under a partial derangement of mind, and views many objects through a disturbed medium. May God grant these mists of the mind may soon disappear—hope it with us my dearest Edward—they have occurred before—although others have not so plainly discovered that they did so. The state of your poor father's health is excellent—nothing appears to tire or fatigue him—and he speaks of you with great kindness.

What can I say further on this anguishing subject? I am staying here at his express desire—he would have Elizabeth to come also, but she would not leave Emmeline solely to wait upon her father, and either James or William will be at Parramatta soon.

The Governor & his family have been residing some time past at the Govt House Parramatta. I have never seen his Excellency—he seems not to pay any visits—and no lady visitors are received at Government House owing to Mrs Bourke's state of health. It is rumoured here—I know not with what truth—that she is deranged. The Governor is very courteous to your father—James and William have seen very little of him. He has said he is desirous to see Camden. Captain Westmacott has been there—you will be pleased to know that your father has had no quarrel with any of the officers, as has sometimes been the case.

I think in the past I have heard your father sometimes expressing himself with greater vehemence than might have been wished—but never unjustly. On the whole my dear Edward, many things are much better & more satisfactory than when your poor father was in an excited state of mind about two years since.

Mrs Bennet was with me the day before I came away. I hope & trust the legacy will be forthcoming without further delay—she needs it. Her husband is dead—he made a will in her favour which is properly attested—but the pension allowed to him ceases—and moreover he had incurred a debt which will absorb most of the little means left her to pay. She at present lives with our old servants John & Nancy Moore. I gave her the copy of the letter you enclosed from Mr Buchanan—other letters of yours since have been received but no mention made of the legacy. Mrs Bennet is truly deserving all the good that can befall her. She was a most faithful, prudent & affectionate wife—and is now quite a pattern of frugal neatness in her appearance. Although she is left solitary & alone, she bears her bereavement of children & husband with a truly pious feeling of meek resignation to the will of God.

I think it better to conclude this rambling letter, that it may accompany Mr Bowman. I may add another letter if time is given. In the meantime accept of our united love & every good wish for the continuance of your health & comfort—believe me to be, my own dear Edward,

Your affectionate Mother
E. MacArthur

I cannot read over what I have written—excuse it—remembrances kind to the Davidsons.

26 May 1832, to her son Edward

Once again Elizabeth is determined to be (or at least appear) optimistic about her husband's mental health, and determined not to dwell on unhappy subjects.

Saturday, May 26th, 1832
from Woolloomullah.
What a name!

My dearest Edward,
I believe it is just a fortnight since I commenced a letter to you, but it was not concluded until a day or two after—this letter was sent by the *Platina* in charge of a Dr Rutherford—this vessel sailed yesterday week. I write now by the *Mary* reported to sail for London about tomorrow.

Since my last, your letter written from East Stoke Park on Xmas Eve has been received and has given us much pleasure—it is just the place I would have wished you to be at that season. Your account of the family is very delightful and highly gratifying to us all. I have had the pleasure of a visit here from your sister Elizabeth since my last—we walked to the Botanic Gardens together with Mary and Mr Bowman. I believe we sauntered about three hours or more and looked at many things you had contributed to the collection and amongst the number the arbutus—it has grown out of my knowledge. It is just now breaking into flower—there has been no plant propagated from it, strange to say. It has been disfigured by repeated & injudicious layering of the branches. But as I intend this to be a short letter I must not let the Botanical Gardens run away with my pen.

You will have heard of poor Frazer's death and that Mr Allan Cunningham who was many years a collector of plants in this country for Kew Gardens is applied for from hence to succeed Frazer. I wish he may have the appointment—he is at present unemployed, as I learn from Dr Cook, who dined here yesterday.

Your two brothers have been here, stayed a night and returned. Your father also paid us a visit for a day and took home Elizabeth with him. He is better dear Edward but still too restless—I think, however, he will gradually become less visionary.

The sitting of the council is postponed to the 20th of July. The Governor continues to be much afflicted by the loss of Mrs Bourke. He still continues at Parramatta.

Here let me stop to tell you that I am keeping house for your sister, who with the Doctor and little James have taken flight to Parramatta purposing to return before it is dark— they set out at half past eight. The infant is left at home. I wish you may have patience to decipher my letters.

I shall look (with some impatience) for letters from you next month, when we may conclude you will have received our letters of last October—I must not revert to the feelings under which those were written. Believe my dear Edward that you occupy my thoughts daily, and although I know you have many kind friends and that you need not be more alone than it is your desire to be—yet do I feel that none of those can be what he was, whom perhaps we selfishly lament!

I hope George continues with you—it is a great comfort to have a domestic to whom we have been accustomed and who is faithful.

I shall now finish for the present—I may add a line on the cover when the travellers return to give you the latest news from Parramatta. Accept my dear Edward of my prayers for your health and comfort.

Your affectionate mother,
E. MacArthur.

2 June 1832, to her son Edward

The original King's School was in Parramatta, so it made sense that John Macarthur, erratic though his behaviour now was, should take his little grandson there each day. What a merciful change in one generation, that an Australian education was now considered good enough, rather than sending children to the other end of the world for an English one.

It sounds from the second part of this letter as though John Macarthur has written to his son Edward in England, and Edward has asked his mother for a reality check. Elizabeth is willing to express her exasperation at her husband's doings quite bluntly here, but also wants to reassure Edward that all is not gloom and doom—a tricky balancing act.

Wooloomoolah
2nd June 1832

I now have the pleasure of addressing you by Dr Cook—he dined here the day before yesterday & promised to call some time today for our letters, believing the *Portland* would sail tomorrow. James was expected from Camden—your father had been taking young Edward to school—there is a King's School established by the Rev Mr Forrest who with his wife arrived about six months since. Edward commenced his schooling on Sunday last—he only goes for a few hours in the day at present—Mr Forrest is much pleased with him & was quite unprepared to find so much intelligence in his young pupil. 'Aunt Eliza' has been very attentive to the little fellow—and you may be sure, she is not a little gratified.

Dr Cook is so kind as to take charge of an opossum skin cloak of native manufacture which perhaps may be a sort of curiosity should it keep…but I am apprehensive the moth has made a lodgement in the fur—in which case, I have told him to throw it overboard. You know the process of making these cloaks. The Natives close the skins together with the sinews of the kangaroo—this one comes from Argyle.

When I think of your <u>noble</u> & kind friends—as those who would be gratified by a little token from a 'far country'— it vexes me that we have not been enabled to dry flowers & collect seeds or plants to send you. We live in hopes of sending more acceptable things than we have done.

Mr Watson Taylor has been a true & tried friend—more than I can find easy to express. I think of him and his affection for our dear dear departed John, until my heart is overflowing with gratitude—and believe me I think of Bridgerule & all our old family.

I shall for the present close this letter—accept therefore of my good wishes and believe me to be, my dearest Edward,

your affectionate mother,
E. MacArthur

Wooloomooloo, 5th June

PS The important improvements your dear father mentions are little other than delusions. The walls of the house have been painted—the two marble chimney pieces brought us by James have been put up, one in the dining room the other in my bedroom, now fitted up as a Library, which it was intended to be when a bedroom wing was added to the present cottage. In the drawing-room the chimney piece was put up during the absence of James. It is much too large for the room but being put up I am as well pleased it has been allowed to remain, instead of being laid about from place to place about this bedroom wing—which is all we really want, or wish for in the way of accommodation.

There have been at least fifty different <u>plans</u>—I know not how many artists consulted & partly employed, the ground marked out in different ways—over & over again—foundations dug out, all sorts of litters & rubbish & still no building begins. Whether it will, I cannot tell—<u>more money</u> has been frittered away than it would have cost to put up the building. Your poor father cannot do anything in a quiet orderly way— the <u>Steam Engine</u> power is applied to the veriest trifle, which in this excited state of mind—he takes very little sleep—keeps every person about him in a state of perplexity—however, this disruption had better be at Parramatta than at Camden—and I hope it will soon be calmed down again.

Be not uneasy for us dearest Edward we have many comforts and consolations & sometimes we vex—& sometimes laugh over odd occurrences.

The conversation to which James alludes, is that your father was under the impression that Major Mitchell <u>had told him</u> (two or three days since, when he was at our house) that the Governor had advised him <u>not</u> to call—as he (your father) was under a mental malady. James has since spoken to Major Mitchell who is quite astonished that any such inference should have been made.

God bless you, dear Edward.

30 June 1832, to her son Edward

Things came to a frightening climax at the end of June. John Macarthur became convinced that his wife was an 'adulteress', that his son-in-law Dr Bowman was poisoning him and that his daughters had robbed him. He declared that he hated 'that woman Lucas' and turned harshly on his son James. He became physically violent, and his wife and daughters were forced to leave the house. Elizabeth went to her daughter Mary's home in Sydney, and her other two daughters went to the cottage near Elizabeth Farm where Mrs Lucas lived.

John Macarthur was restrained, and doctors were called in.

Dr Cook, a family friend, had just sailed for England, and Elizabeth hoped that he'd been able to see Edward and explain in person what was happening, rather than hearing the news in a letter. Elizabeth wrote several times in quick succession, by different ships—this letter and the next. Her confusion and distress are evident, as is her hope-against-hope that things will improve.

Woollahmallah
30th June 1832
half past 3 o'clock

My beloved Edward,
Your brother William has written a hurried letter to be sent by the *London* which is to sail tomorrow. William has only been with us two days. Yesterday Mr Bowman and dear Mary went

170

to Parramatta to see the dear inmates at Mrs Lucas's cottage and to enquire into the state of your poor father. Colonel Lindsay & Major Macpherson went there also—the latter two saw him, you will hear from some one of them, what their opinion is. Mr Bowman does not at present see him, because he is denounced as a 'conspirator' & as one who has aided in poisoning him.

I trust, my dearest Edward, my former letters will in some degree have prepared you for this calamity—let us be thankful to the Almighty that a wholesome restraint was placed upon your beloved father, before his malady had induced him to acts of greater violence. My feelings at this moment will not allow of my entering into details. Of <u>me</u> he has made the most fearful accusations. Your sisters intend promptly to quit the house. Still be not alarmed—his fine mind may yet right itself—he is in the house attended by John Moore our old faithful servant, in conjunction with two or three others, who attend to his personal comforts in every respect, and administer to his wishes, as far as it is deemed practical at present by the medical gentlemen who visit him. These are doctors Hall, Hamilton and Imlay, Bowman and Anderson. The two latter do not press their visits upon him, the three former are well received. Before I left Parramatta, which was at your poor father's most persevering and earnest desire nay <u>even</u> command, he had taken a most unaccountable dislike to our friend Mrs Lucas inasmuch as it caused her to isolate herself altogether to the cottage—after I came here one dislike close followed upon the heels of another, until your sisters were denounced & the house thrown into confusion, pistols, swords

& offensive weapons in his hands!

I need make no further comments. I have written to you so very lately by Dr Cook that there is little of family detail but what you will be in possession of, I hope, before you receive this.

I trust my dear Edward you will receive the painful part of the intelligence our letters now convey with that fortitude which is befitting a Christian—we must bear it—and I pray that we may be enabled all to do our duty.

Dear Mrs & Mr Bowman who is most affectionate together with their three boys are well and join in most affectionate remembrances to you.

Believe me to be
My dearest Edward
Your ever affectionate mother
E. MacArthur.

3 July 1832, to her son Edward

In the days of sail and shipwrecks, no one could ever be sure which of the ships leaving Sydney would be the first to arrive in London, so Elizabeth wrote two letters by different ships to let Edward know what had been happening. It's hard these days to imagine how stressful it must have been, not knowing whether letters had arrived. Still, she sounds a little calmer—the few days between this letter and the last have allowed her to steady herself a little.

Woolloomoolah, Sydney, Wednesday July 3rd 1932

My dearest Edward,

I again sit down to address you—according to my promise in my letter of last Saturday the 30th of June. This letter together with one from each of your sisters was sent by the ship *London* bound for Singapore. She sailed on Sunday morning—this is to go by the *Mary Anne* which is to sail tomorrow, for London direct—by which of these vessels you may first receive our letters is altogether doubtful, as they sail so nearly together.

I hope & trust you will have seen Dr Cook and will understand the letters we sent by him before these come to hand. Under this impression, my dearest Edward, I console myself in thinking you will be in a good measure prepared for the disturbing intelligence of your beloved father—mental aberration—it is even so—and we must endeavour to support ourselves under this heavy affliction with becoming fortitude and an entire resignation to the will of the Almighty & believe also these chastisements are for our good.

I cannot say the blow—severe as it is—has come upon us without long previous apprehension that sooner or later that mighty mind would break down and give way. I cannot enlarge upon this subject—but be comforted, my son, in knowing that the dear object of our solicitude appears to be cheerful, and not at <u>all</u> unhappy, although he believes himself to be under the influence of poison—that his daughters have robbed him—that I have been unfaithful, & that your two brothers have fled to the mountainous passes in Argyle, and he has taken a most unaccountable dislike to our friend Mrs Lucas. Such has been the delusion, or at least some parts of it.

Your poor father occupies the library (formerly my bedroom), a small sleeping room & a small dressing room—all in the East Wing of the Cottage. He is attended by our old servant John Moore and another most respectable man, besides one or two others. One your father thinks to be Dr Hamilton's servant. His medical attendants have been—besides Bowman & Anderson—Dr Hill, Dr Hamilton & Mr Imlay the staff surgeon. The latter is in daily communication with the Governor, having attended the late Mrs Bourke and generally residing in the family.

I learn that Mr Imlay had a couch in the Library prepared for him last night, in order to observe how your poor father passed it. Before I quitted home, his nights were fearfully unquiet.

Your sisters are with Mrs Lucas at her cottage. Elizabeth spent last week here—she looks better than I expected, considering the horrifying time they have had—dear Emmeline also, is I learn pretty well. William has returned to Camden where he expects to find Frederick Thompson. James is just arrived here, and will remain here tonight.

My former letters will show that I came from Parramatta to spend a few weeks here, on the 2nd of May—I believe I have written to you almost every week since I came—therefore there is little of family detail but what you will be in possession of—dear James has had a perplexing time—his feelings and affections wrought upon to an excess, and every day business to be attended to. Such is Life! With dear Mary and Bowman I have had all the comfort and repose which their affectionate care could ensure me.

Fail not, dearest Edward, to remember me kindly to our old friends—& say all that your own heart may suggest. My beloved Edward, I am ever your affectionate Mother,

E. MacArthur

13 September 1832, to her son Edward

Two months later, Elizabeth is still living with her daughter and son-in-law, while her husband is at the family home, in his delusionary state blissfully unaware of any problem.

The Mrs Marsden Elizabeth mentions here is the wife of the Reverend Marsden. He and John Macarthur had been bitter enemies for many years.

My dearest Edward,

I again address you from Sydney after an interval of at least seven or eight weeks since the date of my last letter.

Dr Fairfowl came to us immediately and gladdened us by the good tidings of your father. Your letter to me by him, now lies before me—I hope you had a pleasant excursion to Brighton and that you returned benefited by the change. You tell me of having seen many of our beautiful flowers & shrubs there—just now there are a good variety in high profusion of bloom in their natural abodes on the hills around Sydney— and a great many of the Boronias—<u>all</u> beautiful although I think I still give the preference to the Furze as being my first fancy flower on those well secluded spots—now they are comparatively exposed & laid bare near Sydney, all the high trees having been cut away for firewood. I am not unmindful of your request yet unable at this time to send any seeds or plants. Your own feelings will readily suggest the reason.

It is now more than four months since I left Parramatta and the greater portion of that time has been spent in the house—excepting walks in the garden. Within the last few weeks we have had the benefit of some carriage driving. We drive out on the South Head Road a certain distance and then get out and stroll about (taking a servant with us) to wherever our inclination may lead us.

A great many families have been very attentive in calling upon us and have given very pressing invitations to me to spend a day at their respective houses. Hitherto I have declined so doing on many accounts.

Since Dr Fairfowl arrived your poor father seems to have received James again into favour—he is almost constantly with him, and at his request eats with him, & sleeps at the house— but he still labours under delusions, and is not to be trusted. I had hoped to have dear James here, but he has been unable to leave your poor father. We have hopes of being enabled to engage some respectable person to devote himself wholly to him, as a companion. I very much fear he will not be in a state to be trusted for any length of time.

To dwell on this harassing subject will avail nothing, but tend to disrupt you, my dear Edward, and render me unfit to continue my letter. I am assured your poor father looks exceedingly well—eats & drinks and sleeps—as one who knows of no <u>discomforting</u> circumstance.

I shall leave to James the description of all subjects of business. We are as you may believe, very solicitous for word of the proceeds of the wool, the season for shearing is approaching. William is at Camden making the accustomed preparations.

Mrs Marsden has been staying in Sydney on a visit to her son-in-law and daughter. We have been more drawn together than we have been for many years past—she has gone out with us, in our visitings. We often speak of you.

Dear Mrs Lucas has written to you. She requests me to apologise for her letter & she says she omitted to mention that she had just drawn a bill for one hundred pounds. Mary & Mr B request their most affectionate remembrances—and the two boys send love to 'Uncle Edward'—the little William is just able to walk, being now a year old. Dear little man! We could not trust ourselves to think of his birthday, which was so speedily followed by an announcement which plunged us into so deep a grief.

With my prayers for your health & tranquillity, believe me to be
My dearest Edward
Your Affectionate mother
E. MacArthur

25 September 1832, to her son Edward

The burden of dealing with John Macarthur now fell on his sons
James and William. The female members of the family were still
banished from their home at Parramatta.

Woolloomullah, Sept 25th 1832

My dearest Son

I write a few hasty lines to go by the mail which I see by the
Gazette of Friday is to be made up this evening.

This is merely to say that we are all well. Frederick
Thompson has come from Parramatta to pay us a hasty visit.
He has been living with your poor father at the house, since
James went to Camden which was I think on Wednesday
or Thursday last. Frederick tells me that your father is quite
kind & familiar with him and talks rationally on indifferent subjects—but will not be <u>calm</u> when speaking of his
family—he looks well—eats & sleeps well—uses wine moder-
ately—reads—and seems happy!!

Mrs Lucas & Emmeline are at the Cottage—Elizabeth
here with me. I cannot say all that I feel for Mr Bowman's
kindness to us.

I hope you will have received all the letters I have written
you from hence—I think—my dear Edward, you will not
accuse me of forgetting to write. You are ever kind & lose
no opportunity yourself of writing to us and I am equally
anxious that your solicitude for us should not be increased

179

by our silence. We all send the kindest & most affectionate remembrances to you.

My dearest Edward
Your ever affectionate mother
E MacArthur.

2 November 1832, to her son Edward

Elizabeth has now been at the Bowmans' for five months, in a kind of limbo. I so much admire her strength of character in dealing with a truly awful and seemingly endless situation: not denying her feelings, but not dwelling on them either.

Woolloomala, Friday 2nd November 1832

My beloved son,

Again another ship, the *Waterloo*, is promised to be on the eve of departure for England—I hope she will not be so faithless as was the *Rubicon*, the last ship by which we wrote—she held out promises of sailing five or six weeks & will have occasioned you a great expense of postage if you receive all the letters safe that were written week after week & sent to the Post Office.

I feel that I have very little to tell you worth committing to paper: one <u>great & overpowering</u> cause seems to enervate my faculties. I try to resist the influence, but there are times when I cannot rouse myself. I need not explain that it is the state of your poor father, and perceiving myself and your sisters driven from our home—although we have a most kind & affectionate one here with dear Mary and Bowman, yet still your father maintains his hostile feeling towards us, notwithstanding that he is generally much more rational than he was.

I will not dwell on this subject but endeavour to turn to something else. Your letters dearest Edward are very gratifying to us—it is a great source of our enjoyment to think that you are so respectably and so pleasantly situated.

All the family unite in most affectionate remembrances to you—with
my dearest Edward
your ever affectionate mother
E. MacArthur.

6 January 1833, to her son Edward

The 'bazaar' that Elizabeth mentions here was a charitable fund-raising exercise by Queen Victoria, who is supposed to have made the various articles for sale. Elizabeth is glad to get the items, but doesn't mince words about what she thinks of the 'bazaar', or her scorn for the ladies-who-lunch behind it.

George Watson Taylor's enormous wealth had been based on the slave labour of his Jamaican estates. Enormous though his fortune was, he managed to squander it and by 1832 was so deeply in debt that he had to auction off a great deal of his property.

This is the only letter in which Elizabeth shows, just for a moment, the bitterness she must have felt towards her husband. She was now sixty-seven and should have been enjoying a serene old age.

Sydney 6th January 1833

My dearest Edward,

I write a few lines rather in a tantalized state of mind—the Transport *Ivory* from London arrived this morning & anchored in the cove but it being Sunday, no letters are delivered, and the ship for England is quite ready to sail! Even without having read your letter, I am unwilling to neglect writing a few lines, and fearful to delay doing so, lest the ship should sail.

I am sorry the coldness of General Darling's manner disconcerted you. I must own I feel some kindness towards him myself—perhaps he may not deserve it—but I think he was an honest man and intended well—dull and a <u>formalist</u> in public, a good husband, and a most affectionate father he certainly is. Governor Bourke I have never yet seen, nor indeed any of his family—they are altogether singular in their rudeness, but I do not pretend to find fault, nor trouble myself by motive hunting. Certainly I have not felt myself in circumstances to pay ceremonious visits—it would neither be decorous, not consistent with right feeling that I should do so.

You will observe, my dearest Edward, what James writes of the present apparent amendment in your poor father—and I say how earnestly—how anxiously—I await the intelligence of every day—still it is under the firm belief that the delusions are not <u>all</u> dissipated. James has devoted himself to the painful duty he has had to perform, with the most unwearied assiduity. I trust the next ship will bring you some more certain intelligence. In the meantime, my dearest son, let us trust in the goodness of the Almighty for support under all the misfortunes incident to us poor mortals and be truly grateful for the portion of good we enjoy.

I cannot help mentioning here a remark of your father's on reading the account of Mr Watson Taylor's failure—and speaking of his thoughtless and boundless extravagance he quickly said, 'Why was he not put under restraint for squandering his vast means?' I have forgotten what reply James made, but Mr WT did not abuse his family, nor accuse them of administering poison to him. I will not dwell on this horrifying subject.

I hope all the letters I have written to you from this place will reach you—I think you will be tired of my scribble—I can only say, your letters are of great comfort to me—and I am wishing for one every week to keep up the chain of communication. I have been with you in imagination in the tour you were contemplating to make in Wales with the amiable and good Marquis.

I see that Mr Bannister is still prosecuting his appeal to the Ministers—and persecuting General Darling. Neither is likely to be beneficial to Mr Bannister unless they can give him some employment that may appease his feelings and occupy his time. Miss Harriet Bannister is married at Hobart Town—both sisters are now settled.

I have now to thank you for the letter pocket book, the purchase from the Bazaar—the work of her Majesty is quite an interesting curiosity!!—an exhibition of such little objects wonderfully helps me to fill up conversation in a morning visit. I should hope the money obtained for these ornaments is usefully applied but is it not an odd way to obtain donations? What may be said in answer to this & many other things I suppose is 'that it is the fashion'—and gives occupation and amusement for ladies who are rich, well disposed and have little to do.

I could scribble on—so much is my heart relieved in conversing even in this way with my beloved son—God bless you and with every good wish for your health & happiness in which I am sincerely joined by Mr B and your two sisters, believe me to be

My dearest Edward
Your affectionate mother
E. MacArthur.

9 February 1833, to her son Edward

When this letter was written Elizabeth had been away from home for eight months. She hadn't seen her husband in that time.

Sydney, Saturday Feb 9th 1833

My dearest Edward,

Since my last letter to you by the *Arundel*, we have had the pleasure to receive letters from you and a parcel. Your sisters thank you very much for the muslins—which are decided to be of the new pattern and they arrived at a most useful time of the year to make up, very acceptable for the warm weather. All say 'Edward's gifts are always well-timed.'

Having said that I will briefly sketch our present family position—promising first that we are all pretty well, your poor father in perfect bodily health and very tranquil, Dr Wallace residing with him at the house, Mrs Lucas & Emmeline at the cottage. At present both James and William are at Camden.

Elizabeth and myself are now (as you will perceive) keeping house at Woolloomalah—we have little William left with us, who is able to run about, is quite active & is beginning to talk...I fear I must tire you by my frequent epistles. I can only say I feel so gladdened by the sight of your handwriting that I hope you have something of the same reaction at seeing mine.

God bless you my dearest son Edward—prays
Your ever affectionate mother
E. MacArthur

3 March 1833, to her son Edward

The uncertainty about mail arriving was a constant thread through Elizabeth's letters. Even in the best circumstances, most of a year could pass between sending a letter and receiving a reply. Many of her letters begin, as this one does, with a detailed account of by what ship letters had been sent or received, and to which obliging passenger they'd been entrusted, so that both sides of the correspondence would know if something had gone astray.

As always in her letters to Edward, Elizabeth puts the best face on a bad situation, and is optimistic about her husband's health even when the reality wasn't nearly so rosy.

Why Elizabeth no longer corresponded with anyone in Devon isn't apparent from any of the letters.

Woolloomoolah Sunday 3rd March 1833

Having just been told that the *Mountaineer* is to sail this evening for Singapore, I am induced to write a few lines although I have nothing of a very particular nature to communicate. We have written lately by the *Craigievar,* the *Brothers* and other vessels, but it is always uncertain whether those which first sail will first arrive, and generally speaking those ships which make the shortest passage fail in bringing us letters. I have just heard of the arrival of the *Gulnare* which sailed from England the 7th Nov & that the *Caroline* from Sydney had sailed four days previous.

I am, as you will perceive, still at Sydney, and Elizabeth

also—your dear father, however, is so much better that we hope to return home very shortly—he is becoming daily more himself and delusions are fast subsiding—this I know will be most comfortable intelligence to you.

It is a source of great comfort to me to hear from you through my early friend Mr Kingdon that my dear aged Parent is so well situated—you are of course aware that I have discontinued corresponding with anyone in Devon but it must not be inferred from thence that I am unmindful.

Emmeline spent the whole of the last week with us—she came from Parramatta on Monday evening bringing with her little James. Your brother James came for her yesterday—they are both well—your brother in particular is very much improved since your poor father has become placid & kind to him again.

The *Prince Regent* had the smallpox amongst the passengers on her voyage—which has obliged her to be placed in 'Quarantine'—so that we are pleased that our order was not arranged to be shipped by her. Mr Bowman visited the quarantine ground yesterday, in company with Dr Fairfowl and some other medical men to constitute a Board. Dr Fairfowl breakfasted & dined here—we chatted about you last evening—he promised to take charge of a cockatoo for you—when he sails on the *Sovereign* about the 20th of this month.

I wish you would have the goodness to send us a 'British Peerage'—I often wish to refer to it—make a memorandum of it.

Mrs Bennet is quite well—she often mentions you & your kindness—lives with the Moores—Moore himself waits upon your father.

20 March 1833, to her son Edward

By now, nearly a year after she'd been bundled out of her home, Elizabeth was clearly longing to get back to it. The way forward would be to persuade her husband to go to stay at the Camden property. He was preoccupied with his plans for a grand mansion on the estate, but would need to be induced to go there, as its accommodation was modest—it was a working farm.

Now Elizabeth has come up with a practical plan—for him to stay with their Camden neighbour Matthew MacAlister. Whether moving Macarthur into 'an entire new scene' was really the expert medical view, it was the only possible way for Elizabeth to get back to any kind of normal life.

Woolloomoolah Sunday 20th March 1833

My dearest Edward,
I write a few lines by the *Norfolk*, a ship of Mssrs Buchanan & Lamb—to assure you that we are well and much in the same way with respect to family affairs as when I last wrote. Your poor father, I am told, rails by turns at the house-building at Camden, and then commands, wishing it to be forwarded by all convenient despatch—still he declines going to see what is doing.

If he would be prevailed upon to go to Camden for a short time, I might then return to Parramatta and make there the best arrangement we could. It is the opinion of every person conversant in the nature of your poor father's malady that

removing into an entire new scene would be the most beneficial to him and therefore every inducement has been held
out to make him desirous to visit Argyle. MacAlister has the
means of comfortably accommodating him at his residence at
'Goulburn Plains' from where he might diverge in a number
of directions and visit a variety of other places quite new to
your father, and where he would not be likely to meet with any
thing, or person, to cause any irritable feeling, or any undue
excitement.

He received Frederick very kindly and asked a variety
of questions of him, as to his own affairs, as well as of
Camden—betraying great suspicions of & dislike to persons
without cause. On the whole Frederick says, altho' very much
improved, he perceives that your poor father's delusions are
not set aside—he seems to desire publicity rather than quiet,
which is not the best sign of amendment—still we hope!

I shall here close this—praying that this may find you
well and cheerful—hoping for the best

ever my dearest Edward
Your affectionate mother
E MacArthur

20 April 1833, to her son Edward

Mix-ups about times of ships' sailing must have been common-place, but in this case the cockatoo destined for Edward was part of the cargo and missed the boat. Elizabeth seems to have kept up a steady stream of seeds, cuttings, birds and Indigenous artefacts to friends in England.

Woolloomoolah April 20th

My dearest Edward

I address a few lines to you by the *Wellington,* a brig which its master says will positively sail tomorrow, and may arrive before the *Edward Lombe* which is to sail on Sunday next. On board will be Dr Watt, who has kindly promised to take our letters and those things which were most vexatiously left behind and ought to have gone by Dr Fairfowl in the *Sovereign.*

How this arose I can hardly tell you. Dr F had dined here the evening before this vessel sailed. Mr Bowman accompanied him to the boat & saw him off to the vessel. It was night and the commander said he should not sail before six o'clock in the morning. Mr Bowman, under this impression, desired the hospital messenger to be here for the purpose of taking the cockatoo and parcels at six o'clock, when behold just at that hour the *Sovereign* passed the Bay in fine style!

Our things were sent off by a boat which followed to the Heads—to no purpose, they were all returned. I know not whether the bird will be taken on board the *Edward*

Lombe—and this ends my late and great disappointment. Some preserved Native carrots which Emmeline had prepared were destroyed in the hasty pursuit by the boat—this is a trifle which I should not have noticed, but that you will find a reference to the case of preserves in her letter.

But enough of this—and what have I new to tell you? But that we are all pretty much in the same state as when the *Sovereign* sailed. I have a letter from James today. He says your poor father is in the same way—James devotes himself entirely to him, seldom leaving him an hour.

We are looking out somewhat impatiently for the arrival of the *Lunar*—not exactly for the finery, but for some useful things such as shoes that we are in want of.

I hope poor Mrs Bennet's papers will have reached you safe and no further delay take place with respect to the legacy—she is very well and living comfortably with the Moores—John Moore has been in constant attendance on your poor father for the last six months.

Once again God bless you
E.M.

9 May 1833, to her son Edward

The cockatoo was finally on its way to England, and John Macarthur had finally been persuaded to go to live at Camden. That meant that Elizabeth and her daughters could at last return to their home at Parramatta.

As always, her letter is full of local news that may possibly not have been as interesting to Edward as it was to her. Several times in her letters she describes herself as not being particularly sociable, and says that she tends to keep to home since her husband's disorder became known. Just the same, it's clear from the details of Sydney gossip (much of which I've cut, as it is likely to be of little interest to a present-day reader) that she still had her finger firmly on the pulse of happenings in the wider world of the colony.

I can't say what 'the letters from Devonshire' were about, but the following letter makes it clear that it was something tricky and delicate to do with her mother and her half-sister.

Sydney May 9th 1833

My dearest Edward, I am induced to write to you by the *Mary* because she takes the remainder of the wool of 1832 and I am in the habit of writing by our wool ship—and also there is a chance she may arrive before the *Hashemy* and the *Edward Lombe* by both of which we have written. The *Hashemy* only sailed on Saturday last—Mr Moylan was kind enough to take charge of the cockatoo for you, which should have gone by the *Sovereign* & Dr Fairfowl.

James left this place to return to Parramatta last evening. The last accounts from thence was that your poor father was amusing himself with the building. I do not hear that he makes any enquiries or notices anything in relation to the sheep. He seemed very well and quite cheerful—although complaining of his removal there, to any casual visitor that would listen to him. It was quite a necessary measure and I feel assured he will be much benefited by the change.

James frets under the vehemence of your poor father's expressions of wrath and can hardly be persuaded of the distinction between mental aberration and anger when expressed towards <u>himself</u> in all the bitterness too which your poor father can readily call to his aid.

A meddling person named Dickinson, a man not respected, and a stranger in this colony, was among others invited by your poor father to dinner. He is suspected to be the author of a letter signed 'Observer' which was sent to two of the newspapers for publication last week. Your brother called on the different editors. They all behaved very well. The *Australian* published an edited copy, the *Herald* declined.

Dr Rutherford delivered all your letters immediately on his arrival. I will not say how anxious I am to receive letters from you of a later date when your mind I trust will be more calm and resigned on the subject of your poor father's mental malady—we must bear the affliction.

I assure you my dear, dear Edward, that at times I can hardly believe what has happened. I have been banished from home a year—Elizabeth also—still we have endeavoured to cheer each other, and by frequent communication with the dear inmates of the house and cottage at Parramatta have kept up our spirits. From dear Mary and her kind husband we have had all the support that affectionate kindness could bestow.

It is at present our intention to return to Parramatta in the course of a week or ten days—I do not think it right to hurry home immediately after your poor father had quitted that house and besides there were a few arrangements necessary to be made for our comfort which dear Emmeline is busying herself to do.

Many thanks for your attention in copying the letters from Devonshire. Your replies to them were what I could wish.

I am pleased to learn that Davidson has returned. I hope Mrs Davidson's health will in future be better established. I observe her brother has a better appointment at Ceylon. Mr Bowman has made a purchase from Charles Cowper of that part of the Glebe Land he purchased from the church—37 acres I think. He proposes to commence building on it immediately—indeed it is time Mr Bowman should have a residence of his own near his duties—and not to be put to the expense of renting a house at twenty pounds a year. The archdeacon Broughton and his family are still at Hobart Town—I shall be glad when they return. Mrs Bann is just confined of a daughter—they had before two sons—we hear from India that Colonel MacPherson is returning to England—and that Colonel Lindsay has a command.

Having written you at so much length I shall conclude this little letter by wishing you all the happiness & comfort we poor mortals ought to expect in this changeable world. Mr

Bowman, Mary, Elizabeth and the boys send their affectionate love. We talk of you frequently & think of you still more.

Believe me ever, my beloved Edward,
Your affectionate mother E. MacArthur.

29 September 1833, to her son Edward

In John Macarthur's letters there are recurring references to Elizabeth's headaches (though she didn't mention them in her own letters). Hopefully the spectacles helped—being finally back at home might have helped too.

John Macarthur's nephew Hannibal lived not far away from the Macarthurs. John had no great respect for Hannibal's business sense, and Hannibal had got on the wrong side of his uncle several times, but on this occasion all went well.

Elizabeth's half-sister, Isabella Hacker, seems to have fallen on hard times, and was at least partly supported by the allowance made by the Macarthurs to her mother. Elizabeth wanted to help, while at the same time being cautious about not getting too entangled in a permanent obligation.

Parramatta, Sunday 29th September 1833

My dearest Edward,

I now address you from our beloved home—to which I believe it is three months since my return to it and in this time I have not once written to you, but Elizabeth has, and James also— scarcely any eligible conveyance here in this period offered, and to our annoyance one direct ship departed without our having been apprized of her intention.

We have received the various commissions by the *Sarah*. My spectacles answer exceedingly well—thank you for your trouble in the purchase. The flannel you sent us I think beautiful—it seems to wash well, & is very soft.

Having said this much on orders & commissions—I will turn to other subjects to all of us more interesting—and first let me mention your poor father with whom I have had <u>no</u> immediate communication—nor can I learn that he has made but one enquiry about me—& that was a question to Mr Matthew MacAlister—'whether he had seen me'. He continues to enjoy very good health—only occasionally complaining of rheumatism. Captain King and his son spent a day or two at Camden on their way to & from Argyle. Your father received them very kindly on both occasions—and seemed very much pleased with John King.

Hannibal set out for his establishment in Argyle on Wednesday last, he called to take leave of us the evening before and seemed very apprehensive about going to Camden. However he determined to make the experiment, and we have the pleasure to hear by a letter from dear William that he was well received & that your father talked to him a great deal on various subjects—and that after having spent one day at Camden in this agreeable & satisfactory manner he proceeded on his journey much cheered and gratified.

Elizabeth & her nephew Edward are reading in the drawing room whilst I am sitting apart scribbling, my hand shaking to such a degree that I am fearful I cannot make myself intelligible to you—the weather is very warm and enervating and very dry—the country suffering from want of rain.

I perceive I have omitted to name dear Mrs Lucas—she would be very much annoyed to know that her kind & affectionate regards were not presented to you—and therefore let me tell you how frequently you are the subject of our conversation—and particularly when we two old folks retire into a corner to gossip.

I cannot rally my sprits to write much to you in the way of news. I believe I wrote to you from Sydney thanking you for the reply you had given to the letters from Devonshire—it was prudent and feeling also. I do not think under all circumstance that I should write—it is the family connection which causes me to be silent. My mother is a truly surprising woman & I thank God that I have been enabled to assist her by such an addition to her income which made her truly comfortable in her advanced age and assisted her <u>own</u> people. I would wish to continue, for a time, the same allowance to my sister when it please God to take my Mother, as the poor soul will then be deprived, I appreciate, of all income. Dearest Edward—I know your delicacy of mind will let you know the embarrassment I feel. Say everything for me to the Kingdons—Mr Broughton told me Miss Kingdon was married—is it so?

Marriages are rather prevalent here just now. Miss Bourke is married to Mr Deas Thompson. There have been many others but none of course of such conspicuous notoriety—I was going to say illustrious!

We were gratified to learn your noble friend was well—thank the Marquis for his remembrance of me. I shall conclude this rambling epistle by prayers for your health and well-being, and saying that I am ever,

Your most affectionate mother, E MacArthur.

28 January 1834, to her son Edward

When Elizabeth was writing her letters, bulk was always an issue. To save paper, it was common to 'cross-write'—that is, to write a page in the normal way, then to turn the page at right angles and write across what had already been written. Needless to say, this increases the already-considerable difficulties of reading idiosyncratic handwriting.

Writing a letter involved finding paper (a relatively expensive commodity, only available in New South Wales as an import), making the ink, getting the blotter ready, preparing the sealing wax (which had to be melted and then impressed with a seal), and shaping a quill for a pen. In Elizabeth's case, with her poor eyesight, it would also have been necessary to make sure the page was well lit, which would have involved candles or lamps being brought and arranged, and of course finding the spectacles Edward had sent her.

Parramatta January 28th 1834

My dearest Edward,
You will have thought it long since you have been trusted to decipher my scribbles—I have not been enabled to write to you so frequently since my return to dear home—as when I was sojourning at Sydney—partly on account of a slight inflammation in my eyes, and also that I am not so aware of the sailing of ships—and old people require some time to collect all the materials together for writing a letter.

Hannibal has commenced building a house on a very extensive scale annexed to the present cottage. I have not been to see it—having not yet had resolution to move about to make any visits. I have plenty of exercise within the limits of our estate—and the looking about the garden and grounds keeps me amused.

I think of your poor father at Camden and am pleased that he is now in the way of seeing a few persons. But the effort to make visits abroad, and the apprehension of coming in contact with strangers, I have not been able to combat. People in the world would think this dread a foolish thing, and perhaps it is so.

Elizabeth & Emmeline have each been staying with Mary, who, it is expected, will soon add to the number—we wish for a girl. Little James has been staying with us several weeks—he is a fine frolicsome little fellow. I am vexed to have crossed my writing—it confuses my own sight and it will be an infliction on your patience I fear—but I had determined on a letter of chit-chat or gossiping details.

12 March 1834, to her son Edward

After a time of relative calm, John Macarthur's disorder now returned more severely than ever and required him again to be 'restrained'. Whether his violence was only directed towards others, or was also turned on himself, isn't known.

Parramatta Wednesday 12th March

My dearest Edward,

I am altogether ignorant whether or no either of your brothers will write by the present opportunity. William is now in Sydney—he came from Camden on Saturday, leaving James there quite well.

I wish I could say the same of your poor father whose bodily health is nevertheless very good but his mental aberration has again manifested itself to the great grief of us all, and to the more immediate disquietude of James & William. It has been found absolutely necessary to impose a system of restraint again. The cottage is relinquished to his use, your brothers making use of a room or two at the back. A part of the new house will soon be habitable—William's business at Sydney is to order some furniture for use in three rooms there.

By the vessel about to sail (the name I really have forgotten) the Archdeacon, Mrs Broughton and their two daughters are passengers, also your friend Dr Price who has visited us two or three times. These are the only passengers. The Archdeacon & his family called to take dinner of us last week, where Mrs

Broughton expressed the wish to be remembered to you. I write this therefore for that purpose. He expects to return again shortly.

I will conclude this for the present—believe me I am your affectionate mother,
E MacArthur.

23 March 1834, to her son Edward

Elizabeth always makes sure to be attentive to her son's activities and travels, and to respond to his news with lively interest. Closer to home, she's very aware of the technological changes—telegraph, steamships, and public coaches—that were transforming the world.

Sydney Sunday March 23rd 1834

My dearest Edward, I have the pleasure to acknowledge your letter to me of the 1st of November and to communicate the news that yesterday your dear sister Mary was safely delivered of a fine little girl! To the great satisfaction of both parents—& I have the pleasure to add the mother & infant are doing as well as can be expected.

Your brother James has written to you—he will have told you that he left your brother William at Camden well, and your poor father also in bodily health, but the mind sadly astray. Such is the will of God & we must submit.

What an interesting tour has yours been through the north of England, and what a cheering picture your narrative gives of the wealth, opulence, spirit, talent and industry of the agricultures and manufactures of respected, and respectable old England! I shall look for your more detailed account with considerable impatience.

Dr Evans breakfasted with us yesterday morning and went to Parramatta by the evening coach—you would be surprised at the number of these coaches between Sydney & Parramatta!! They travel to Windsor, to Bathurst, to Liverpool, to Campbell Town & to Goulburn Plains—you will perceive how we are also increasing in bustle & importance.

I wrote you very lately by Archdeacon Broughton and also by Mr Price who was a passenger in the same ship—I made rather a bulky packet for the latter, I hope it may not be an excessive one. It occurred to me rather suddenly to send you such letters written from Camden as I had preserved— as better calculated to explain how matters stood—than any account I could give.

17 May 1834, to her son Edward

*Elizabeth's husband was now kept in seclusion and, when neces-
sary, restraint at Camden. As well as his sons James and William
he had other attendants, including William Wetherman, a free
settler fallen on hard times.*

*John Macarthur died at Camden, aged sixty-seven, in April
1834.*

Parramatta Saturday 17th May 1834

What can I add to the sad details which the letters from your
beloved brothers will communicate? I am assured, very little
more than which will arise in your own filial bosom when
the first impression of the awful yet natural event which has
deprived you of a much loved and reverenced father has given
place to resigned & tranquil reflections.

I know you will weep—dearest Edward—and indeed
the fountains of my eyes which I believed to have been nearly
dry have been opened anew. I seemed only to want to have
mingled my tears with yours conjointly with your dear
brothers & sisters—and yet why should I have desired this?
We ought not to expect our vain wishes to be accomplished.

It is now just five weeks since the mortal remains of your
dear father were consigned to its last earthly tenement—his
immortal spirit is I humbly hope & trust, in a state of bless-
edness. Under this impression, my dearest Edward, I am
resigned, and can look around me for sources of consolation

now that the shock arising—or rather increased—by the suddenness of the event, has in some measure subsided.

I had freely indulged myself with the hope that it will have pleased God to restore the dear departed for a more sane state of mind. I think he might have been at peace with his family—that he was restored to reason for a few minutes I have no doubt—more was not granted. Let us say thy will be done on Earth O God as it is in Heaven.

Your dear brothers have had a melancholy duty to perform, and well they sustained it. You will learn that James had only quitted Camden for a day or two previous to your father's death—the active duties each had to perform will readily arise to your mind. I was at Sydney, where I had been for more than a fortnight staying with dear Mary in her confinement, which took place on Saturday the 22nd March, when she was safely delivered of a fine little girl.

Your sister Elizabeth came to us at Sydney immediately the melancholy event was known at Parramatta. Hannibal accompanied her down & returned again immediately. Dear Mrs Lucas was left with Emmeline who young Edward & little James were staying with then. The former was only just recovering from a severe illness with which he was seized suddenly & which exhibited for many hours a very dangerous aspect. I mention this because you will see some notice of it in some of the notes I mean to pack up—I am happy to say he is better, and I hope gaining strength. He rides three or four miles every fine day on a nice little pony.

I wander from my little narrative—on Tuesday the 14th of April when James came to us at Sydney he left Hannibal and Frederick Thompson at Camden. The latter remained there about a week, when your dear brother William came to us also, leaving for a while the scene where so many objects could not but recall painful associations. Elizabeth remained a week longer with Mary. James paid a quick visit to Camden. Thus have I hastily sketched our position for the first time in six weeks—thinking that you will be comforted to know all that can be told of our movements. Every person has been attentive and many families of the middling class of inhabitants at Parramatta, have put on mourning as a token of grateful respect to your dear departed father.

Now let me close this narration—whilst writing the within, we received by the coach from Sydney your various packets we had long expected by the *Craigievar*—thanks dearest Edward for your letters to me—I will leave the other members to say as much for themselves. Sir Edward Parry will take charge of the packet in which this will be enclosed. I trust you will meet. He will be enabled to communicate much information, which it will be very desirable you should be acquainted with.

It was only on the 25th March that Mr Wetherman's decease took place at Camden. He died of apoplexy—he had been much esteemed by Sir Edward Parry, and by your poor father who respected him and pitied his fallen fortune, and had welcomed his arrival at Camden about a fortnight before—and seemed greatly pleased with the prospect of having him for a companion. This good feeling did not continue until death removed the object. The shock of this awful event William had also to encounter alone.

A well educated medical gentleman named Fotheringham, highly recommended, was thought an eligible person to succeed Mr Wetherman. He was staying with MacAlister at Bathurst, from whence he hastened to meet dear James at Parramatta or Sydney. James left Camden for the purpose of this meeting on the 6th or 7th of April. I need say no more on this melancholy subject. Nor should I have written so much, but in some measure to relieve James of some detail of painful reminiscence.

Believe me to be, my beloved son
Your ever affectionate mother
E. MacArthur.

24 October 1834, to her son Edward

Elizabeth's mother was now in her eighties, a remarkable age for those times. She died two years after this letter was written.

My beloved son,

I cannot let our friend Dr Fairfowl depart without a few lines addressed to you by myself. I took leave of him yesterday—he walked over from the Vineyard soon after breakfast and stayed about an hour. He seemed to look forward with pleasure to the thought of meeting you in London immediately on his arrival.

Mr MacAllen has hired a cottage in Parramatta. I like his appearance—and I am told Mrs MacAllen is a very pleasant person. They have dined at Woolloomalluh—Mary is pleased with them. As you know, she is not very apt to be pleased with strangers.

You will observe a note from James written at Camden. They have seen a great deal of company of late and perhaps rather more than their sober-minded friends think prudent, where there are so many young girls.

You will observe that I have not yet been to Camden—in truth there has been such a demand made upon the little cottage that I have felt discouraged from going. I want to be quiet and alone with my family when I make this first visit, which must excite feelings I would not forgo, but of too solemn a nature for publicity. I wish there was an inn in the vicinity of Camden to accommodate ordinary guests.

I have on a former occasion written to you, what were my wishes in case of the demise of my poor aged mother—which was that the annuity allowed her should be continued to my sister, who would otherwise, I fear, be left destitute. Of this event I cannot but expect to hear at no very distant period. I trust to your discretion & kind feelings to do every thing for her, much as I might myself. Pray thank Mr Kingdon for all his good and kind attentions. Perhaps an all gracious and divine Providence may allow of our meeting in another state of existence.

Believe me to be my dearest Edward
Your affectionate mother
E MacArthur.

10 November 1834, to her son Edward

Elizabeth was very conscious of Edward's distance from his family, and that distressing news had to be conveyed to him by letter, months after it had happened, and—what could cause great distress—that letters might not arrive in the order in which they were sent.

Parramatta, Nov 10th 1834

My dearest Edward, I write a few hasty lines to go by the ship now about to sail. I am not aware if either of your brothers have written. They are both at Camden, busily engaged in supervising the sheep shearing and in preparations for the approaching harvest. It was mine and Elizabeth's intention to have been at Camden at this time—we have however been prevented by a variety of causes, not worth enumerating, and now we are all more or less suffering from an epidemic sort of influenza, which our newspapers call a catarrh, which will prevent our journey for some time longer.

William writes to me that the shearing is proceeding rapidly & that the sheep wash well, and although from the sudden severe heat & consequent drought some dust unavoidably will be collected in the fleece after washing, yet he promises it to be in very good order. It is a great privation to me, not to be there at this time. I am so fond of seeing the operation.

I hope we shall have letters from you again soon. I await

the arrival of your response to the intelligence you will receive by James, which oppresses my mind and causes me to feel a melancholy which I would willingly suppress. Dearest Edward, your blessed father I humbly hope is reaping the reward of the many benefits he bestowed on this community—to his foresight and zeal may be attributed much of its present prosperity. Excuse the poor writing which is all I am capable of at this moment—accept the affectionate love of your sisters and believe me ever my dearest Edward your affectionate mother

E. MacArthur

20 February 1835, to her son Edward

The grand house John Macarthur planned at Camden wasn't finished when he moved there in 1833, but one part of it had been quickly made habitable and furnished.

Elizabeth's praise of this house can only be described as faint.

Edward's 'young namesake' was Elizabeth's grandson Edward Bowman.

Parramatta, Friday February 20th 1835

My beloved Edward,

I have just put up for your perusal—at a leisure hour—that of the Camden correspondence as I thought might amuse, and give you a more lively account, of some things than a mere letter of detail.

You will be glad to learn that I have at length been enabled to visit Camden with some degree of comfort for myself—and that we spent three weeks there in the last month with more cheerfulness than I had anticipated. Elizabeth and your young namesake Edward were my companions—the latter was delighted with everything he saw—the scene was altogether new for him, and dear William devoted himself to amuse and divert the boy.

Your brother James was in Argyle when we first went, but returned from thence about a week after our arrival looking all the better for his trip, and the general aspect of things being satisfactory for him. James and Frederick Thompson went to Sydney this morning, the former for the purpose of dispatching the business connected with the embarkation of the year's wool, which I am pleased to say is all safely embarked (the first load of lambs' wool). It has always been an anxious time for me, to see the wool being safely shipped, and I rejoice that the object has been accomplished.

Frederick is in very good health & spirits, only complaining of the heat, which is indeed oppressive and has been for several weeks past. It makes me so tremulous that I can scarcely write.

You will expect me to say something of the new house at Camden. It is a handsome building, more of a classic character than any other I have seen—spacious on the ground floor and indeed sufficiently so on the chamber floor. But you will not need to be told, dearest Edward, that one wing was planned & furnished long before the other part, for a particular purpose. Alas, the destined and beloved occupant is I fervently hope and trust reaping a rich harvest of reward for all that his benevolent spirit originated and all that it contemplated to effect. I cannot pursue this train of thought. You may be sure that when weeping over his tomb, I thought of and prayed for you also, my dear son.

I shall conclude this and sign myself, your affectionate mother E. MacArthur.

July 1840, to her daughter Mary

Mary's son Edward, Elizabeth's grandson, had travelled to Camden for a visit. He was fourteen. The doting grandmother remembered how much a mother wants news of an absent child, and hastened to reassure Mary.

Uncle William is Elizabeth's son William, who lived at Camden and (with James) was chiefly responsible for the flocks. Emily is probably her youngest daughter, Emmeline Emily.

Camden, Friday, 2 o'clock, July 1840

My dearest Mary,

I know you will be anxious to hear how dear Edward is after his journey—and after having passed the first night after it—I scribble a few lines to say that 'Uncle William' and his nephew safely arrived about 3 o'clock yesterday.

As I was not quite prepared to expect Edward, you may judge of my surprise and pleasure at his appearance and I assure you of Emily's also. We had been sauntering about in the morning—mutually expressing a wish that he <u>might</u> come with William. Emily and I were on the verandah holding a parley with some natives and administering to a sickly infant amongst them, all connections of Brodberry, as the travellers alighted in the yard. They walked in & took us quite by surprise.

Edward was not so much tired, but that after having taken some refreshment, he was nothing loth for a ramble, accordingly we all set out to see what was to be seen about the town & garden—we returned to dinner, where the dear boy was very prudent in what he ate. We all retired to rest at 10 o'clock, having previously arranged that Edward should sleep in my dressing-room, where there is a comfortable bed and a constant fire, besides being immediately opposite the room I sleep in—so that by keeping both doors open & the lamp in the passage he is quite at ease & free from nervous apprehension.

I gossiped with him last night after he was in bed until he fell asleep—in the night he walked into my room to tell me how 'beautifully bright the stars shone in the window' and that he had just heard the clock strike five. Dear child, he returned to his bed and soon fell asleep again. Today they have been fully occupied in seeing the contents of the newly arrived plant cases. As I have written to the end of my paper I can only add our united kind & affectionate remembrances to yourself, Mr B and the children.

Ever—my dearest Mary
Your affectionate mother
E. MacArthur.

18 December 1840, to her son Edward

Elizabeth's half-sister, Isabella, had married Thomas Hacker and they'd now emigrated to Prince Edward Island in Canada. Exactly why Isabella was 'my poor sister', and why Elizabeth's feelings needed to be spared, is unknown.

The Mr Kingdon to whom Elizabeth refers here was one of Bridget Kingdon's younger brothers. He'd have known Elizabeth well during their young days.

The vicarage that Elizabeth remembers was one of the places I was especially interested in during my visit to Bridgerule in 2016. At that stage I hadn't read this letter, but my day in Bridgerule was dominated by a ferocious wind—rude gusts indeed—from the sea.

The vicarage is exposed to that wind because it's on a hill above the village. The muddy lane leading from the village is extremely steep. When, in the novel, I pictured Elizabeth Macarthur doing her best to rid herself of an unwanted pregnancy, I remembered the pitch of that lane, up which a desperate woman might have forced herself to run.

Parramatta
Dec 18th, 1840

My beloved son,
I am now more especially induced to write to you to thank you my dear Edward for a letter received the evening before last. It is little more than a copy of one from Mr Kingdon, so kind, so

full of tender recollections that I was overcome by the perusal. Well indeed do I remember the old Vicarage House, its aspect towards the sea, from whence rude gusts would frequently shake and assail the apartment above more especially. Those scenes of my childhood and youth cannot be easily forgotten, nor will the memory of dear friends departed, nor of those that still remain once my young playfellows be effaced from my memory whilst it pleases God that I retain that faculty. Mr Kingdon forgets my age, when he speaks of my return to my still dear native land. The time is too far past.

Thanks dearest Edward for all that you have done for my poor sister Mrs Hacker!! I pray that she and her family may establish themselves in comfort in the land of their adoption, where there is, I trust, a field for virtuous industry to exert itself. I can only say once <u>for all</u> that I am abundantly thankful to you my son for all you have so considerately done to meet my wishes, and at the same time to spare my feelings on this and also on former occasions.

We had three boys, Edward, James & Willy Bowman last night—Willy stays here—poor little fellow—he had the misfortune to fracture his left arm, & has been at Lyndhurst under his father's care for several weeks, until a few days since—the arm is now pronounced to be quite well—I have not seen him yet. He has however been staying at Camden and frequently at Lyndhurst.

I would willingly write of various persons, but in truth it bewilders me—Mr Frederick Bigge has not returned from Swan River—none of his friends knew of his expedition—I believe he has been gone nearly two years—perhaps I may be mistaken as to the time—a gentleman from Swan River who was at Camden a week or two since, said Mr Bigge was waiting to return by the *Beagle*, Her Majesty's surveying Ship commanded by a very worthy man Capn. Wickham—engaged to Annie MacArthur.

I must conclude my dearest Edward with prayers for your continued health and everlasting happiness.

Your ever affectionate mother,
Elizabeth MacArthur.

5 October 1841, to her son Edward

By the terms of John Macarthur's will, Edward, the eldest son, stood to gain the greatest control over the various family enter-prises. Not surprisingly, this created difficulties with his brothers, who'd been the ones shearing the sheep and sorting the wool for so many years while Edward was pursuing military advancement on the other side of the world.

For a long time the sons kept their disagreement from their mother, but she was finally told of it. William had written a letter to Edward in which he made the case for having a greater share in the estate, and Elizabeth had been asked to confirm the truth of what he said. In this letter you can hear the pain of a mother who's caught up in a disagreement between her equally beloved children.

As was usual at the time, Elizabeth, as John Macarthur's widow, didn't inherit anything, in spite of the years of work she'd put into the family business. All the property had always belonged to her husband. She was allowed to go on living in the family home until she died, but she never owned anything.

My dearest Edward,

I have carefully perused the accompanying letter, and can fully concur in the <u>accuracy</u> and <u>truth</u> of the statements in it. Often has your dear and respected father held conversations with me, hoping and praying that our children would be satisfied with the disposition of his property, and that his greatest consolation was founded on the belief that the family were so strongly united in the bonds of mutual confidence and affection—and in the desire to carry out his plans for the general good—as would lead them hereafter to act, each individual, for the benefit of the whole, and for the attainment of the objects he had through life ardently devoted himself to, rather than for any views of individual or separate advantage. I do assure you, my dearest Edward, this dissatisfaction of yours has given great pain—I was only apprized of it a short time since and only within the last two days saw your letter announcing your displeasure, which was to me as an Electrical Shock, having been assured by James on his last return from England in answer to my enquiry that all had been arranged with you in accordance with the proposed plan submitted to me before he left the colony and in the justice and propriety of which I entirely agreed. I certainly did strenuously urge you to come out and <u>see</u> for yourself, knowing how impossible it is to judge of the state of things without seeing. This I still urge you to do, as the proper course in every point of view, for it will enable you, if you prefer returning to England, to speak from your own knowledge, and thereby add great weight to your <u>statements</u> and <u>representations</u> on behalf of the colony.

9 November 1845, to her son Edward

Even in old age, Elizabeth still took a keen interest in what was happening in the colony she'd known almost since its first days, including the visit of the famous Caroline Chisholm, 'The Emigrant's Friend', who worked to protect female emigrants who would otherwise have been vulnerable to exploitation. (Dickens wrote about Caroline Chisholm too—the character of Mrs Jellyby in Bleak House *is based on her.)*

Captain Logan is the central character in The Commandant, *a novel by Jessica Anderson that portrays him in a much less golden light than Elizabeth does here.*

Parramatta, November 9th 1845

My dearest Edward,

The departure of a vessel for England gives me the pleasure to acknowledge your letter from Sligo by the July packet, which I received on Thursday. I am in hopes from your account that the change of scene cannot but be agreeable to you. The Mrs Logan you mention must be the widow of Captain Logan who unfortunately lost his life at Moreton Bay—by the natives—it was a sad disaster and very much lamented. Mr Bowman knows the family, having been to Moreton Bay on a medical tour at the time poor Captain Logan commanded there, and I have often heard him spoken of in terms of great commendation.

The July packet was expected to bring important

intelligence for the colony—but was long on her passage so that we had public intelligence conveyed to us from India prior to her arrival. However it is a most satisfactory conveyance for letters—and <u>especially</u> for <u>family</u> letters. I look out for one from you, my dear son, with an assurance you will not fail in writing to me by each monthly conveyance. I hope I shall not tire you by my frequent letters—it is scarcely a fortnight since I wrote to you and also to Lady Brisbane.

I received a letter from Camden yesterday. The family are all well & busily engaged in sheep shearing. William has returned from Argyle, but James had made a beginning before & had some fleeces got up under his supervision, which are indeed very beautiful.

Emmeline writes of a Mrs Chisholm having paid them a visit—a sort of inspection, to collect information—she is an extraordinary person, very intelligent I have understood—and has, I believe, effected good here by untiring perseverance, to forward female emigrants to the interior parts of the colony—getting some assistance from the govt and contributions from private persons which she has passed on to them. She obtained service for these women. I believe she is about to publish some work on the subject of emigration. Emily says she took samples of soil and went to the vineyard & garden and had visited all parts of the estate & proposed looking in upon those on the other side. In short she is an extraordinary woman—her husband is an officer serving in India—are you not tired of Mrs Chisholm?

Hannibal & his daughter Emmeline stopped at Camden two nights on their way south & they have paid a visit to the Gordons, at their residence, with which they are much pleased. I am well and the little family are much as usual. I have not had a letter from Mary at Ravensworth since this day fortnight. Mary I am sorry to say has not regained the use of her leg. The Bishop has made a stay at Ravensworth in his journeying to and from New England. I sent your last letter to Camden last evening.

I so much like to have a chat with you my dear Edward, and too many things crowd upon my mind to say—and I fear I make a very uninteresting selection. I hope to write again soon, accept my prayers for the continuance of your health & welfare, and believe me to be

your affectionate mother
E. MacArthur.

31 May 1849, to her son Edward

This is one of Elizabeth Macarthur's last letters. She was eighty-four when she wrote it, and had just returned from a visit to Sydney to her home of sixty years, Elizabeth Farm. Elizabeth Farm is now open to the public as a wonderfully well-planned and accessible museum. When I was researching for the novel I visited it many times, and felt very close to Elizabeth as I sat on the verandah she'd have enjoyed, looking out to the garden, and as I stood in the room where she'd have written many of the letters in this collection. It's a lovely house, modest in scale and style but comfortable and welcoming—a real home. No wonder she loved it so much.

My dearest Edward,

I am once again at Parramatta, in that home endeared to me by its having been my abode so many years and in such a variety of circumstances—some indeed of a very painful nature—some of serene happiness—and surrounded by many blessings conferred on me which I pray to God I may be sufficiently thankful.

Elizabeth Macarthur died on the ninth of February 1850. She was eighty-five. In her long life she had watched New South Wales develop from a struggling, hungry settlement clinging by its fingernails to a tiny part of an unknown continent, to a thriving powerhouse for the production of wool and wheat.

Nothing in her letters shows that she had any awareness of what this meant for the Indigenous people. In this she was like most of her contemporaries—though not all. Perhaps, as I imagine in the novel inspired by her, she did come to understand that she was on stolen land. On the other hand, like many then and now, she might have preferred not to look too hard at that uncomfortable reality.

The descendants of her son James still live at Camden, in the grand house that John Macarthur planned but never saw finished. Elizabeth and her husband are both buried nearby, on a hill over-looking the land that changed their lives.